The Cromwellian Pr

MANCHESTER
UNIVERSITY PRESS

NEW FRONTIERS IN HISTORY

series editors

Mark Greengrass
Department of History, Sheffield University

John Stevenson
Worcester College, Oxford

This important series reflects the substantial expansion that has occurred in the scope of history syllabuses. As new subject areas have emerged and syllabuses have come to focus more upon methods of historical enquiry and knowledge of source materials, a growing need has arisen for correspondingly broad-ranging textbooks.

New Frontiers in History provides up-to-date overviews of key topics in British, European and world history, together with accompanying source material and appendices. Authors focus on subjects where revisionist work is being undertaken, providing a fresh viewpoint, welcomed by students and sixth-formers. The series also explores established topics which have attracted much conflicting analysis and require a synthesis of the state of debate.

Published titles

David Andress French society in revolution 1789–1799

Jeremy Black The politics of Britain, 1688–1800

Paul Bookbinder The Weimar Republic

Michael Braddick The nerves of state: taxation and the financing of the English state, 1558–1714

Michael Broers Europe after Napoleon

David Brooks The age of upheaval: Edwardian politics, 1899–1914

Carl Chinn Poverty amidst prosperity: the urban poor in England, 1834–1914

Conan Fischer The rise of the Nazis (2nd edition)

Bruce Gordon The Swiss Reformation

T. A. Jenkins Parliament, party and politics in Victorian Britain

Neville Kirk Change, continuity and class: Labour in British society, 1850–1920

Keith Laybourn The General Strike of 1926

Frank McDonough Neville Chamberlain, appeasement and the British road to war

Alan Marshall The age of faction

Evan Mawdsley The Stalin years, 1929–1953

Alan O'Day Irish Home Rule 1867–1921

Panikos Panayi Immigration, ethnicity and racism in Britain 1815–1945

Daniel Szechi The Jacobites

David Taylor The New Police

John Whittam Fascist Italy

The Cromwellian Protectorate

Barry Coward

Manchester University Press
Manchester and New York

distributed exclusively in the USA by Palgrave

The right of Barry Coward to be identified as the author of this work has been
asserted by him in accordance with the Copyright, Designs and Patents Act 1988.

Published by Manchester University Press
Oxford Road, Manchester M13 9NR, UK
and Room 400, 175 Fifth Avenue, New York, NY 10010, USA
www.manchesteruniversitypress.co.uk

Distributed exclusively in the USA by
Palgrave, 175 Fifth Avenue, New York,
NY 10010, USA

Distributed exclusively in Canada by
UBC Press, University of British Columbia, 2029 West Mall,
Vancouver, BC, Canada V6T 1Z2

British Library Cataloguing-in-Publication Data
A catalogue record for this book is available from the British Library

Library of Congress Cataloging-in-Publication Data applied for

ISBN   0 7190 4316 6 hardback
        0 7190 4317 4 paperback

First published 2002

10 09 08 07 06 05 04 03 02   10 9 8 7 6 5 4 3 2 1

Printed in Great Britain
by Bookcraft (Bath) Ltd, Midsomer Norton

Contents

v

Contents

Acknowledgements

My principal debt in writing this book is to all those historians on whose work I have drawn in order to formulate my own views of the Cromwellian Protectorate. My thanks go to all those people whose writings are listed in the endnotes and in the bibliographical essay. I am especially indebted to Professor Chris Durston and Professor Mark Greengrass, both of whom read and commented on a draft of the whole book. I have benefited greatly from their advice. I am also grateful to the Department of Coins and Medals at the British Museum for permission to reproduce the 1655 medallion. Finally, I have nothing but praise for Alison Whittle, Jonathan Bevan and Rachel Armstrong at Manchester University Press for their help and support in transforming my typescript into print. My thanks too go to Jane Raistrick, who has used her considerable skills as a copy-editor to iron out inconsistencies in my text and (above all) to make it very much clearer than it was when I first sent it to her.

Introduction

The historical study of the 1650s, particularly the Protectorates of Oliver and Richard Cromwell from 1653 to 1659, has reached a very interesting stage. Whereas research on seventeenth-century England before and after the 1650s has led to major reinterpretations of both those periods, in contrast long-accepted views of the 1650s have not been fundamentally revised. This is not to say that no new work has been done on the 1650s or that historians have not mounted challenges to accepted views of the decade. The books, articles and theses cited in the notes of this book and in its bibliographical essay demonstrate that the former is not the case; and two wide-ranging articles by Austin Woolrych and Derek Hirst in the 1990s are examples of work that has suggested new ways of looking at the 1650s in general and at the Cromwellian Protectorate in particular.[1] Yet the predominant view of the period remains that reflected in the chapter entitled 'the retreat from revolution' in the first edition of my book *The Stuart Age 1603–1714* (1980).[2] Along with many other historians at that time, it seemed to me that after 1649 – a year which saw a revolutionary transformation of England brought about by the execution of Charles I, the abolition of monarchy and the House of Lords, and the establishment of an English republic – the main theme of the 1650s was a drift back towards traditional constitutional and ecclesiastical structures, climaxing in the collapse of the republic and the restoration of the old monarchy and Church in 1660. What makes the historical study of the Cromwellian Protectorate so interesting at present is that recent work on it, as well as

1

on the period before and after it, makes it possible to suggest an alternative view of the regime. The main aim of this book is to show that the depiction of the regime as a 'retreat from revolution' is very misleading indeed.

Instead the Cromwellian Protectorate will be portrayed in this book as a regime that tried to resolve the tensions between divisions in the country that it inherited when it was established in December 1653. These divisions had deepened and widened during the English Civil War from 1642 to 1646. Although the war ended decisively from a military point of view, with Charles I's armies totally defeated, there was no similar decisiveness about the constitutional and religious post-war settlement. This is not surprising, since historical research on the period before 1642 during the last decade or so has made it clear once more that, whatever the short-term causes of the war (Charles I's political ineptitude, the impact of events in Scotland and Ireland, and so on), the Civil War conflict in England was rooted in fundamentally different attitudes among English people about what kind of government and Church they wanted in their country.[3] This in turn explains another feature of the Civil War that has been confirmed by recent research: these competing ideologies drove supporters of both sides to fight so ferociously that the war had a major impact on the social and economic rhythms of people's lives.[4] Consequently, though the defeat of the royalist armies in 1646 brought the war to an end, the divisive issues for which it had been fought were not resolved.

In the later 1640s the vast majority of people in the country wanted a settlement that restored Charles I with the kinds of limitations on his power that had been imposed on him by laws passed by the Long Parliament in 1640 and 1641, and a restoration of the type of post-Reformation Church that had existed before Charles I's attempt to impose Laudianism on it after 1625. This was a vision of a post-Civil War settlement that can be seen in the manifestos of the Clubmen movement in the last months of the war in southern counties of England and Wales, and in the programme of the Presbyterian 'counter-revolutionaries' at Westminster, led by Denzil Holles, in 1646–47. This programme received powerful support from people at all levels of English society. Yet the history of England between 1646 and 1649 demonstrates that a minority in England had alternative, more radical visions of

2

what post-Civil War England should become, and since that minority secured the support of the parliamentary New Model Army, it succeeded in quashing the more conservative plans for settlement in 1648 and in bringing about the English Revolution of 1648–49.[5]

These more radical visions for the settlement of England will be discussed in the first chapter of this book, which also makes clear that tensions between the advocates of these and alternative visions remained very much alive during the Commonwealth period of republican rule of the Rump Parliament (1649 – April 1653) and Barebone's Parliament (July–December 1653). The argument of the first chapter is that the establishment of the Cromwellian Protectorate came about as a direct result of the persistence of these tensions that were rooted in the existence of conflicting aspirations for the future of the British Isles.

The main aim of the next four chapters (2–5) is to portray the Cromwellian Protectorate as a regime led by men whose main concern was to resolve these tensions. What makes the Protectorate such a fascinating regime is that it was not one primarily intent on bringing the country back to traditional ways. For its leaders, the quest for godly reformation was at least as important as the quest for settlement.

The remaining chapters (6–8) and the conclusion examine the impact that this attempt to square the circle of the quest for seemingly incompatible ends had on England and Wales, Scotland and Ireland, and on England's international role. These chapters also show that the impact of the Cromwellian Protectorate, as well as its aims, do not justify its portrayal as a 'retreat from revolution'.

Notes

1   A. Woolrych, 'The Cromwellian Protectorate: a military dictatorship?', *History*, 75, 1990; Derek Hirst, 'Locating the 1650s', *History*, 81, 1996.

2   In the 2nd edition of the book published in 1994 I re-titled the chapter on the 1650s 'the failure of revolution', which is at least nearer to my current view.

3   For criticisms of the views of many historians (often called 'revisionists') who emphasised short-term, at the expense of long-term, causes of the Civil War, see R. Cust and A. Hughes, 'Introduction: after revisionism' in *idem*, eds, *Conflict in Early Stuart England: Studies in*

Religion and Politics 1603–42 (London, 1989); R. Cust and A. Hughes, 'Introduction' in *idem*, eds, *The English Civil War* (London, 1997).

4 See, for example, C. Carlton, *Going the Wars: The Experience of the British Civil Wars 1638–51* (Stroud, 1991); S. Porter, *Destruction in the English Civil Wars* (London, 1994); M. Bennett, *The Civil Wars Experienced: Britain and Ireland 1638–51* (London, 2000). All these build on the path-breaking article by Ian Roy, 'England turned Germany? The aftermath of the Civil War in its European context', *Transactions of the Royal Historical Society*, 5th series, 28, 1978.

5 The best books on the later 1640s are D. Underdown, *Pride's Purge: Politics in the Puritan Revolution* (Oxford, 1971) and A. Woolrych, *Soldiers and Statesmen: The General Council of the Army and its Debates, 1647–48* (Oxford, 1987). But see also Robert Ashton, *Counter-Revolution: The Second Civil War and its Origins, 1646–8* (New Haven and London, 1994).

Part I

The Protectorate and the quest for reformation

1

The establishment of the Cromwellian Protectorate, December 1653: 'a conservative reaction'?

A common view of the Cromwellian Protectorate is that it was a conservative, reactionary regime and that its establishment in December 1653 put the British Isles on a road which led from the high point of the English Revolution in January 1649 to the restoration of the traditional monarchical constitution in May 1660.[1] The main aim of this chapter is to contest that view.

However, as will be seen in the first part of the chapter, this task has not been made easy by recent work on Barebone's Parliament, the institution that was forcibly removed to make way for the Protectorate. It is now apparent that it was in many respects a much more effective, reforming regime than has often been suggested. Nor is there any doubt that it was brought to an end by the threat to use military force on 12 December 1653, after a minority of its members, in collusion with officers in the New Model Army, principally John Lambert, abdicated power to Oliver Cromwell. Whether or not Cromwell knew the details of the planned coup in advance is not known, but it is certain that he was more than happy to see the end of Barebone's Parliament. Only four days after its forcible dissolution Cromwell was installed as Lord Protector of Britain and Ireland by virtue of the Instrument of Government, a paper constitution drafted by Lambert and other senior army officers. Ostensibly the expulsion by military force of a regime that was intent on bringing about reform supports the view that in December 1653 there was 'a conservative reaction' effected by men who wanted to prevent further change.

The second part of this chapter casts serious doubts on this assumption. Neither those who planned the coup to send Barebone's Parliament packing nor Oliver Cromwell were opposed to bringing about change in Britain and Ireland. As will be seen, those both inside and outside the army who supported the establishment of the Protectorate had been strongly committed to instituting reforms between 1649 and April 1653 during the rule of the Rump Parliament, the remnants of the Long Parliament that had survived the army purge of December 1648. During that time they had become increasingly frustrated by the failure of the Rump to carry these out on an extensive scale. There is considerable doubt about the exact reasons why Cromwell decided to use military force to expel the Rump on 20 April 1653, but it is highly likely that what primarily drove him to act was seething anger at the unwillingness of most members of the Rump to push forward with the reforms that he and many others in the army wanted to bring about. It will also be seen that, although Cromwell and others welcomed the meeting of Barebone's Parliament in July 1653 in the hope that it might achieve what the Rump had not, events soon convinced them that unless it were brought to an end, the cause of further reformation would be irreparably damaged. A key question about the establishment of the Cromwellian Protectorate is why had its promoters been driven to that conclusion?

Barebone's Parliament, July–December 1653

One of the most important recent discoveries by historians working on mid-seventeenth-century Britain is that Barebone's Parliament was in fact very different from its customary image. There are three outstanding features of that image. The first is that its origins are to be found largely in the millenarian ideas of Major-General Thomas Harrison and his Fifth Monarchist friends, who believed that, following the demise of the four great monarchies of Babylon, Persia, Greece and Rome and the papacy that had ruled down to their own day, there would soon be established the Fifth Monarchy, King Jesus's thousand-year reign on earth. It was a commonplace of Fifth Monarchist thought that in the brief period before Jesus's return to earth, there was a need to establish the rule of an interim body of godly men who, like the Jewish

Sanhedrin, would rule according to the biblical laws of Moses.[2] Therefore it was widely assumed that when the Council of Officers announced on 30 April 1653, ten days after the dissolution of the Rump, that power was to be devolved to a Council of State and an assembly of 140 nominated men of 'approved fidelity and honesty' from all parts of Britain and Ireland, it was putting the Fifth Monarchy plans into effect.

As a consequence, a second characteristic of Barebone's Parliament was assumed to be its composition by men who were largely unfitted to rule, either because they came from outside the ranks of the traditional governing elite of the country or because they were religious fanatics, like Praise-God Barebone, from whom the assembly gained its nickname. It was assumed that the membership of Barebone's Parliament was largely determined by religious congregations which recommended men from their number who were noted more for their godly lifestyle and views than for their experience of government. The sneering jibe of Clarendon in his *History of the Rebellion* that Barebone's Parliament was 'a pack of weak, senseless fellows; much the major part of them consisted of inferior persons, of no quality or name, artificers of the meanest trades, known only for their gifts in praying and preaching' was long taken as an accurate assessment of those who sat in the assembly.[3]

Not surprisingly, therefore, a third feature of Barebone's Parliament was said to be its tendency to be a talking shop that discussed reforms that were too wild, idealistic and impractical to have any chance of working. Thus its origins and composition meant that it could not be an effective vehicle to bring about reformation.

In recent years the work of historians, such as Austin Woolrych, has shattered each of these components of the hostile image of Barebone's Parliament.[4] It is true that in the wake of the dissolution of the Rump Parliament Cromwell and many of his fellow senior army officers were desperate to find a means of achieving the kind of reform that the Rump had failed to carry out, and they had high hopes that Barebone's Parliament would be able to oblige. Their enthusiastic expectations of the new assembly are most vividly illustrated in Cromwell's speech when it assembled on 4 July 1653:

I confess I never looked to see such a day as this is – it may be nor you either – when Jesus Christ should be so owned as He is, at this day and in this world ... I say you are called with a high call. And why should we be afraid to say or think, that this may be the door to usher in the things that God has promised; which hath been prophesied of; which He hath set the hearts of His people to wait for and expect? ... Indeed I do think something is at the door; we are at the threshold.[5]

Yet, although parts of the speech read as though Cromwell had decided to use military force to impose a full-scale, Fifth Monarchy-style millenarian rule of the saints, other evidence suggests that he and his allies had no clear idea what to do after the precipitate dissolution of the Rump.

They were more certain about what they did not want to do. They very soon vigorously denied that they intended to establish a military dictatorship. In a printed letter, dated 3 May 1653, written by a journalist employed by Cromwell, the charge that the use of naked military force had stifled 'the liberty of the people' was countered by the declaration that 'it [parliamentary power] is only suspended, 'tis a sword taken out of a mad mans hand, till he recover his senses'.[6] Such claims need, of course, to be treated with some scepticism, but they receive support from the fact that, according to Edmund Ludlow, immediately after 20 April Cromwell and his senior army officers spent a lot of time discussing with civilian ex-Rumpers, including Oliver St John, means of drawing up 'some instrument of government that might put the power out of his [Cromwell's] hands'.[7] They realised that to have called an elected parliament at this stage would inevitably have resulted in a large anti-army majority and the permanent collapse of their hopes of reform. But they made it clear that they were in favour of calling elected parliaments in the future, as also later did members of Barebone's Parliament. Shortly after they assembled they declared that 'our posterities ... we expect still to be governed by successive parliaments'.[8]

It soon also became clear that Cromwell and the senior officers had decided not to take the Fifth Monarchy route advocated by Major-General Thomas Harrison, who in the weeks after the dissolution of the Rump floated the proposal that an assembly of 70 men, appointed by Independent gathered churches and modelled on the Jewish Sanhedrin, should rule until Jesus's earthly kingdom was established. It is true that the decision announced by Cromwell and the Council of Officers on 30 April that the new assembly would consist of 140 men nominated for their godly qualities was interpreted by Major-General John Lambert as a victory for Harrison, his rival in the high command, and as a defeat for his own proposal for the temporary appointment of a small council of 12 men to fill the power vacuum. But he was wrong. In reality, Harrison was just as unhappy about the outcome as Lambert, and both men withdrew temporarily from the political stage in high dudgeon. The proposal might have passed power to an assembly of godly men, but their selection was not left to the gathered churches, who probably directly recommended only 14 members of Barebone's Parliament. The selection process was kept strictly in the hands of members of the Council of Officers, who bore in mind that godliness was one, but not necessarily the only, qualification for selection.[9]

As a result, the membership of Barebone's Parliament was very different from the image projected of it by Clarendon and others. It is true that those chosen were generally of slightly lower social status than those normally elected to parliaments in the seventeenth century, but the vast majority were gentlemen. These included two titled noblemen (Lord Eure and Viscount Lisle), representatives of leading county landed elites, like Sir Charles Wolseley, and three future earls, including Anthony Ashley Cooper, future Earl of Shaftesbury. Most members were from the lower end of the gentry, but very few were tradesmen. Moreover, few of them lacked some education or political and administrative experience. Around 60 had been educated at a university or Inn of Court, 14 or 15 were barristers, 119 were justices of the peace (JPs) (including 89 who had been JPs before 1650), and even more had served on parliamentary commissions in their localities.[10]

Not only was Barebone's Parliament not 'a rabble as never had hopes to be of a Grand Jury', but most of its members cannot be described as 'religious fanatics'. Detailed work by Woolrych and Capp has uncovered only 12 or 13 Fifth Monarchists in Barebone's Parliament and many of them (including Harrison) played only a small part in its proceedings. Most members were moderate religious Independents, who wanted liberty for individual consciences within a broad national Church.[11]

What is also surprising to those accustomed to the image of
Barebone's Parliament as a complete flop is both the efficiency
with which it went about its business and its practical achievements. In some respects it acted like a normal seventeenth-
century parliament. It met in St Stephen's Chapel in Westminster,
the home of Stuart parliaments; it chose as its Speaker Francis
Rous, who had sat in every parliament since 1626; and its Clerk
was Henry Scobell, who had held that post in the Rump. In other
respects it acted with more efficiency than normal parliaments,
few of which regularly met (as did Barebone's Parliament) from
8 a.m. and on six days a week. Nor did its habit of occasionally
setting days aside for prayer (which was another thing it had in
common with the Long Parliament) interfere with its business,
which was streamlined by a structure of standing committees,
devised by 'a committee of committees'.

In this context its impressive legislative record is not surprising.
In just over five months it passed 30 statutes, and many others
were in the pipeline when it ended in December 1653. Most
progress was made on law reform. Acts were passed for the relief
of creditors and poor prisoners, and for civil marriage carried out
by JPs. Even more wide-ranging law reforms were being considered, encompassing many of the recommendations made by the
Hale Commission on law reform that had fallen on deaf ears in
the Rump Parliament. Measures were also proposed to rationalise
the revenue system, including abolition of the hated excise, and
an act was passed to regulate the conditions under which idiots
and lunatics were kept. Barebone's Parliament also continued the
Rump Parliament's work in bringing Scotland further under English control, making the government of 'Britain' a reality for the
first time since the union of the crowns in 1603.

Despite these achievements, Barebone's Parliament was
brought to a precipitate end on 12 December, an event that
spawned different explanations in pamphlets at the time, as will
be seen. But, although they differ on why it happened, all the
sources broadly agree on how it happened.[12] After a divisive vote
on a report from a committee on religion on Saturday 10 December, a few members met privately on the next day and arranged,
with the collusion of the Speaker, to meet even earlier in the
morning than usual on Monday 12 December. In a sparsely
attended assembly, one of the members of the Council of State, Sir

Charles Wolseley, made a speech fiercely critical of some of the proceedings of Barebone's Parliament during the previous few months. Other speakers supported him, those who attempted to argue the opposite case were silenced by the Speaker, and the majority of those present (probably about 40, including the Speaker) decided to leave St Stephen's Chapel for the Palace of Westminster to abdicate power to Oliver Cromwell. *En route* they considered a short document that stated: 'the sitting of this Parlament any longer as now Constituted, will not be for the good of the Commonwealth; and that therefore it was requisite to deliver up unto the Lord General Cromwell, the Powers which they received from Him'.[13] This was signed by those members who had left with Speaker Rous, together with about 40 more members who had turned up later (i.e. about 80 in all). A much smaller number (contemporary estimates vary from 27 to 35) objected to these proceedings and remained in St Stephen's Chapel. Within a very short time, however, two army officers, Colonel William Goffe and Lieutenant-Colonel Francis White, appeared with some soldiers and gave the remnant of Barebone's Parliament no alternative but to leave. The doors of the chapel were barred behind them.

The establishment of the Protectorate, December 1653

A common explanation for the coup of 12 December 1653 and for the establishment of the Protectorate four days later is that these events were the work of men anxious to put a stop to the process of radical political and religious change. What makes this extremely unlikely is that most of the key actors in the events of 12–16 December were men who were keen to bring about radical change in Britain. As will be seen, what in fact drove them to put a sudden end to Barebone's Parliament was their belief that if it were allowed to continue not only would the existing social and political order collapse and religious anarchy ensue but the chances of bringing about any reform in the future would all but disappear.

Who were the key actors in the events that led to the establishment of the Protectorate and did they have reforming ideas in common? It is impossible to know the names of all those who were involved in the coup and/or who promoted the establishment of the Protectorate, but the names of most of the prominent people involved are known. The two most well known of these, Oliver Cromwell and John Lambert, were too politically skilful to leave any evidence of involvement in the coup, but the balance of probability is that Lambert did know of it and was implicated in it, since, as will be seen, he had been working for weeks on a new constitution, the Instrument of Government, on which the Protectorate was to be based. Cromwell may have been strictly correct when in September 1654 he claimed that 'I did not know one tittle of that resignation, until they all came and brought it, and delivered it into my hands'.[14] But, although there is no evidence that he knew the precise details of the coup in advance, he was aware that secret discussions were taking place about a constitution to replace Barebone's Parliament and it is stretching credulity a long way to believe that a man with such acute political antennae was unaware that at some stage soon a move would be made to end sittings of Barebone's Parliament. What is beyond doubt is that he welcomed the end of Barebone's Parliament and the abdication of power to him. Whenever he referred to the assembly in later years his contempt for it was undisguised. Its continued existence, he said in 1657, would have led to 'the subversion of the laws and the liberties of this nation, the destruction of the Ministry of this nation, in a word the confusion of all things'.[15] If he had any doubts about accepting the Instrument of Government, these were quickly overcome. Only four days after the coup he was inaugurated as Lord Protector.

In addition to Cromwell and Lambert, the key people in the establishment of the Protectorate also included those who were directly implicated in the coup. These have been identified by Austin Woolrych as Sir Charles Wolseley, William Sydenham, Sir Gilbert Pickering, Edward Montague, Colonel Philip Jones, Sir William Roberts, Anthony Ashley Cooper, Henry Lawrence, Colonel John Desborough, Colonel John Hewson and Colonel John Clarke.[16] Unfortunately some of these men are very shadowy figures and it is consequently very difficult to say anything about their beliefs. Yet it is striking that most of those for whom there is some information seem to have been religious Independents who shared Cromwell's zeal for liberty of conscience and godly reformation. This is certainly true of Pickering and Sydenham, who are characterised by Woolrych as 'markedly religious men', closely associated with prominent religious Independents like John Owen. Wolseley 'was to remain a devout Independent throughout the rest of his long life'. Hewson was closely associated with the Baptists in Ireland during the Protectorate. Although after the Restoration Montague was to show no signs of his earlier religious enthusiasm, 'as the youngest colonel in the New Model Army and for some time after he had the reputation of a strong Independent or even a sectary'. Moreover, although Ashley Cooper is difficult to categorise as a man driven by deep religious beliefs – he appears as someone who had his 'eye more on the main chance than on the New Jerusalem' – running through his career even in the 1670s and 1680s is a concern to protect liberty of conscience for Protestants against militant religious intolerance.[17] The same too can now be said of Lambert. Although he did not share Cromwell's fierce religious passion, Dr Farr's recent analysis of his beliefs reveals a man who was fiercely committed to the toleration of a broad range of religious standpoints.[18]

Most of the promoters of the Protectorate probably shared Cromwell's yearning for a programme of reformation of which liberty of conscience was the centrepiece; in none of them, though, was it as intensely apparent as it was in the man chosen to be the new Protector. It is, of course, possible to argue that Cromwell's zeal for a godly reformation was merely a cloak for other aims. This was certainly the view of Richard Overton, who in 1649 sneered that 'You shall scarce speak to Cromwell about anything, but he will weep, howl and record, even while he doth smite you under the first rib'.[19] But the consistency and fervour with which Cromwell expressed his views make it difficult to sustain the idea that Cromwell's religious zeal was insincere. It would be wrong to fall into the trap of categorising him as *either* a head-in-the-clouds idealist *or* a Machiavellian hypocrite aiming merely at self-advancement. There are times when Cromwell acted with calculated ruthlessness and low political cunning. But the view taken in this book is that the exercise of political cunning is not incompatible with the pursuit of high ideals: on most occasions when Cromwell acted ruthlessly he did so primarily to advance his hopes of bringing about a godly reformation in Britain.

What was Cromwell's vision of 'a godly reformation'?[20]

Unfortunately, a full answer to that question will never be possible since Cromwell lacked the intellectual frame of mind that might have led him to write a tract detailing his blueprint for a hoped-for new Jerusalem. Yet it is possible to reconstruct from scattered references in his letters and speeches the main features of the kind of Britain that Cromwell wanted to see. The first feature was a restoration of social and political stability after over ten years marked by civil war and military and political violence. As will be seen in succeeding chapters, 'settlement' was the word Cromwell used to describe this aim of 'healing and settling' the social and political wounds brought about by this traumatic period in the nation's history. But for Cromwell this was not sufficient by itself. With 'settlement' Cromwell wanted 'reformation'. In part this was a desire to bring about social justice. With the restoration of social and political order should come the rooting out of corruption. Efforts should be made to ensure that the rich carried out the duties that came with the privileges of wealth and power, and that institutions like the law be reformed so that they should operate fairly. The most stirring statement of this aspect of Cromwell's hopes of reformation is in the letter that he wrote to the Speaker of the Commons on the day after his great victory over the Scots at the battle of Dunbar on 3 September 1650:

> We pray you own His people more and more, for they are the chariots and horsemen of Israel. Disown ourselves, but own your own authority, and improve it to curb the proud and the insolent, such as would disturb the tranquillity of England, though under what specious pretence soever; relieve the oppressed, hear the groans of poor prisoners in England; be pleased to reform the abuses of all professions; and if there be anyone that makes many poor to make a few rich that suits not a Commonwealth.[21]

But there was more to Cromwell's 'reformation' than just the achievement of social justice. Central to his hopes was the concern that had been voiced by generations of godly men and women in England since the early years of the reign of Elizabeth I for what they called 'a reformation of manners', which was essential if the Reformation that had begun in the sixteenth century should be developed and eventually completed. For Cromwell, as for other godly men and women, that process had made scant progress so far. It is true that during the late 1640s and early 1650s more progress had been made than ever before in ridding church

16

liturgy and government of traces of Catholicism. 'Popish' officials like bishops and practices like the celebration of Christmas had been abolished by parliamentary ordinances passed in the 1640s; the iconoclastic tearing down of 'popish' images in churches was legalised. But for Cromwell and the godly, 'further reformation' would not be achieved until there was a transformation in the ways people lived their lives. For this to happen people had to purify their lives of drunkenness, swearing, adultery, fornication and all other sins.

As will be seen in later chapters, Cromwell came to place more and more importance on achieving this 'reformation of manners' as each year passed, as he came to identify this as the main thing required of him and the nation by God. It was a mission that had been indelibly impressed on him by his military experiences, during which he had equated victories on the battlefield with God's support. In return, he was convinced, God demanded 'reformation'; if it were not striven for, God would remove his support. This was the message that Cromwell drew from other battles in 1650–51 than Dunbar. Lambert's victory at Inverkeithing in July 1651 was followed by demands to members of parliament (MPs) in the Rump Parliament that they get on with the reforms necessary to retain God's support. After 'the crowning mercy' at Worcester on 3 September 1651 Cromwell again urged the Rump to see 'that justice and righteousness, mercy and truth may flow from you, as a thankful return to our gracious God'.[22]

After Worcester Cromwell returned from the battlefields to Westminster, desperately trying to prevent an open breach between Rump and army. But during 1651 he became more and more frustrated by the Rump's failure to reform. Significantly, on 13 August 1652 he allowed an army petition deeply critical of the Rump's arid record on reform to be sent to parliament from the Council of Officers over which he presided. The petition called for measures to encourage godly ministers, to reform the law, to root out financial corruption and vagabondage, and to ensure that MPs elected in future parliaments would be 'pious and faithful to the interests of the Commonwealth'.[23] Eight months later, his anger at the Rump drove him to get rid of it altogether. There is considerable uncertainty about Cromwell's exact motives for dissolving the Rump by military force on 20 April.[24] But the most likely explanation is that by this time Cromwell had come to the conclusion that any parliament elected without imposing qualifications on new members would be hostile to the kind of reforms he wanted.

Significantly, on the day before the dissolution he and his fellow officers had had a long meeting with some MPs to consider a plan to replace the Rump by a council of 40 MPs and army officers who would hold supreme authority until a new parliament should meet at an unspecified future date. Although not all the MPs present supported this proposal, Cromwell believed that most had agreed that parliament should not proceed with a constitutional bill until further discussions had taken place. In these circumstances, whether (as Cromwell and his fellow officers later alleged) the bill that the Rump began to rush through on 20 April proposed to perpetuate the Rump in power by providing only for by-elections, or whether (as now seems more likely) it provided for a general election in the autumn with new MPs vetted by the outgoing parliament, is irrelevant in explaining what happened next. For if either of these measures had been put into effect, power would have slipped away from the army and Cromwell and would have been put more firmly than ever in the hands of civilian Rumper republicans like Sir Arthur Heselrige and Thomas Scot for whom liberty of conscience and godly reformation were not the highest priorities. From the point of view of Cromwell and the army officers, the inescapable conclusion was that unless they took steps to seize power for themselves, the chances of bringing about a Cromwellian reformation would be gone for ever.

By December 1653 Cromwell and his allies had come to believe that this was also true of Barebone's Parliament. How was it that an institution which had set about the task of reformation with a zeal and efficiency that had been absent in the Rump came to be seen as a threat to reformation? The broad answer is that in the eyes of some, Barebone's Parliament seemed to be more concerned with tearing down rather than reforming the political, social and religious order. As such it came to be considered by some to be as dangerous a threat to the army and the cause of religious liberty as the Rump had been.

Ironically, although the vast majority of its members were not low-born revolutionaries intent on subverting society, many of the things that Barebone's Parliament did made it *seem* as though it was a major threat to the hierarchical social order. When

Cromwell later said of Barebone's Parliament, 'what did they? Fly at liberty and property', he was reflecting a common view of it that gained substance especially from attempts by radicals in the assembly to push forward reform of the law and to abolish tithes and the right of laymen to appoint ministers to church livings (advowsons).[25]

Although there was much common ground among members of Barebone's Parliament on the need to reform the law as the Hales Commission had recommended, a few radicals pressed for more fundamental radical changes, some even proposing the Fifth Monarchist idea of the replacement of English common law with the biblical Mosaic law. To some the vote on 5 August in favour of abolishing the Court of Chancery was seen as a terrifying move in that direction. Despite the claim made by Samuel Highland in *An Exact Relation*, one of the most effective contemporary defences of Barebone's Parliament, that there was no intention to destroy the law, other pamphleteers pilloried the principles of some in the assembly that 'led them to a pulling down all and establishing nothing: so that instead of the expected Settlement, they were running into meer Anarchy and Confusion'.[26]

Even more horrendous to conservative opinion were the proposals to abolish tithes and advowsons, which were considered by many landed gentlemen to be an inalienable property right, not as Highland called advowsons 'one of the strong holds of Satan'.[27] The vote on 10 December that prompted some to initiate the coup to bring an end to the assembly was a narrow defeat by 56 votes to 54 of a proposal from a committee on religion that had also recommended the retention of tithes. 'Though we called our selves a Parliament', Wolseley is reported as saying in his speech urging the abdication of power on 12 December, 'yet we acted most unlike unto it: and that appeared in our endeavours to destroy Proprietie in attempting to take off the power of Patrons to present to Church-livings.'[28] This was a charge that did not go unchallenged: 'Was it a destroying of property', asked Highland, 'for the former parliament to take away the lands, and to sell many of the lands of bishops, deans and chapters?'[29]

When Barebone's Parliament continued the wide-ranging purges of the commissions of the peace begun by the Rump, ejecting many wealthy men from what they considered to be their rightful places on the bench, the fears that some in the assembly were intent on turning the social order upside down were strengthened. Moreover, even though the assembly demonstrated its conservatism by arresting and bringing to trial the Leveller leader John Lilburne, the huge popular demonstrations in London that greeted Lilburne's acquittal were slotted into the image of an assembly intent on destruction rather than reformation.

What made this image also appear to be a reality to some was the threat that Barebone's Parliament seemed to pose to the army and religious liberty. It was only with some difficulty that defeat was secured for proposals in the assembly to abandon the assessment tax, the main source of army funding, and to make army officers forgo part of their pay. In the main official condemnation of Barebone's Parliament, *A True State of the Case of the Commonwealth*, Marchamont Nedham claimed that these moves endangered the nation's security. If the proposals had been taken up, 'all supplies must have been cut off likewise from the Navy, and our Affairs and friends left to sink or Swim in Ireland and Scotland; yes, and all this at such a time of unusual danger and necessity. When Scotland was unquiet [and] the Commonwealth engaged with Enemies abroad.'[30] This claim is not without some force, since during the second half of 1653 England's military control in Scotland, established in the aftermath of Cromwell's campaigns there in 1650–51, was seriously threatened by the outbreak of Glencairn's Rebellion in the Scottish Highlands. Negotiations to end the Anglo-Dutch war that had begun in 1652 might also have been endangered by the assembly's attacks on the army.

But it is likely that what caused more concern about these attacks is that they coincided with a challenge from a minority inside and outside Barebone's Parliament to the principle that was most dear to the army's heart: religious liberty. Nedham in *A True State* put at the head of his list of reasons why Barebone's Parliament had to be brought to an end the habit of some of its members of 'fastening a name of Antichristianism upon every thing they liked not'. They 'un-sainted every man, whose conscience was not of the same size with their own, and condemned all as Enemies to Reformation, who kept not an even peace with Themselves in the House'. As will be seen in later chapters, one of the consistent features of many radical Protestant groups in the 1650s was their refusal to extend the toleration they enjoyed from the regime to fellow Protestants with whom they disagreed. This was especially true in 1653 of Fifth Monarchist preachers in London like Christopher Feake and Vavasour Powell, who (in Nedham's words) 'pronounced all the Reformed Churches as the Out-Works to Babylon'.[31] As has been seen above, support for the Fifth Monarchy movement in Barebone's Parliament was small, but the assembly's image nevertheless came to be tarnished, as Cromwell's efforts to persuade radical preachers to cease their attacks on fellow Protestants fell on deaf ears.

Only just over a month after the first meeting of Barebone's Parliament Cromwell had begun to despair at the behaviour of some of his 'Christian friends' who, he wrote to Charles Fleetwood on 22 August, 'being of different judgements, and of each sort most seeking to propagate their own, that spirit of kindness that is to them all, is hardly accepted of any'.[32] In November he received a letter of intelligence from someone who echoed his own fears: 'If you take a survey of all the factions now displayed under the notion of religion … every one of them drives at an establishment of their owne, their owne members, their owne principles and opinions'.[33] One of the main conclusions of this chapter is that it is likely that, for many of those who engineered the fall of Barebone's Parliament and its replacement by the Protectorate, a concern to safeguard liberty of religious conscience was as important as a concern to safeguard property.

Notes

1 See W. Lamont, 'The Left and its past: revisiting the 1650s', *History Workshop Journal*, 23, 1987, for a critical assessment of the view of the Protectorate as 'years of retreat, the successive stages in the process of sell-out, by which the monarchy is restored in all but name well before 1660'. The quotation is from p. 142.

2 B.S. Capp, *The Fifth Monarchy Men: A Study in Seventeenth-Century Millenarianism* (London, 1972).

3 Edward Hyde, Earl of Clarendon, *History of the Rebellion* (ed. W. Macray, 6 vols, Oxford, 1888), vol. 5, p. 282.

4 Austin Woolrych, *Commonwealth to Protectorate* (Oxford, 1982). Much of this chapter relies on this excellent book.

5 Ivan Roots, ed., *Speeches of Oliver Cromwell* (London, 1998), pp. 23, 25.

6 John Hall, *A Letter to a Gentleman in the Country*, May 1653, quoted

in Woolrych, *Commonwealth to Protectorate*, p. 110.

7   C.H. Firth, ed., *Memoirs of Edmund Ludlow* (2 vols, Oxford, 1894), vol. 1, pp. 357–8. This source, too, is problematical. See Blair Worden, *Roundhead Reputation: The English Civil Wars and the Passions of Posterity* (London, 2001), chapters 1–4, which shows that Ludlow's 'Memoirs' were probably heavily edited by John Toland in the 1690s. On p. 11 Worden goes so far as to call the *Memoirs* 'a forgery; or rather a semi-forgery'. I take the view that, although Toland diluted Ludlow's religious zeal, he had no reason to tamper with Ludlow's account of episodes like the aftermath of the dissolution of the Rump.

8   Quoted in Woolrych, *Commonwealth to Protectorate*, p. 154.

9   Woolrych, *Commonwealth to Protectorate*, especially pp. 115–29, is the most persuasive account of the choice of members of Barebone's Parliament.

10   *Ibid.*, chapter 6: 'The quality of the House'.

11   *Ibid.*, chapter 7: 'Moderates and zealots', *passim*, especially pp. 209–17; Capp, *Fifth Monarchy Men*, p. 68.

12   The main contemporary accounts are *The Names of the Members of Parliament … Which Began on Monday the 4th of June [sic] 1653 … with the Severall Transactions Since That Time*, 1654, in *The Somers Collection of Tracts* (ed. W. Scott, 1811), vol. 6, pp. 255–7; *An Answer to a Paper Entitled a True Narrative*, 4 January 1654 (British Library, E725(21)); and two accounts from radical members of Barebone's Parliament, *A True Narrative of the Cause and Manner of the Dissolution of the Late Parliament up to 12 of December 1653* (British Library, E725(21)) and Samuel Highland, *An Exact Relation of the Proceedings and Transactions of the Late Parliament* in *Somers Tracts*, vol. 6, pp. 266–84.

13   Marchamont Nedham, *A True State of the Case of the Commonwealth*, 1654 (reprinted by the Rota Press, Exeter, 1978, from British Library, E728/5), p. 22.

14   Roots, ed., *Speeches of Oliver Cromwell*, p. 45.

15   *Ibid.*, p. 151.

16   Woolrych, *Commonwealth to Protectorate*, p. 343.

17   *Ibid.*, pp. 189–209; the quotations are from pp. 200, 201, 202–3.

18   David Farr, 'The military and political career of John Lambert 1619–57' (unpublished PhD thesis, University of Cambridge, 1996), chapter 4.

19   D.M. Wolfe, ed., *Leveller Manifestoes of the Puritan Revolution* (New York, 1944), p. 370.

20   For a fuller answer than is possible here, see Barry Coward, *Oliver Cromwell* (Harlow, 1991), especially pp. 105–14.

21   W.C. Abbott, ed., *The Writings and Speeches of Oliver Cromwell* (4 vols, Cambridge, Mass., 1937–47), vol. 2, p. 325.

22   *Ibid.*, vol. 2, p. 463.

23 *To the Supreame Authority the Parliament*, 12 August 1653, quoted in Peter Gaunt, *Oliver Cromwell* (Oxford, 1996), p. 136.

24 The fullest discussions are in B. Worden, *The Rump Parliament* (Cambridge, 1974), pp. 345–8; Woolrych, *Commonwealth to Protectorate*, chapter 3; and Sean Kelsey, *Inventing a Republic: The Political Culture of the English Commonwealth 1649–53* (Manchester, 1997), pp. 165–89.

25 Roots, ed., *Speeches of Oliver Cromwell*, p. 111.

26 Highland, *An Exact Relation*, p. 278; Nedham, *A True State*, pp. 13–14.

27 Highland, *An Exact Relation*, p. 278.

28 *A True Narrative*, p. 2.

29 Highland, *An Exact Relation*, p. 280.

30 Nedham, *A True State*, p. 19.

31 *Ibid.*, p. 14.

32 Abbott, ed., *Writings and Speeches*, vol. 3, p. 89.

33 Thomas Birch, ed., *A Collection of the State Papers of John Thurloe Esquire* (7 vols, London, 1742), vol. 1, pp. 591–2.

2

The first year of the Cromwellian Protectorate, December 1653 – January 1655

What kind of regime was the Protectorate during the first few months of its life? Since it was the only government in British history to have had a written constitution, this is an easier question to answer than it might otherwise have been. As will be seen in the first part of this chapter, an analysis of that constitution, the Instrument of Government, provides an important part of the answer. Yet, a fuller answer requires an examination of how the government worked in practice. Accordingly this chapter also addresses the question of who actually held power and made policy decisions in the early months of the Protectorate. It also aims to determine the priorities and intentions of the people at the centre of power in the Protectorate as they took up the reins of government. Did they follow a consistent programme in the period before the meeting of the first Protectorate Parliament in September 1654 or were they, like most other early modern regimes in Britain before and after them, merely responding to day-to-day pressures by a series of *ad hoc* decisions? And, if there was any consistency in what they did, was this merely to return to traditional ways of governing by promoting Cromwell as 'a king in all but name'?

Whatever the answer to those questions, it is certain that the Protectorate government before September 1654 was much more successful than it was during the meeting of the Protectorate Parliament between September 1654 and January 1655. As will be seen in the second part of this chapter, it is possible to exaggerate the 'failure' of this parliament. But the dominant theme of its brief history is the conflict between most MPs and the Protector and his Council. This raises the last major question that is discussed in this chapter: what were the causes of this troubled relationship that climaxed with Cromwell's abrupt and angry dissolution of the parliament in January 1655?

The Instrument of Government and rule by Lord Protector and Council, December 1653 – September 1654

The process by which the Instrument of Government was drafted is shrouded in secrecy. Just a few things are known about it. Even though the source is open to criticism, there seems little reason to question Edmund Ludlow's report of John Lambert's speech to the Council of Officers on 13 December 1653 when a draft of the Instrument of Government was read to them; it had been, according to Lambert, 'under consideration for two months past'.[1] Nor is there much doubt that Lambert, probably with the advice of a small group of fellow army officers, played a central role in the drafting process. But it is not possible to reconstruct the detailed negotiations that led to the final version of the new constitution that was made public after the installation of Cromwell as Lord Protector. Even the assumption that the early drafts of the constitution included the provision that Cromwell should be given the title of King has recently been questioned.[2] Yet the fact that Cromwell's recollection just over three years later, that seven army officers brought the Instrument of Government to him 'with the name of King on it', went unchallenged suggests that the offer was made.[3] But it had been dropped by the time the draft was read to the Council of Officers on 13 December, no doubt because Cromwell's objections to becoming King Oliver were as strong and decisive as they were to be in 1657. During the next few days further work was done amending the draft constitution 'in a clandestine manner carried on and huddled up by two or three persons'. It was, concluded Ludlow, 'a work of darkness'.[4] Consequently the ways in which the Instrument of Government was amended can only be the subject of speculation. It is not even certain when the drafting process was completed; it may have continued after the installation of Cromwell as Protector on 16 December, since the Instrument was not made available in print until 2 January 1654.[5]

Although there is great uncertainty about the way in which the Instrument of Government was drafted, there is very little about the content of the document.[6] Its drafters clearly drew directly for some of the details of the new constitution from two of the major constitutional proposals emanating from the army in the late 1640s, the Heads of the Proposals of 1647 and the Officers' Agreement of the People of 1649, as well as from the Rump's abortive 'Bill for a New Representative' of 1652–53. Most of the provisions in the Instrument of Government relating to the franchise, notably that voters should be non-Catholic males over the age of 21 who had at least £200 in real or personal possessions and who had not opposed parliament since 1642 or taken part in the Irish Rebellion, were taken from these three documents. The distribution of 400 seats to English counties and 30 seats each to Ireland and Scotland was also similar to the provisions of the 1649 version of the Agreement of the People and the Rump's Bill, marking a great reduction in the extent of borough representation and an increase in county representation compared with earlier parliaments. The central provision of the Instrument of Government – that the supreme legislative authority should be shared by 'a single person' (albeit a Lord Protector not a monarch) and 'the people assembled in parliament' – was also an echo of the aspirations of the drafters of the army proposals of 1647 and 1649.

But events that had taken place since 1649 also had a marked influence on the shape of the new constitution.[7] The Instrument of Government demonstrates a marked bias against 'over-mighty' parliaments, of the kind which its drafters clearly thought had ruled between 1649 and 1653. Their views are reflected in Marchamont Nedham's official defence of the new constitution, published in February 1654, *A True State of the Case of the Commonwealth*, which is peppered with diatribes against parliaments like the Rump Parliament. Although, as will be seen below, parliaments were given a far from insignificant place in the new constitution, it does not take a long examination of the Instrument of Government to see that many of its clauses put major limitations on parliamentary influence. According to Nedham, even the decision to separate the executive and legislative powers, which is one of the key features of the Instrument of Government, was made because of what had happened when both powers had been held by the Rump Parliament (document 1). Not only were parliaments stripped of executive power, but even the legislative powers given them by article 24 of the new constitution were more limited than they seem at first sight to be. By that article the Lord Protector was only given the power to veto parliamentary legislation for 20 days, after which it would automatically become law. But since this 'suspensive veto' was not to cover bills on important matters, like provisions for religious liberty, the maintenance of an army of 30,000 men and a large navy, and the frequency with which parliaments met and the length of time they sat, the scope of parliament's legislative freedom from the veto of the Lord Protector was very limited.

Moreover, three other articles of the constitution made inroads into the independent power of parliaments. Article 30 gave the Protector and Council the right to legislate before the first parliament met, a right that was used energetically, as will be seen. Article 12 stipulated that sheriffs acting as returning officers in parliamentary elections should send in returns that everyone elected 'shall not have power to alter the government as it is hereby settled in one single person and a Parliament', thus attempting to forestall the right of MPs to amend the new constitution. Finally, Protector and Council only needed to call parliaments once every three years and were empowered to dissolve parliaments after they had sat for only five months. If Peter Gaunt is right in suggesting that in the final drafting process the minimum duration of parliamentary sessions had been reduced from three years and the date for the first meeting of parliament had been put back from February to September, this would give even more emphasis to the mistrust of parliaments among the founders of the Protectorate than is apparent in the final constitution.[8]

Yet the Instrument of Government also clearly shows that they had not abandoned the aspirations of the 1640s. Three of these are reflected in it: a desire to give protection to a much wider range of Protestant religious views than ever before; a determination to ensure that parliaments should meet regularly, even if their powers were limited; and an eagerness to prevent the single person (albeit now a Lord Protector not a monarch) from having unbounded prerogative powers. The desire to prevent people from imposing their religious views on others is as strong in the Instrument of Government as it had been in the Heads of the Proposals in 1647. The Instrument decreed that 'the Christian religion, as contained in the Scriptures, be held forth and recommended as the public profession of these nations'. But like the drafters of the Heads, the authors of the Instrument made it illegal to use coercive powers against 'such as profess faith in God by Jesus Christ (though differing in judgment from the doctrine, worship or discipline publicly held forth)'. Such people were not to be 'restrained from, but shall be protected in the profession of the Faith, and exercise of their religion'. As in 1647, the main qualification to this religious 'liberty' was the exclusion from it of those who disturbed the peace and who practised 'popery', 'prelacy' and 'licentiousness'.

Similar strands of continuity can be seen in the Instrument's constitutional provisions. The drafters' mistrust of parliaments did not prevent them from making provisions for regular parliamentary sessions. Article 7 laid down that parliaments should meet once every third year; article 8 made it illegal for parliaments to be dissolved without their own consent until each session had lasted five months; and, more remarkably, article 11 made provisions that, if the Protector failed to call a parliament, then the Commissioner of the Great Seal would issue parliamentary writs. The drafters of the Instrument were also as careful to put limitations on the powers of the Lord Protector as had been the drafters of the army's constitutional proposals in 1647 to check those of the monarch. Indeed both used the Council as the main way of doing this. The main difference was that in 1653 the powers of the Council were much more extensive. Not only did various articles of the Instrument decree that the Protector should 'govern ... by the advice of the Council' (article 3) and that the Council should have a major say in the appointment of new councillors (article 15), but another made it compulsory for the Protector to make both orders regarding the army and navy and decisions about peace and war when parliament was not in session 'with the advice and consent of the major part of the council' (article 4). Furthermore, on the death of Oliver Cromwell, the Council was empowered to choose his successor (article 32).

The above analysis tells us a lot about the fears and intentions of the founders of the Protectorate. But it does not answer one of the most obvious questions that arises from it: how effective were these limitations on Cromwell's power *in practice*? Did Cromwell rule with the Protectorate Council? Unfortunately, the existing conciliar records, which merely record the decisions made by the Council, not how they were arrived at, do not provide a definitive answer. Yet, when taken together with other evidence, they do suggest two conclusions.

The first is that it is easy to exaggerate the limits that the Council put on Cromwell's exercise of power. Whatever the paper constitution said, the reality was that Cromwell dominated the political world at the start of the Protectorate to an extent that he had not done at any time previously, certainly not before April 1653. Historians have sometimes been guilty of overestimating Cromwell's influence and importance in the later 1640s and early 1650s, giving too little attention to the roles of people like Henry Ireton in the events that led to the revolutionary episode of 1648–49, and to major politicians like Sir Arthur Heselrige, Thomas Scot and Henry Marten who moulded events during the Commonwealth of 1649–53. But Cromwell's dissolution of the Rump by the use of military force demonstrated the decisive political power of the army and this fact had been confirmed, if that were necessary, by the coup that had led to the end of Barebone's Parliament. Although, as will be seen, a few soldiers opposed this political use of military might, they were exceptions and their opposition was ineffective. Most of the leading generals in the army were tied to Cromwell by family or other influences; for example, John Desborough was his brother-in-law and Charles Fleetwood his son-in-law. Within the Council, too, were many men who had similar close connections with the Protector; for example, Henry Lawrence and Edward Montague were related to him by blood or marriage. Even John Thurloe, who came to have a position at the heart of the Protectorate as its Secretary of State, had been Cromwell's legal agent since at least 1647, when he was steward of the estates granted to Cromwell by parliament.[9] The only potentially effective focus of opposition to Cromwell within the army and Council was John Lambert, and he, as yet, showed no signs of challenging Cromwell's supremacy. The prime fact of political life in these circumstances was that Cromwell held the key to power. It is unlikely that any major decision was ever made without his approval.

But the work of Peter Gaunt has authoritatively established a second conclusion: that the Protectorate Council was far from being a rubber stamp.[10] Certainly this was Cromwell's own view.

When parliament met in September 1654, he told it, approvingly:

> The council are the trustees of the Commonwealth, in all intervals of Parliaments, who have as absolute a negative voice upon the supreme officer in the said intervals, as the Parliament hath whilst it is sitting. It cannot be made use of, a man cannot be raised nor a penny charged upon the people, nothing can be done without the consent of Parliament; and in the intervals of Parliament, without the consent of the Council it is not to be exercised.[11]

Later he had obviously become less happy with the situation, judging by the acerbic tone of his complaint in 1657 that under the 1653 constitution 'I was a child in its swaddling clouts. I cannot transgress by the [Instrument of] Government. I can do nothing but in ordination with the Council.'[12] Cromwell's comments exaggerate the power of the Council, but it was not only Cromwell who believed that the power given to the Council by the Instrument of Government was not a sham. The Dutch ambassadors, after receiving in March 1654 a document containing proposals as part of the peace negotiations designed to end the Anglo-Dutch war, sent it back. They would not consider it, they insisted, until it had been 'signed in a clearer form by the Council of State'.[13] What seems to have happened during this early part of the Protectorate, at least, is that although all major policy decisions were finally approved by the Protector, he was content to leave the day-to-day government to the Council, attending only 39 of its 202 meetings between December 1653 and September 1654. This gives substance to claims that the Council's power and influence were more extensive than those of the royal Privy Council in the political world of Stuart rule in the early and later seventeenth century. This was one way, but (as will be seen) not the only way, in which the Protectorate government differed from the government of Stuart monarchs.

Who, then, were the Protectorate councillors who contributed with Cromwell to the making of policy in the first year of the Protectorate and did they have anything in common? The original 15 members named in the Instrument of Government in addition to Cromwell were Henry Lawrence, John Lambert, Charles Fleetwood, Philip Skippon, John Desborough, Edward Montague, William Sydenham, Sir Anthony Ashley Cooper, Sir Charles Wolseley, Sir Gilbert Pickering, Francis Rous, Richard Major, Philip Jones, Walter Strickland and Philip Sidney, Viscount

Lisle. Of these, only Lambert, Fleetwood, Skippon and Desborough were still serving soldiers, and with the later addition in February, April and June 1654 respectively of Humphrey Mackworth, Nathaniel Fiennes (younger son of Lord Saye and Sele) and Edmund Sheffield, Earl of Mulgrave, the Council took on an even more 'civilian' complexion. Yet it is probable that any divisions in the Council between its 'military' and 'civilian' members are not significant, since, after all, some of its 'civilian' members, like Ashley Cooper, had been soldiers in the Civil War.

Rather than any dubious 'military–civilian' differences between them, it is more important to emphasise that what most of them had in common was their close personal and family connections with Cromwell, as well as the shared political experience of attempting to make government work in the aftermath of the expulsion of parliament in April 1653. Most of them had been members of either the Council of State between July and December 1653 or Barebone's Parliament, and, as such, had become increasingly frustrated at the obstacles that had been put in the way of achieving the twin causes of reformation and liberty of conscience during these months. All of them shared a desire to push ahead with reform as rapidly as possible. This may have been given further impetus by the reappearance of Oliver St John as Cromwell's informal adviser; St John had been closely associated with Cromwell in the 1640s in the pursuit of godly reformation, but had broken with him at the time of the King's trial and execution. Throughout the Protectorate he was (according to Derek Hirst) 'at the Protector's elbow'.[14] Consequently, in a manner not unlike that of modern governments made up of politicians who take up the reins of power after having spent years of frustration in opposition, the Protector and Council seized the opportunity of the moment to such an extent that it is possible that many historians have underestimated the scale and significance of what they attempted and achieved in the months before the first Protectorate Parliament met in September 1654.

In the space of just eight months the Council discussed over 200 draft ordinances, of which over 80 became law. This was done under the terms of article 30 of the Instrument of Government, which allowed the Protector and Council to issue ordinances before the meeting of the first Protectorate Parliament in September 1654 'for the peace and welfare of these nations, where it shall be necessary, which shall be binding and in force, until order shall be taken in parliament for the same'. In his important study of these ordinances Ivan Roots wrote: 'that anyone visualised using this clause as an opportunity to bring in a great programme of reform seems doubtful. Nor in the event was there one.'[15] Most historians have followed that view, making the assumption that the drafters of the Instrument of Government merely intended to allow the Protector and Council to pass routine measures necessary to enable the government to continue until parliament met. Undoubtedly some of the ordinances passed and the decisions made by Protector and Council between December 1653 and September 1654 can be classified in this way.[16] Many (but not all) of the financial ordinances were essential measures to ensure that customs duties, excise, assessments and other taxes continued to be collected. Ordinances were also passed (like one in December 1653 that authorised the use of the title of 'Lord Protector' in legal proceedings) to ensure that the business of the law courts was not interrupted by the change of regime. Foreign affairs, too, had to be dealt with and the Council accordingly concluded treaties with the Dutch in April 1654 and with other European powers shortly afterwards.[17]

However, the character of many other ordinances, together with other government decisions that were made at this time, suggests that the new Protectorate was not simply a government intent on dealing with business on an *ad hoc* basis, but rather that it was attempting to begin a longer-term programme aimed at 'settlement' and 'reformation', a programme which it did not believe parliament could be trusted to carry out.

Of these two central aims of the new Protectorate, the first has generally been given greater attention and emphasis in accounts of this period. There is no doubt that those at the centre of power were anxious to cultivate the support of as many people as possible. When the first Protectorate Parliament met, as will be seen, it became clear that the events of 1653 had alienated many of the supporters of the British republic. But even before September 1654 those in power were already aware of the unease many felt towards a regime that depended so heavily on military force. Not surprisingly, therefore, major efforts were made by the new regime to woo support by making the regime seem as traditional as possible and one that, unlike Barebone's Parliament, was not a threat to the existing social and political order.

Consequently, one of the early decisions of the Council, made at its first meeting on 16 December 1653, was to order all sheriffs to publish a document 'proclaiming His Highness Oliver Cromwell Lord Protector of the Commonwealth of England, Scotland and Ireland'. The choice of 'Commonwealth', which, like 'His Highness', was a familiar word used in contemporary political discourse, was surely meant to reassure anxious conservative opinion. So too was an ordinance approved by Protector and Council on 19 January 1654 repealing an act passed by the Rump in 1650 that had made it compulsory for all adult males to take the Engagement, an oath of allegiance to the republic that included a public acknowledgement of the legality of the abolition of monarchy and the House of Lords. Oaths like these, the Council conceded, had 'proved burthens and snares to tender consciences'.[18]

No doubt, too, the regime's rapid adoption of regal ceremonies, iconography and practices during the first weeks of its existence was done in part in order to convince these 'tender consciences' that it was a bulwark against anyone who threatened property and the traditional social order.[19] With this intent the Council ordered that all former royal palaces be given to Cromwell, and he and his family soon moved into Whitehall Palace and Hampton Court; these were refurbished and some of the tapestries that had hung there during the residence of Charles I were restored. There too, as Roy Sherwood has shown, the Protector established a Cromwellian Court that was regal in style.[20] What is more, Cromwell's visit to the City of London on 8 February followed the ceremonial precedents of monarchs. Cromwell himself even underlined the traditional nature of the occasion by knighting the Lord Mayor. There also seems to have been a conscious effort to follow royal precedents in the way the regime conducted its diplomacy. The Protectorate's conduct of its foreign affairs was as formal as that of any early modern European monarch. It is arguable that Roy Sherwood is justified in claiming that all this indicates that Cromwell was 'a king in all but name', anxious to make the Protectorate a carbon copy of the Stuart monarchy.[21] Yet it is more likely that what it reflects is simply a regime intent on 'settlement' and anxious to gain as wide an acceptance in the country as possible.

The new regime soon made it clear that it had other aims than transforming itself into a Stuart-style monarchy. 'Reformation', as well as 'settlement', was high on its agenda, and in order to set it in motion the Council delegated tasks to small groups of councillors who were ordered not only to respond to petitions that flooded in but also to draft ordinances. An examination of their work suggests that they interpreted their brief to pass ordinances that were essential 'for the peace and welfare of these nations' as a green light to begin to undertake fundamental reforms. In particular, two sets of ordinances passed in 1654 deserve to be seen as much more than emergency measures to meet short-term problems: those that were intended to effect fundamental change in the way the British Isles were governed, and those that tackled the problems of reforming the law and the Church.

The Protectorate inherited a unique legacy from its republican predecessors. Never before had any regime been in effective control of all the British Isles. By December 1653 only the Highlands of Scotland, which were in the grip of a revolt led by the Earl of Glencairn and Lieutenant-General John Middleton, remained to be conquered and occupied by English troops. The situation was reflected in the Instrument of Government's provision that MPs from Scotland and Ireland should sit in Protectorate parliaments that met in London. The intentions of those at the centre of power during the early years of the Protectorate regarding these conquered nations were threefold: that the military conquests of Scotland and Ireland should be made secure by the maintenance of large standing armies of occupation; that those in both countries who had opposed the English in the 1640s and early 1650s should be punished; and that both countries should be reformed on English lines. In these respects the Protectorate adopted the British policies of the Rump. Also like the Rump, the Protector and Council intended to impose these policies much more severely and uncompromisingly on Ireland than on Scotland.

The outlines of the punitive Irish settlement were set out in the Act for the Settlement of Ireland passed by the Rump in August 1652. It is difficult to imagine a more draconian measure. Although the Act began by declaring that 'it is not the intention of the Parliament to extirpate the whole Nation', the terms that followed provided for the executions of large numbers of Irish people and for the confiscation of the land of most Catholic landowners, who were to be transported to land in the west of

Ireland (document 25). The extent to which these terms were fully implemented during the Protectorate will be discussed in chapter 7, but there is much evidence to suggest that Cromwell and the Council *initially intended* to pursue fully the Rump's punitive Irish policies. This is the conclusion to be drawn from the appointment of Charles Fleetwood, a man who had no compunction in riding roughshod over the interests of the native Irish, as Lord Deputy of Ireland early in 1654. Henry Cromwell, the Protector's son, visited Ireland in the spring of 1654 and advised the Council to conciliate Irish Protestant opinion. But the Council chose to ignore this advice and instead favoured Fleetwood's approach. During the first months of the Protectorate Fleetwood and his Council in Dublin began to carry out vigorously the transplantation policy. In June 1654 the Council also issued an ordinance to 'encourage' the settlement of English adventurers who had been allotted land in Ireland since the early 1640s.

There is even more evidence that the Protectorate initially adopted the broad thrust of the Rump's policies for the settlement of Scotland. These policies had been made clear in a declaration of October 1651 offering union with England to the Scots (document 24). It is true that this reflected the less severe attitude that most English Protestants held towards Presbyterian Scots than towards Catholic Irish. Cromwell was no exception when he said in 1649 that 'I had rather be overrun with a Scottish interest than an Irish interest; and I think of all this is most dangerous'.[22] During his Scottish campaigns in 1650–51 Cromwell had made great efforts to win the Scots over by argument, only resorting to military force and conquest when this failed. This attitude accounts for the fact that, in marked contrast to the Act for the Settlement of Ireland, the declaration regarding Scotland offered union to the Scots. But within the velvet glove was an iron fist. The declaration decreed that all who had assisted the Stuarts in the wars of 1648 and 1650–51 were to have their estates confiscated. Moreover, in reality the offer of union was one that the Scots could not refuse. It was also one that, unlike the union of 1707, was an explicit threat to the independence of Scottish government, law and the Kirk. This was the union that was legalised by a Protectorate ordinance in April 1654.

While there were reforming aspirations as well as coercion in the Protectorate's British policies, these can hardly be said to amount to a 'British vision' designed to create a new British state from the separate kingdoms of England, Ireland and Scotland. What the regime seems to have intended was the anglicisation of the British Isles. Judging from the statements that Cromwell made during his military campaigns in Ireland in 1649–50, what he had in mind was the exportation to Ireland of the kind of changes aimed at social justice and godly reformation that he wanted to bring about in England. In 1649, shortly after he landed in Ireland, he wrote that under English rule it would be possible to establish in Ireland

> a way of doing justice amongst these poor people, which, for the uprightness and cheapness of it, may exceedingly gain upon them, who have been accustomed to as much injustice, tyranny and oppression from their landlords, the great men, and those that should have done them right, as, I believe, any people in that which you call Christendom ... they having been inured thereto. Sir, if justice were freely and impartially administered here, the foregoing darkness and corruption would make it look so much the more glorious and beautiful; and draw more hearts after it.

Shortly after, he compared Ireland to a 'clean paper':

> capable of being governed by such laws as should be found most agreeable to justice; which may be so impartially administered, as to be a good precedent even to England itself; where when they once perceive propriety preserved at an easy and cheap rate in Ireland, they will never permit themselves to be so cheated and abused as now they are.[23]

These aspirations may have still been in his mind in the early years of the Protectorate. At that time, though, more thought seems to have been put into how the 'benefits' of English justice and reform could be brought to Scotland. Three Scottish ordinances issued by the Council in April 1654 granted the Scots free trade within the British union, and abolished feudal dues, servitude and vassalage, and hereditary sheriffdoms. In the spirit of the 1652 declaration, which promised that the Scots within the union would live 'like a free People, delivered (through Gods goodnesse) from their former slaveries, vassalage and oppressions', the ordinances decreed that tenants should have security of tenure and justice dispensed by English judges, justices of the peace and courts baron freed from the corrupting influence of Scottish nobles. A fourth ordinance 'for Pardon and Grace' exempted all but 24 named individuals and those implicated in Glencairn's Rising from the penalties decreed in 1651, marking a move away from the punitive policies of the Rump. As will be seen in chapter 7, this moderation would later be taken further in Ireland as well as in Scotland. But as yet there were few signs that the Protectorate intended to deviate from policies designed to impose an English uniformity on the whole of the British Isles.

The timing of the Scottish ordinances was no doubt determined by the imminent conclusion of the Anglo-Dutch peace, which meant that the Council could turn its full attention to the problems of subduing and then governing Scotland. It is no coincidence that the appointment of General George Monck as a strong commander-in-chief in Scotland, with the resources to suppress Glencairn's Rising that had been denied to his predecessor, Robert Lilburne, was also made in April 1654. But this ought not to obscure the fact that these Scottish ordinances were the result of nearly four months of meetings of a sub-committee of councillors that had been working since 26 December 1653.

Similar concerted and detailed planning lay behind the ordinances that were intended to bring about major changes in the financial structure of the British government. In particular, two financial ordinances of 21 June and 2 September 1654 were designed to simplify the Protectorate's revenue system by remodelling the Exchequer as the main institution responsible for collecting the regime's income, which derived from the excise tax, the confiscated estates of royalists and Catholic recusants, as well as the assessment tax. The complex structure of overlapping bodies that had been established to administer these new sources of income since the start of the Civil War was simplified, and the reconstituted Exchequer was to be run by treasury commissioners who were supported by a paid secretariat.

The same effort, attention to detail and zeal to expedite government efficiency on the part of the Council at this time can also be seen in the work resulting in the ordinance of September 1654 that reformed the postal service, the gestation of which has been revealed by Peter Gaunt's impressive research.[24] By the ordinance the Council granted the contract to run the postal service to John Manley for two years on payment of £10,000 p.a. But the Council was careful to establish in the ordinance such details as the routes that Manley was to service, the speed at which inland letters should be conveyed and charges for posting private letters.

The Council's efficiency and reforming energy in matters relating to the way the British Isles were governed is a great contrast to the Rump's foot-dragging on reform.[25] The contrast between the achievements of the early Protectorate and the Rump is even greater with regard to the law and the Church. This is largely accounted for by the fact that Cromwell, while leaving the day-to-day details of business to the Council, played a key role in determining the shape of legal and ecclesiastical reform and in ensuring that the reform process did not stagnate or get sidetracked through the efforts of its opponents. There is no better witness to this than the man who probably had more daily contact with Cromwell than anyone else. John Thurloe, soon to become the Secretary of State in the Protectorate, was in no doubt that 'the great things his highness sets himself to [are] the reformation of the law and the ministry'.[26]

Cromwell's initiative can be clearly seen in influencing the course of reform of the law. As with most topics it discussed, the Council set up a sub-committee for the reform of the law, consisting of William Strickland and the newly appointed councillor and lawyer Humphrey Mackworth. Potentially ominous for the prospect of legal reform, however, was the decision (reported by Thurloe to Bulstrode Whitelocke in January 1654) to commit the crucial matter of reform of Chancery to 'the learned of the profession', i.e. Sir Thomas Widdrington, a Chancery commissioner, Edmund Prideaux, the Attorney General, and Chaloner Chute, a barrister who practised in Chancery. Not surprisingly, this vested interest group had failed to produce any reform proposals by the time that the law courts resumed their sitting in May after the Easter recess. By July Fleetwood was extremely gloomy about the situation. 'It is much to be wondered at that the regulation of the law goes on slowly', he wrote to Thurloe from Dublin. 'I know your hands are full, and fear that we may be too hasty in expectation; but the eyes of all are upon my lord, and if ever these considerations [law reform and tithes] come before a parliament, where there will be such a diversity of interests, I fear it may prove as fatal as both have been in the last two parliaments.'[27]

By this time, however, Cromwell had taken two initiatives to push ahead with reform before parliament met: on 18 June he met the conciliar committee stressing the urgency of making progress, and, of more importance, he brought William Sheppard to London to act as his legal adviser. Sheppard's main law book, *England's Balme*, was not published until 1656, but already Sheppard had made a name for himself in Gloucestershire as a proponent of legal reform and as a champion of religious Independency. As such he fitted in well with the circle around the Protector and it is likely that he had a major role in drafting the 67 articles of the Chancery ordinance that was presented to the Council and given two readings on 13 July, and then sent to the conciliar sub-committee for final drafting before being approved by the Protector and issued on 21 August 1654.

The ordinance made many procedural changes aimed at avoiding the delays for which Chancery was infamous. For example, article 8 enabled JPs to act as Chancery officials to take depositions from litigants locally without waiting for them to travel to London, and article 41 made provisions for the court to sit in the afternoons as well as mornings to ensure that cases were held on the appointed days. It also restricted the scope for corruption by making it illegal for judges to sell court offices (article 67); and major steps forward were made to improve the court's fairness and efficiency by establishing an appeals court that consisted of common law judges as well as Chancery commissioners (article 63) and by restricting the scope of Chancery's jurisdiction (articles 49–53, 66–8). To Cromwell the latter was worthy of note when he opened the first Protectorate Parliament in September 1654: 'the things depending there [in Chancery] which made a burden of the work of honourable persons entrusted in those services beyond their ability, it hath referred many of them to those places where Englishmen love to have their rights tried, the courts of law at Westminster'.[28] Historians may have underestimated the importance of these changes; contemporaries did not. The bitter reactionary opposition of Whitelocke, Widdrington and other lawyers to them when they were put into effect in 1655 is an indication that the Chancery ordinance was a significant measure of law reform.[29]

The spring and summer of 1654 also saw the Protector pushing the Council to take significant steps towards making a Cromwellian religious settlement. As has been seen, the aspirations of Cromwell and those around him to extend religious liberty to 'such as profess faith in God by Jesus Christ (though differing in judgement from the doctrine, worship and discipline publicly held forth)' had been set out in the Instrument of Government. This aim was probably strengthened by the stream of petitions received from local congregations by the Protector and Council in these early months asking for 'godly' ministers to be confirmed in their posts, and even more by the addresses of 'congratulation' sent in from some localities.[30] These urged the regime to realise their hopes for effecting a godly reformation by an alliance of sympathetic magistrates and ministers (see document 2).

The basic outline of a scheme to fill this need was at hand in the Humble Proposals. This document, submitted to the Rump in February 1652 by religious Independents, including Cromwell's chaplain, John Owen, and Philip Nye and Thomas Goodwin, advocated a national Church controlled by commissioners who would examine candidates for the ministry and eject existing ministers who were deemed to be unfit. On 1 March 1654 Nye and Goodwin, assisted by William Sheppard and four councillors, met to draft an ordinance that was published three weeks later establishing a London-based commission for the approbation of ministers (popularly known as triers). The commission included religious Independents, Presbyterians and a few Baptists, illustrating the breadth of Cromwellian religious liberty. In August 1654 the second part of the Cromwellian Church structure was put in place by an ordinance establishing ejectors: local commissions to investigate ministers in post and, if necessary, to eject those found to be ungodly. On 3 September another Church ordinance was published encouraging the union of parishes to meet the demand for preaching ministers. A conciliar committee tried to find alternative means of paying ministers other than by tithes. Sheppard's comment in his *The Parson's Guide; or the Law of Tithes* (published on 15 June 1654) illustrates the aspiration of many around Cromwell as well as the magnitude of the task they faced: 'I wish they [tithes] were taken away, so that … a more convenient way of maintenance thereof be provided for the ministers; but this I will suppose will ask time'.[31] That was an understatement to say the least, for it was a problem that was never resolved. But within a few months the Council had at least succeeded in laying the foundations of a new Church settlement.

It would be wrong to exaggerate the scale of the reformation achieved by Protector and Council between December 1653 and

September 1654. Moreover, one gets the distinct impression that as the time for the calling of the first Protectorate Parliament drew nearer, the Council's reforming zeal gradually became blunted by the sheer weight of business with which it had to deal.[32] But in contrast to the Rump Parliament, the Protector and Council had made an efficient and energetic start towards reformation. When in the summer of 1654, under the terms of the Instrument of Government, they issued writs for parliamentary elections, they must have hoped that their work would be continued by the first Protectorate Parliament when it met in September.

The first Protectorate Parliament, September 1654 – January 1655

In his keynote speech at the opening of parliament on 4 September 1654, Cromwell trumpeted the achievements of the previous months. To make the most of these he skilfully painted a dark picture of

> what condition ... these nations were, when this government was undertaken ... Every man's hand almost was against his brother ... Was not everything almost grown arbitrary ... The magistracy of the nation, was it not almost trampled under foot, under despite and contempt by men of Levelling principles? ... Indeed in spiritual things, the case was more sad and deplorable ... The prodigious blasphemies, contempt of God and Christ, denying of him and his ordinances and of the Scriptures ... The axe was laid to the root of the Ministry, it was Antichristian, it was Babylonish.

Protector and Council, he argued, had saved the country from this dire situation, this 'heap of confusions', which was exacerbated by foreign war, 'consuming our treasure, occasioning a vast burden upon the people'. Peace had been made with the Dutch, treaties concluded with France, Denmark and Portugal, and the work of reformation had been initiated at home. Significantly, he highlighted this point by referring to what the government had done on legal and religious reform. 'It hath called together persons, without reflection of as great ability and as great integrity as are in these nations, to consider how the laws might be made plain and short, and less chargeable to the people ... And those things are in preparation and Bills prepared ... The Chancery hath been reformed.' Steps had been taken to ensure that only

41

'men of piety' were appointed to the ministry and that all those 'who are scandalous, and who are the common scorn and contempt of the administration' were expelled from it. But this, he made clear to MPs, must be only the beginning. 'These are but entrances and doors of hope, wherein through the blessing of God you may enter into rest and peace. But you are not entered.' Referring to the sermon that had preceded the opening of parliament, he went on to emphasise the point by reference to a biblical parallel that (it will be seen) he was to use often. 'You were told today of a people brought out of Egypt towards the land of Canaan, but, through unbelief, murmuring, repining, and other temptations and sins, wherewith God was provoked, they were fain to come back again, and linger many years in the wilderness, before they came to the place of rest.' The lesson was obvious: like the Israelites the people of Britain needed to regain God's blessing by undergoing a period of reformation. Then, he went on, echoing the phraseology of the addresses he received from the godly in the localities, 'if the Lord's blessing and his presence go along with the management of affairs at this meeting, you will be enabled to put the top-stone to this work'.[33]

It would have been difficult for any assembly to live up to these high expectations, and the first Protectorate Parliament spectacularly failed to do so. It is true that it was not quite as barren of achievements as many in the past have imagined. It did set about the task of drafting and discussing bills, as well as dealing with local petitions and day-to-day matters. It is also true that, when it set about amending the Instrument of Government, the MPs were not in conflict with Protector and Council on every clause of the constitution.[34] But there is no real reason to dispute the familiar picture of this parliament spending more time on opposition to and amendment of the Instrument of Government than on anything else. So engrossed did it get in this task that in December it decided not to proceed with any legislation until an amended constitution in the form of a Government Bill had been concluded. By the time it was dissolved it had put not one item of new legislation on the statute book. Cromwell's charge when he sent this parliament packing on 22 January 1655 is not without some truth: he told MPs that they had not passed 'the good and wholesome laws which the people expected of you and might have answered the grievances ... proper to you as a Parliament'.[35]

To what extent and why did relations between the Protector and his Council and the first Protectorate Parliament become so soured?

Cromwell and the Council were not unwilling that parliament should discuss and if necessary amend the Instrument of Government, and they may well have invited it to do so. But they expected that this would be a short process involving only minor constitutional revisions, before parliament moved on to what they considered to be the more important work of reformation that they had begun before parliament met. That it was unlikely that this would happen became apparent from the first few days' parliamentary proceedings. Although the prime source for these, the journal of the MP for King's Lynne, Guibon Goddard, is very sparse, it reflects the ferocity of the attack made by MPs between 5 and 11 September on the basic principle of government by a single person and a parliament, led by those who had been leading members of the Rump, particularly Sir Arthur Heselrige and Thomas Scot. For these so-called 'Commonwealthsmen' the Protectorate was an illegal regime ruling solely by a military force that had violated parliamentary sovereignty on 20 April 1653 (document 3).

Until this point Protector and Council had made no extensive attempt to use the right given them by the Instrument of Government to exclude MPs. Probably only as few as eight had been prevented by the Council from sitting before the session began. But the bitterness of the Commonwealthsmen's attacks on the Protectorate now stung it into making a much more extensive purge of MPs. When MPs came for the start of the parliamentary session on 12 September they were subjected to an angry speech by the Protector, in which he picked out four 'fundamentals' of the constitution that should not be tampered with.[36] One of these – government by a single person and a parliament – was included in a document ('the recognition') that all members who wished to continue sitting were forced to sign. Eventually between 50 and 80 MPs refused to do so, including most of the Commonwealthsmen.[37]

But the purge, which was on a much smaller scale than that in the second Protectorate Parliament, had little real effect. During the next few weeks criticism of the Instrument of Government continued to dominate parliamentary proceedings, demonstrating that opposition to the new constitution was not confined to the Commonwealthsmen, but was shared by many people, including a few within the army. In November 1654 the petition of three colonels, Thomas Saunders, John Okey and Matthew Alured, which was probably drafted by the former Leveller John Wildman, pilloried the drafters of the Instrument of Government for putting the control of the army into the hands of one person, who, if corrupt, would be able to 'destroy Parliament and bring us under vassalage' (document 4).[38] This view was also rife among opinion outside the army and was voiced by MPs in the first Protectorate Parliament who survived the purge of September 1654.

Consequently the predominant theme of the entire parliamentary session was the attempt to redraft the Instrument of Government and replace it with a 'Government Bill'. Day after day from morning to night MPs debated every clause of the Instrument of Government, attempting to revise many of them in order to increase the powers of parliament at the expense of those of Protector and Council. Their aim was nothing short of replacing Lambert's constitution with a new one of their own. Goddard's notes of the speeches record condemnations of the arbitrary power of Protector and Council with ringing declarations of the need to restore parliamentary rights and liberties. In the debates on 2 October, in demanding a greater parliamentary voice in the making of peace and war in articles 52 and 53 of the Government Bill, MPs condemned the authority given to Protector and Council in the Instrument as 'an arbitrary power' that amounted to 'a power over our estates, our persons, and our lives. And this was an undoubted right of Parliament, that no tax can be made, no man's person impressed, nor their lives exposed to arbitrary martial laws but by consent of Parliament.'

Later in the month MPs made even more fundamental claims for parliamentary power by drafting a clause in the Government Bill (article 2) that gave parliament (in co-operation with the Protector) the right to alter the constitution (whereas the Instrument had made no provision for any alteration to it) and by claiming in article 3 of the new bill that the election of future Protectors should be in ways 'such as parliament shall think fit' (whereas the Instrument had given that right to the Council alone). 'It was a fundamental right inherent in the Parliament, to choose their supreme officers', Goddard records one MP saying. 'Something of authority was alleged, in all ages, even from Caesar's time, downwards, how kings have been elected, or approved and confirmed by Parliaments … The original rights of the people, being intrusted with the Parliament, they cannot depute or delegate the trust to another.' In the debate on 2 December in support of articles 39 and 40 of the new bill giving parliament a greater voice in Council elections, one MP claimed that this would ensure that the Council was 'the Council of the Commonwealth and the Parliament's Trustees'.[39]

It is not difficult to imagine the anger and frustration of Cromwell and the Council at the way precious parliamentary time was being used in constitutional revision at the expense of what they considered to be the more important work of reformation. What must have intensified this attitude was the growing evidence that most MPs were as hostile to the cause of religious liberty and to the army as were many of those who had sat in the Rump and Barebone's Parliaments (and indeed in the Long Parliament before it was purged in 1648). On 12 September 1654 Cromwell had spelled out to MPs aspects that were in his view 'fundamental' to good government: government by a single person and a parliament; frequent election of parliaments avoiding the 'evil' of perpetual parliaments; liberty of conscience in religion; and the shared control of the army by Protector and parliament.[40] MPs had been bludgeoned into accepting the first. They accepted the second by approving the Instrument of Government's provision for triennial parliaments. But it gradually became clear in the debates on the Government Bill that the opposition of most MPs to the last two of Cromwell's 'fundamentals' of government was much more intractable.

By mid-November 1654 the gulf between most MPs and the Protector and Council over the extent of religious liberty that could be allowed was already so great that Cromwell refused to co-operate with a Commons committee on religion about the religious clause in the Government Bill. The Protector, it was reported, 'was wholly dissatisfied with the thing … and that the Parliament had already taken the [Instrument of] Government abroad (in pieces was meant) and had altered and changed it, in the other articles, as they pleased, without his advice; and therefore, it would not become him to give any advice … as to this article'.[41] By 7 December, when the committee's report was published, the gulf on the religious issue had become even greater. The committee recommended that parliament should have a greater control over the kind of religious beliefs that were to be tolerated and the subsequent debates soon made it clear that most MPs had a much more limited definition of 'religious liberty' than did the Protector and those around him. MPs and Council were not all that far apart on the parliamentary decision to order that John Biddle's anti-trinitarian book, *His Twelve Arguments Refuting the Common Opinion of the Deity of the Holy Ghost*, be burned by the common hangman. But as the force of parliamentary religious intolerance gathered pace, Cromwell and Council held back from fully endorsing the condemnation of Biddle. In the day-long parliamentary debate on 11 December 1654 'damnable heresies' were enumerated that, if they were made liable to punishment (as a minority of MPs pointed out), 'might expose the godly party, and people hereafter, to some danger of suffering under the law'.[42] Articles 42 and 43 of the Government Bill proposed significant parliamentary control over religious beliefs that were to be tolerated and some MPs even demanded that the laws restricting religious liberty should be excluded from the Protector's right to veto legislation. Cromwell's disillusionment is well captured in his reaction to a petition from London in support of parliamentary religious intolerance: 'Where shall we have men of a Universal Spirit? Everyone desires to have liberty but none will give it.'[43]

What reinforced this concern among Cromwell and the Council was the sustained attacks on the army that accompanied this erosion of religious liberty. Parliamentary demands for the reduction of the monthly assessments to pay for the army from £90,000 to £30,000 and for a large reduction in the standing army and the establishment of local militias were met by conciliar concessions to lower the assessment to £60,000. But Protector and Council realised that they could concede nothing to meet MPs' demands that parliament should control the army. To do so, said a Cromwellian supporter in a debate on 20 November, 'would be to give up the cause, that eminent and glorious cause, which hath been so much and so long contended for since Parliaments might hereafter be chosen as would betray the glorious cause of the people of God'. But this was a view that received only minority support, and the majority of MPs voted that after Cromwell's death control of the army should pass to parliament (articles 45–7 of the new bill), since it was argued that otherwise parliament would be a mere 'Jack-a-Lent ... For, give any single person in the world but power, and you give him a temptation to continue and engross that power wholly to himself, and an opportunity to effect it.'[44]

A combination of reasons led to Cromwell's impulsive decision to dissolve the first Protectorate Parliament on 22 January 1655 after it had sat for only five lunar months (even less than the minimum five months' period decreed in the Instrument of Government). Among these was the disappointment of the hopes that it would continue the work of reformation begun so energetically by Protector and Council before it met. But more important, even than parliament's failure to carry out reforms and maintain liberty for tender consciences, was its hostile attitude to the army. As Cromwell pointed out in his dissolution speech, if control of the army

> should be yielded up at such a time as this when there is as much need to keep the cause by it ... what would become of all? ... It [the army] determines his [the Protector's] power, either for doing the good he aught, or hindering Parliaments from perpetuating themselves, or from imposing what religions they please on the consciences of men, or what government they please upon the nation.[45]

Nothing could more clearly indicate that, as in April and December 1653, the first Protectorate Parliament was dissolved in the belief that if parliament had been allowed to continue, not only would the cause of reformation have made no further progress while it sat, but the chances of bringing it about at any time in the future would have gone for ever.

Notes

1   C.H. Firth, ed., *Memoirs of Edmund Ludlow* (2 vols, Oxford, 1894), vol. 1, p. 369. See chapter 1, note 1, above for doubts about the authenticity of Ludlow's *Memoirs*.

2   David Farr, 'The military and political career of John Lambert, 1619–57' (unpublished PhD thesis, University of Cambridge, 1996), p. 289.

3   W.C. Abbott, ed., *The Writings and Speeches of Oliver Cromwell* (4 vols, Cambridge, Mass., 1937–47), vol. 4, p. 418. The contemporary evidence suggesting that the first drafts of the Instrument of Government included the kingship proposal is examined in A.H. Woolrych, *Commonwealth to Protectorate* (Oxford, 1983), pp. 354–5.

4   Firth, ed., *Memoirs of Edmund Ludlow*, vol. 1, p. 371.

5   Peter Gaunt, 'Drafting the Instrument of Government: a reappraisal', *Parliamentary History*, 8, 1989, *passim*. See also G.D. Heath, 'Making the Instrument of Government', *Journal of British Studies*, 6, 1967.

6   For the text of the Instrument of Government, see J.P. Kenyon, ed., *The Stuart Constitution: Documents and Commentary* (2nd edn, Cambridge, 1986), pp. 308–13, and S.R. Gardiner, ed., *Constitutional Documents of the Puritan Revolution* (3rd edn, Oxford, 1906), pp. 405–17.

7   Woolrych, *Commonwealth to Protectorate*, pp. 366–79 and especially p. 377.

8   Gaunt, 'Drafting the Instrument of Government', pp. 34–5.

9   David Farr, 'Oliver Cromwell and a 1647 case in Chancery', *Historical Research*, 71, 1988, pp. 344–5.

10   Peter Gaunt, 'The Councils of the Protectorate from December 1653 to September 1658' (unpublished PhD thesis, University of Exeter, 1989); *idem*, '"The single person's confidants and dependants"?: Oliver Cromwell and his protectoral councillors', *Historical Journal*, 32, 1982.

11   Ivan Roots, ed., *Speeches of Oliver Cromwell* (London, 1998), p. 53.

12   *Ibid.*, p. 150.

13   Gaunt, 'The Councils of the Protectorate', p. 88.

14   Derek Hirst, *England in Conflict: Kingdom, Community, Commonwealth* (London, 1999), p. 284.

15   Ivan Roots, 'Cromwell's ordinances: the early legislation of the Protectorate' in G.E. Aylmer, ed., *The Interregnum: The Quest for Settlement* (London, 1972), p. 145.

16   All the ordinances are printed in C.H. Firth and R.S. Rait, eds, *Acts and Ordinances of the Interregnum* (2 vols, London, 1911), vol. 2, pp. 823–1029.

17   See chapter 6.

18   Firth and Rait, eds, *Acts and Ordinances*, vol. 2, p. 830.

19   One of the many unresolved questions about the Cromwellian Protectorate is whether the ceremonies and iconography of the regime represented a desire to cultivate an image that, while appropriating some monarchical forms, was intended to emphasise the Protectorate's distinctiveness from monarchy. Suggestive discussions relating to this point can be found in K. Sharpe, '"An image doting rabble": the failure of republican culture in England' in K. Sharpe and S.N. Zwicker, eds, *Refiguring Revolutions: Aesthetics and Politics from the English Revolution to the Romantic Revolution* (Berkeley and Los Angeles, 1998) and

L.L. Knoppers, *Constructing Cromwell: Ceremony, Portraits and Print, 1645–61* (Cambridge, 2000), chapters 3 and 4.

20   Roy Sherwood, *The Court of Oliver Cromwell* (London, 1977), *passim*.

21   Roy Sherwood, *A King In All But Name 1653–58* (Stroud, 1997), pp. 16–19, for an account of Cromwell's visit to the City on 8 February, and *passim* for the regal-like ceremonial at Cromwell's receptions of foreign ambassadors.

22   Abbott, ed., *Writings and Speeches*, vol. 2, p. 38.

23   *Ibid.*, vol. 2, pp. 187, 273.

24   Peter Gaunt, 'Interregnum government and the reform of the post office, 1649–59', *Historical Research*, 66, 1987.

25   G. Aylmer, in *The State's Servants: The Civil Service of the English Republic 1649–60* (London, 1973), p. 47, describes the Protector's and Council's legislation as 'the great series of reforming ordinances passed from January to September 1654'. For a different view, see Roots, 'Cromwell's ordinances'.

26   Quoted in N. Matthews, *William Sheppard: Cromwell's Law Reformer* (Cambridge, 1984), p. 37. The following two paragraphs rely a lot on this book.

27   Thomas Birch, ed., *A Collection of the State Papers of John Thurloe Esquire* (7 vols, London, 1742), vol. 2, p. 445.

28   Roots, ed., *Speeches of Oliver Cromwell*, p. 36.

29   See chapter 3.

30   Many of these are printed in the *Calendar of State Papers, Domestic Series*, 1654, as well as in newsbooks, e.g. congratulatory addresses from Buckinghamshire and Poole in Dorset in *Mercurius Politicus*, 4–11 May 1654, pp. 3467–8, 3474–5.

31   Matthews, *William Sheppard*, p. 117.

32   I am grateful to Dr Peter Gaunt for a discussion on this point.

33   Roots, ed., *Speeches of Oliver Cromwell*, pp. 28–40.

34   Peter Gaunt, in 'Law making in the first Protectorate Parliament' in C. Jones, M. Newitt and S. Roberts, eds, *Politics and People in Revolutionary England* (Oxford, 1986), p. 165, does his best to pick out 'positive and constructive' aspects of this parliament. So, too, does David L. Smith, 'Oliver Cromwell, the first Protectorate Parliament and religious reform', *Parliamentary History*, 19, 2000. I have relied a lot on both these articles in what follows.

35   Roots, ed., *Speeches of Oliver Cromwell*, p. 59.

36   See p. 45 for these 'fundamentals'.

37   Peter Gaunt, 'Cromwell's purge? Exclusion and the first Protectorate Parliament', *Parliamentary History*, 6, 1987, p. 18; Peter Gaunt, 'Oliver Cromwell and his Protectorate Parliaments: co-operation, conflict and control' in Ivan Roots, ed., *'Into Another Mould': Aspects of the Interregnum* (Exeter, 1998), p. 88.

38 Derek Massarella, 'The politics of the army and the quest for settlement' in *ibid.*, p. 119.

39 J.T. Rutt, ed., *The Diary of Thomas Burton Esquire* (4 vols, London, 1828), vol. 1, pp. xlv, liii, cv.

40 Roots, ed., *Speeches of Oliver Cromwell*, pp. 51–4.

41 Rutt, ed., *Diary of Thomas Burton*, vol. 1, p. lxxix.

42 *Ibid.*, vol. 1, p. cxiv.

43 Barry Coward, *Oliver Cromwell* (Harlow, 1991), p. 122.

44 Rutt, ed., *Diary of Thomas Burton*, vol. 1, p. lxxxiii.

45 Roots, ed., *Speeches of Oliver Cromwell*, pp. 69–70.

3

The crisis of the Cromwellian Protectorate, February 1655 – June 1656

The dissolution of parliament on 22 January 1655 plunged the Protectorate into a period of deep crisis. What particularly alarmed the Protector and his Council about the parliamentary session was that it had provided unqualified confirmation of just how few people shared their own visionary ambitions. One effect might have been to cause them to lose faith in these hopes and to abandon them. In fact, the opposite proved to be the case. The consequence of the disillusioning parliamentary experience was to strengthen their commitment to godly reformation and to reinforce their view that they were an embattled godly minority who had a duty to show the unregenerate, ungodly majority the errors of their ways. A main aim of this chapter is to show how this 'siege mentality' brought about an extraordinary shift in the politics of the Protectorate that lasted for about 16 months after Cromwell's impetuous dissolution of the first Protectorate Parliament. Protector and Council did not renounce totally their ambitions to bring about settlement by cultivating the support of mainstream political opinion in the country. But, as will be seen in the second part of this chapter, the Protectorate government responded to the crisis situation in ways that revealed it to be more than ever committed to bringing about reformation, if necessary by means that flouted what Cromwell once called 'the ordinary rules' of law and constitutional practice. But, first, it is important to tackle the question of why Protector and councillors, none of whom were militant social or political radicals, were driven to take such desperate measures that went against their instincts to follow paths of legal and constitutional respectability.

The Protectorate's siege mentality

The hostility of most members of the first Protectorate Parliament to the regime's constitution, its conception of religious liberty and its close connections with the army undoubtedly alarmed the Protector and Council; but it probably did not surprise them. Cromwell and most of the councillors were godly people, or, as they are more commonly called, Puritans, who were very accustomed to being a minority group in English society.

A great deal of excellent historical research has established the fact that from the time Puritans first appeared in the later sixteenth century they shared many of the beliefs of other Protestants.[1] Like most other members of the English Church after the Reformation, they were firmly attached to the theology of predestinarianism, the belief that an individual's fate after death was preordained by the grace of Jesus Christ and owed little or nothing to his or her good works during life. Puritans too shared the general Protestant concern that everyone should read and study the Bible and that the central point of church services should be to help everyone to do that through sermons clearly expounding the teachings of the Scriptures. They also put as much emphasis as other Protestants on the importance of having educated clergymen who were able to spread the Gospel into 'the dark corners of the land' and thereby counter the forces of Catholicism. Despite the tiny numbers of committed Catholics in England by the mid-seventeenth century, most Protestants, including Puritans, were convinced by millenarian views popularised in influential books like John Foxe's *Book of Martyrs* that European Protestantism was in danger of being engulfed by a rising tide of Counter-Reformation Catholicism that they considered to represent the forces of Antichrist. This battle was believed to be part of a long-running contest between the forces of Christ and Antichrist that biblical prophecies foresaw would one day end in the vanquishing of Antichrist and the establishment of the Millennium, the thousand-year reign of King Jesus on earth.

But the same research has also clearly demonstrated that during the course of the later sixteenth and early seventeenth centuries Puritans did develop some beliefs and attitudes that distinguished them from most other Protestants. These have been well-described by Patrick Collinson as differences 'of degree, of theological temperature, so to speak, rather than of fundamental principle'.[2] Puritans had a much more intense attitude towards predestinarianism (described by one historian as a belief in 'experimental' rather than 'credal' predestinarianism) that led them to indulge in long periods of anguished introspection and self-examination in order to convince themselves that they were one of the Elect.[3] They also took much further than other Protestants the importance of studying the Bible, which became a central feature of life in godly households. They were, too, much more influenced by anti-Catholicism than other Protestants, adopting a firm conviction that the English were an Elect Nation chosen by God to lead the cause of international Calvinism against the machinations of Antichrist. Above all, though, what set the godly apart from other Protestants was their zeal for further godly reformation of the kind that it has been seen was central to the visionary aims of the Protectorate since its foundation.

Puritans were acutely aware that these attitudes and beliefs set them apart from their fellow countrymen, most of whom were unsympathetic to these aspirations. Richard Baxter's famous description of his youth in the Puritan household of his father in Shropshire in the 1620s well captures the sense of isolation and ostracism that this could lead to. As a child, he recounts in his autobiography, he was sometimes tempted to leave the godly Baxter household with its incessant routine of Bible-reading in order to join those outside who were making 'the great disturbance of the tabor and pipe and noise in the street'. But, he concluded, 'when I heard them call my father Puritan, it did much to cure me and alienate me from them; for I considered that my father's exercise of reading the Scriptures was better than theirs, and would surely be better thought on by all men at the last; and I considered what it was for that he and the others were so derided'.[4]

The alienation Cromwell and many councillors felt at the end of the first Protectorate Parliament needs to be seen against this historical background. It explains the force of the Protector's complaint to a parliamentary committee at the end of 1654 that 'the major part [of the people], a great deal, are persons disaffected and engaged against us'.[5] Yet it is important to stress that at this time, as in the past, this feeling of isolation and realisation of how different they were from many others did not demoralise the godly. On the contrary, it became for them a source of great strength, because like similar minorities in other societies at other times, the perception of Cromwell and those around him that they were an embattled minority gave them a bond that unified them and made them determined to remain constant in their beliefs and aspirations.

In the wake of the dissolution of the first Protectorate Parliament this unity and determination among the Protectorate's supporters was very strong. Furthermore it was reinforced early in 1655 when they perceived that the ranks of those who opposed them had grown alarmingly. There was ample evidence that many of their one-time allies were now utterly opposed to them. Thomas Harrison, on being called before the Council on 15 February 1655 along with John Carew, Colonel Rich and Quarter-Master General Courtney, 'appeared stiff in opinion' (in the words of the editor of *Mercurius Politicus*), 'justifying themselves, and refusing to give assurance of their peaceable behaviour under the Government'.[6] This followed hard on the heels of the publication of a tract by the Leveller John Wildman called *A Declaration ... Against the Tyrant Oliver Cromwell*, for which he and a Leveller sympathiser, Lord Grey of Groby, were arrested and sent to prisons in Chepstow and Windsor Castles respectively. Perhaps more worrying was the growing evidence of disaffection in the army. In November 1654 three colonels, Matthew Alured, Thomas Saunders and John Okey, who had circulated a petition hostile to the Protectorate, were arrested. A harsher fate was suffered by Major-General Robert Overton, Governor of Hull, who was believed to be sympathetic to English soldiers in the army in Scotland who were said to be organising anti-government petitions. Although no firm evidence against him was discovered, Overton was kept in prison for five years.[7] Swift action was also taken against two other army officers, Colonel Eyers and Major General Allen, in January 1655.

Moreover, early in 1655 intelligence reports indicated that the threat to the Protectorate from royalists was apparently also becoming more serious. 'Apparently' is the key word in that last sentence, because just how serious the royalist threat was has been a question at the centre of a long-running controversy.[8] With hindsight it is possible to argue that the regime exaggerated the scale and seriousness of royalist conspiracies early in 1655. As can be seen from many reports in government newspapers at this time, the Protector and Council were far from unwilling to release details of people arrested on suspicion of plotting in order to smear all royalists with charges of sedition and subversion. Moreover, the Protectorate's efficient counter-espionage system organised by Thurloe revealed most of the details of royalist conspiracies long before they came to fruition.

In January and February 1655 some London merchants said to be illegally importing arms were arrested, as were prominent royalists sympathisers who were alleged to have been the recipients of the arms, like Sir Henry Littleton, the Sheriff of Worcestershire, and Sir John Packington. Accurate information about the activities of the Sealed Knot, an underground royalist organisation headed by a council of six men and formed at the end of 1653 to co-ordinate plans from the court of the exiled Charles II, was fed to Thurloe through a network of spies. This allowed rigorous counter-measures to be taken. Troops were recalled from Ireland and Scotland to England in anticipation of an uprising, and on 15 February 1655 a commission was issued ordering three foot regiments to be raised in London. Two days earlier the Protector had met the Lord Mayor and other leading members of the City government and laid the ground for their acceptance of this by showing them a copy of a letter written in July 1654 by Charles II, giving his full support for an uprising in England. On 24 February 1655 a Protectorate proclamation forbade the holding of horse race meetings, which might have been the cover for such a rising, and rigorous efforts were taken to arrest 'idle persons' in and around London.

Prospects of a successful royalist rising were made even dimmer by the shambolic nature of royalist planning and disputes between the Sealed Knot and other royalist factions, and it is not surprising that when the rebellion took place early in March 1655 it went off like a damp squib. Meetings of small groups of armed royalists at Morpeth in Northumberland, Marston Moor in Yorkshire and Rufford in Nottinghamshire quickly dispersed as it became clear how few people had come out to support them. Other areas in which there were supposed to be armed uprisings saw no activity at all. Only in Wiltshire did anything worthy of the name of a 'rising' occur, when on 12 March 1655 Colonel John Penruddock and others arrested two assize judges, Chief Justice

Rolle and Baron Nicholas, and the Sheriff of Dorset, in Salisbury. They gained more supporters as they rode further west, but, as news of the appointment of John Desborough as Major-General of the West on 12 March and the issue of new militia commissions ordering the requisitioning of arms and horses on 14 March spread, most potential rebels stayed at home. Penruddock and his pathetic force were soon overcome in Devon and he and his fellow leaders and many of their supporters were imprisoned in gaols in Exeter and elsewhere.

Ought one, then, to conclude from all this that the Protector and Council did not believe that the royalist plots of the spring of 1655 were a serious threat to the regime? To do so would be to underestimate the impact that the plotting and risings had on the history of the Cromwellian Protectorate. Inept though many of the royalist plans for uprisings in England were, their very existence served to confirm the view of Protector and councillors that their regime was being threatened from every direction. One of the major effects of Penruddock's Rebellion was to bolster the siege mentality among government supporters and those at the centre of power in the Protectorate in the early months of 1655.

What also contributed to this mentality was news that broke two months after the defeat of Penruddock's Rebellion that seemed to suggest that the godly cause was being threatened not only at home but abroad as well. On 24 May 1655 news filtered to London of a massacre committed a few weeks earlier by troops of the Catholic Duke of Savoy against communities of Protestants, known as the Vaudois or Waldensians, in some Alpine valleys in Piedmont in northern Italy to the west of Turin. The Vaudois had been tolerated by the dukes of Savoy since the mid-sixteenth century (a toleration confirmed as late as 1653 by an edict issued by the current Duke of Savoy, under the influence of his mother, Duchess Christina, the sister of Charles I's wife, Henrietta Maria). But as their communities had spread from the Alpine valleys into the more fertile and wealthy lowland areas of Piedmont, outside the regions allowed by the toleration edicts, the Duke of Savoy and his mother were able to justify the massacres on those grounds.

The impact of the news on the Protectorate government was dramatic. Like the Irish Rebellion of 1641, the Vaudois massacre of 1655 was seen by Protestant English opinion as an example of evil

Catholic atrocities against innocent Protestant communities, confirming their millenarian world-view of the Antichristian nature of Catholicism. Reports received by the government drew explicit comparisons with the Irish Rebellion. 'Let the blood of Ireland be fresh in your view, and let their treachery cry aloud in your eyes', wrote one correspondent.[9] The similarities with Ireland and the early 1640s were reinforced by the reports of Catholic Irish soldiers among the Duke of Savoy's troops (document 27), and, no doubt, also by the fact that Henrietta Maria's sister had played a major role in initiating the massacre. The implication was clear: it was England's duty as an Elect Nation to take the lead in seeking revenge and in securing a halt to further oppression by the Antichristian forces of popery. 'Avenge, O Lord, thy slaughter'd saints, whose bones / Lie scatter'd on the Alpine mountains cold', wrote John Milton in a famous sonnet.

But the point is that it was not just the Vaudois who were at risk. Significantly the proclamation of Protector and Council calling for a day of humiliation and fasting for the Vaudois explained that this was necessary also for 'the future Danger upon all the Protestant Churches in general' (document 5). Protector and Council therefore acted swiftly. On the day after receiving the news of the massacre, Samuel Morland was sent with letters of protest to the Catholic powers of Europe and letters urging intervention by Protestant princes. The Protector contributed £2,000 from his own pocket to a fund to help the Vaudois. As will be seen in chapter 6, because of the state of international relations between the Protectorate and France at this time, Cromwell's intervention on behalf of the Vaudois was remarkably successful in halting the punitive policies of the Duke of Savoy against them. But for a few months in mid-1655 the Vaudois episode made a vital contribution to the development of the siege mentality of those at the heart of the Protectorate government.

One final component of that mentality needs to be considered. As has been pointed out already, the impact of opposition and adversity on the godly prompted activism and not resigned passivity. One essential element in explaining this response is that in times of trouble the godly often saw glimmers of hope which they were able to interpret as providential signs that (great though the opposition to them might be) they still had God's support to help them in crises. In the first half of 1655 such signs were found and pointed out to encourage the godly. Public letters distributed to local magistrates in southern England and south Wales in late March 1655, urging them to take careful security measures in the wake of Penruddock's Rebellion, all began by pointing out that it was 'the hand of God going along with us' that had defeated 'the late rebellious insurrection'.[10] Similarly, a letter of congratulation to Admiral Blake from Cromwell on 13 June 1655 for a successful attack on the navy of the Governor of Tunis in the Mediterranean referred to 'the success it hath pleased God to give', and he gratefully acknowledged 'the good hand of God towards us in this action, who … was pleased to appear signally with you'.[11]

There were two major consequences of the development of this siege mentality for the Cromwellian Protectorate during 1655 and much of 1656. The first was that the regime came to see the need to rely more than ever on godly minorities in the localities. Significantly, as Professor Durston has recently pointed out,[12] the government press in the spring of 1655 focused on the vital part played by the godly in putting down the royalist uprisings (document 6). These were the kind of men to whom the Protectorate government came to look increasingly for support. The second consequence of the crisis-ridden siege mentality of those at the heart of the regime was that they were pushed more and more to the conclusion that they and their godly allies must adopt extraordinary – if necessary unconstitutional and illegal – measures if their vision of godly reformation was ever to be achieved.

Godly rule

The Protectorate did not change direction totally in 1655. There are signs that it still tried to cultivate the support of the bulk of the political nation, while at the same time pursuing plans to reform the country in ways that most people found unacceptable: conflicting aims that were the source of many of the regime's problems seen in chapter 2. One of its first decisions after the dissolution of parliament was to adopt a measure proposed by a majority of MPs a few weeks earlier, to reduce the annual assessment to be levied in England and Wales to pay for the army from £90,000 to £60,000. As will be seen also, one of the Protectorate's major innovations of this period, the rule of the major-generals, while giving renewed impetus to the Protector's and Council's drive for reformation, was also in part at least an attempt to appeal to conservative demands for reduced taxation to support the army. Yet 'settlement' is only a sub-theme of the history of the Protectorate in the mid-1650s. The *main* themes are the pursuit of reformation more zealously than ever before in alliance with godly minorities in the localities, and the replacement of attempts to conciliate unsympathetic and hostile opinion with harsh repression.

On 15 February 1655 Protector and Council published a proclamation on religion that was meant to be a clear signal to the godly in the country of the Protectorate's commitment to pursuing its visionary ambitions (document 7). This is not the only possible interpretation of it. Professor Hutton, for example, calls it 'a proclamation to restrict religious liberty', because of the ban it imposed on religious groups like Quakers and Ranters.[13] But (as is apparent from the provisions of the Instrument of Government) the Protectorate had never stood for unlimited religious liberty. Its religious objectives were not to promote the kind of religious freedom that would encourage the growth of sects which, as recent events had shown, were as intolerant of the views of others as had been the Laudian bishops in the 1630s. The central religious objective of the Protectorate was, on the contrary, to promote religious unity not diversity. This had long been Cromwell's ambition and it is likely that it was shared by his fellow rulers in the regime. 'I have waited', he wrote to his friend and cousin, Robin Hammond, in November 1648, 'for the day to see union and right understanding between the godly people (Scots, English, Jews, Gentiles, Presbyterians, Independents, Anabaptists and all)'.[14] This was still the case in 1655, when he commissioned a pamphlet which prophesied 'a glorious vision of the people of God, made to be of the same spirit'.[15] The February 1655 proclamation emphasised that the regime's aim was 'to preserve and continue the freedom and liberty to all persons in the Commonwealth fearing God, though of differing judgements'. One of the most noticeable absences from the proclamation, as from all the Protectorate's pronouncements on religion, was the prescription of specific forms of worship. This is what Professor Davis in one of the most important articles on the topic has called the 'antiformalism' of Cromwell and many of his allies, like John Owen and Peter Sterry, the Protector's two spiritual advisers in the 1650s.[16] What lay behind this antiformalism was the hope that it would provide a framework broad enough to enable the godly to join with all believers in building a truly national Church in which the godly were no longer an ostracised minority; they would be at its epicentre.

Despite the ban on their activities in the February proclamation, even groups like the Quakers and Fifth Monarchists were not given up as lost causes. Just before and after the proclamation was drafted and published, major efforts were made by the Protector to try to convince prominent members of these groups to accommodate themselves within the broad Cromwellian Church; his personal involvement suggests that Cromwell took an even greater role in the Protectorate's affairs than he had done earlier. In the last days of 1654 he had long conversations with the Fifth Monarchists John Simpson and Christopher Feake. Newspapers reported his discussions with another Fifth Monarchist, John Rogers, on 6 February 1655. The Quakers too were subjected to Cromwell's personal blandishments. On 26 February 1655 one of the Quaker leaders, George Fox, had a long meeting with the Protector, who attempted to convince him (as he had the Scottish Presbyterians in 1650) that 'religion [is not] wrapped up in that or any one form ... in the bowels of Christ, think it possible you may be mistaken'.[17] His appeals to the Fifth Monarchists and Quakers met with as little success as did those to the Scots five years earlier. But his efforts are significant indicators of Cromwell's desire to bring about a 'union and right understanding between the godly people'. The same is true of Cromwell's attitude to 'Prayer Book Protestants' at this time.[18] Although a proclamation in November 1655 forbade anyone from employing those clergy who persisted in using the Book of Common Prayer after 1 January 1656, Cromwell had meetings with Archbishop Ussher and other 'Prayer Book Protestants' in the first weeks of 1656, trying to find ways of allowing them to worship on the condition that they gave assurances that they would not support plots against the regime.

The most remarkable example of all the plans to bring together 'the godly people' at this time was the attempt to secure the readmission of the Jews to England at the end of 1655.[19] Nothing better illustrates the extent to which visionary ambitions had come to have a central place in the concerns of the Protectorate during the middle years of its history. It is also an episode that provides confirmation that the Protector played a major personal role in ensuring that this was so. *The Humble Address of Menasseh ben Israel,* an Amsterdam Jew, was published in London on 5 November 1655 and immediately gained Cromwell's interest. Shortly after that, when ben Israel submitted a request that Jews might live in England practising their worship and trade free of the penal laws against them, it was on Cromwell's insistence that the petition was put before the Council. Cromwell also overcame an attempt to reject the petition outright and enthusiastically supported the suggestion that a conference of four councillors (Lawrence, Lisle, Wolseley and Pickering), church ministers and lawyers be held at Westminster to discuss it. He also attended every session of the conference that was held between 4 and 18 December 1655, and there, according to the major accounts of the conference, he took a leading role in countering objections to the readmission of the Jews. One reported speech of the Protector that took issue with the objection of London merchants to Jewish commercial competition is rich with irony: 'Can you really be afraid that this mean despised people should be able to prevail in trade and credit over the merchants of England, the noblest and most esteemed merchants of the world!'[20] Despite Cromwell's oratory and influence, the Council refused to allow ben Israel's petition and the Protector had to use his power behind the scenes to allow the unofficial entry of the Jews into England in the following months.

Why was Cromwell so anxious to overcome opposition to the readmission of the Jews? The answer lies in Cromwell's belief that, as had been prophesied in the Bible, the conversion of the Jews to Christianity was an essential precondition to the establishment of the millennium. 'Was it not … our duty, in particular, to encourage them to settle here, where alone they could be taught the truth.' 'He had no ingagment to the Jews [he was reported to have said] but what the Scripture held forth, and since there was a Promise of their Conversion, means must be had to that end, which was the preaching of the Gospel.'[21] For Cromwell the conversion of the Jews was necessary to fulfil biblical prophecies that would propel the nation towards the creation of the new Jerusalem.

By this time, however, Protector and Council had decided that a more immediate way of bringing this about was by forging closer links than ever with those who were already within the ranks of the godly. The petitions from these people that flooded to the Protectorate Council in the wake of the dissolution of parliament must have left its members in no doubt about the sense of purpose they shared with them. A typical example is a petition drafted only four days after the publication of the February proclamation from the mayor, aldermen and 118 inhabitants of Harwich (document 8). Pleas like these must have confirmed the belief of Protector and Council that they must work closely with and support the 'British Jerusalem', the community of the godly, in their common campaign against ungodliness.

The best illustration of this intention is the relationship between the Protectorate and ruling groups in towns in 1655–56. Those who have written about this in the past have been divided about whether or not the regime had a coherent policy to interfere with the government of boroughs in order to promote to power men loyal to it.[22] The most recent study of the topic concludes that 'at no time did Cromwell's regime encourage boroughs to surrender their charters in order to renew them on terms the government might favour'.[23] It is likely, however, that this comment underestimates the initiatives taken by the Protectorate in this regard. It would be anachronistic to argue that the Protectorate had a 'policy' aimed at remodelling borough charters in favour of its supporters. But there is no doubt that the Council was very willing to respond to (and to encourage) requests for help from godly urban magistrates who felt that their position was being undermined by 'ungodly' opponents.[24]

In September 1655 it seemed as if a major means by which the government could do this was about to disappear. On 28 September a parliamentary act of 1647 that had been extended for a further three years by the Rump Parliament in 1652 was due to lapse. The act had barred delinquents from being elected to municipal offices and from voting in municipal elections. A fortnight before the act was to expire the Council made clear its fears of the consequences, when it commented that not only was the forthcoming municipal election in Newcastle-upon-Tyne 'like to be in danger through choice of ill-affected persons but the evil may become general and can better be prevented than redressed'.[25] To do this Protector and Council decided to ignore legal niceties and to make law by issuing on 21 September a proclamation that kept in force indefinitely the provisions of the 1652 Act (document 9). Moreover, as will be seen in chapter 8, during the next few months steps were taken to use these provisions to purge town corporations of men considered to be hostile to the regime. In addition, the godly officials who were left in power were given every encouragement to petition for new charters that would make their positions secure. By April 1656 the Council had established a committee charged specifically with dealing with municipal charters, and two months later the committee had appointed a permanent sub-committee of four lawyers headed by William Sheppard, who were to consider 'the renewal of all charters the renewing of which is prayed and draw up all the alterations proposed to be made with such variations as they think best for religion and good government and the discouraging of vice'.[26]

It would be hard to exaggerate the contrast between the efforts made by the Protectorate in 1655–56 to forge close comradely links with the godly in these kinds of ways and the excessive harshness that was meted out at the same time to those whom it considered the opponents of the godly cause. Not surprisingly, those who took part in the rebellion of March 1655 were given little mercy. Penruddock and his fellow leaders of the rebellion were executed and many of their supporters (whether or not they were found guilty of treason) were transported to servitude in the West Indies. Penruddock claimed at his trial in Exeter on 19 April 1655 that the indictment against him was illegal since the Protectorate treason ordinance was not valid and existing statute law only covered treason against kings. But these arguments were swept aside with scant regard for legal precedent. There is some justice in Penruddock's complaint at his trial that 'treason in this age [is] an *individium vagum*; like the wind in the gospel, which bloweth where it listeth; for that shall be treason in me today, which shall be none in another tomorrow, as it pleaseth Mr. Attorney'.[27] This was a view shared by the two judges Francis Thorpe and Richard Newdigate, who were sent to York to try those involved in the March royalist plots in the north. Both judges questioned the validity of the Protectorate treason ordinance and, after being interrogated by the Council, were sacked from their posts in a display of iron-fisted authoritarianism.

An even more blatant display of unwarranted interference in the legal process by Protector and Council is the infamous case of

George Cony, which early in May 1655 came before the Court of Upper Bench (as the Court of King's Bench was now known) (document 10). Cony had been imprisoned and fined in November 1654 for refusing to pay customs duties on silk he had imported and for forcibly preventing customs officials from seizing his property. He subsequently refused to pay the fine and was again imprisoned. When his lawyers brought his case to court they claimed (paralleling the legal attack on the Protectorate treason ordinance) that the financial ordinance which authorised the levying of customs duties was not valid, since it had been issued in March 1654 and had not been approved by the first Protectorate Parliament. In response to this blatant attack on the validity of the Protectorate constitution, the Council responded on 12 May 1655 by imprisoning Cony's lawyers, and a week later Lord Chief Justice Rolle was brought before the Council and reprimanded for allowing the case to proceed, under which pressure he resigned.

A month later on 6 June 1655 Bulstrode Whitelock and Thomas Widdrington, two of the commissioners of the great seal, were also forced to resign because of their refusal to put into effect the 1654 ordinance for reforming the Court of Chancery. The same kind of bullying tactics were also used in July 1655 against Sir Peter Wentworth, a republican Commonwealthsman from Warwickshire, who had refused to pay the assessment tax on the grounds that it had not been approved by parliament. He had also persuaded the Sheriff of Coventry to arrest the local assessment commissioners. He too was subjected to a conciliar interrogation and forced to withdraw his objections. Moreover, not only were critics of the regime slapped down in these kinds of ways, but Protector and Council tried to ensure that any hostile or critical views of the regime would be suppressed. In August and September 1655 by order of Council a three-man censorship committee was appointed, and by late September 1655 all newspapers had been suppressed apart from the weekly *Mercurius Politicus* and *The Public Intelligencer*, which were under the editorship of Marchamont Nedham and firmly under government control.

This chapter ends with a consideration of the most famous decision made by the Protector and Council in the middle years of the Protectorate's history: the appointment in the late summer of 1655 of a number of major-generals to take command in the provinces of England and Wales.[28] The decision to inaugurate the rule of the major-generals underlines three of the major characteristics of Protectorate government in 1655–56 that have already been identified in this chapter: a fear of the royalist security threat; a willingness to use harsh, extra-legal measures against opponents; and an overriding commitment to godly reformation in league with godly allies around the country.

The first of these characteristics, the regime's belief that it faced a major security threat from royalist conspirators both at home and abroad, was deeply entrenched. The decision to appoint the major-generals was a direct response to this siege mentality, which continued to grip those at the centre of power in the government despite the comprehensive defeat of Penruddock's rebels in March 1655. Maintaining the security of the regime remained a high priority, but the problem facing the government was to find means of doing that while at the same time keeping military expenditure at (and, if possible, below) the reduced level that had been announced in February. This problem was not new; nor was there much that was novel about the immediate attempt to solve it. Like earlier regimes in the later 1640s and early 1650s and like a committee of MPs in the first Protectorate Parliament, the Protectorate considered plans to reduce the size of the standing army and with it the burden of national taxation, while raising local volunteer militias that would be funded by local taxation.[29] In response to a request by the Council to consider the problem, a committee of army officers spent three weeks discussing it, after which in April 1655 it came up with a recommendation that savings be made by reducing the pay of regular soldiers and by forming a new horse militia of volunteers to be kept in readiness for times of emergency. By the end of May the Council had accepted this advice and it began to appoint officers to command a new 6,520-strong volunteer militia, which was to be raised throughout England and Wales, consisting of 64 county troops of horse and two troops of foot in Norwich. Late in July the Council then announced cuts in the standing army in England and Scotland from its December 1654 level of over 30,000 to around 21,000 men. Although it dragged its feet in implementing these cuts, the Council made rapid moves to raise the militia. On 2 August Desborough was appointed to command the 12 militia troops in south-west England and a week later the rest of England and

Wales was divided into nine other regions, each commanded by a senior New Model Army officer appointed to carry out the same task. It was not until later that these officers were given the title of 'major-general' and that the regional districts commanded by them were amended to 12.[30] But by the end of August 1655 the skeletal framework of the rule of the major-generals was in place.

The next decisions taken by the government illustrate the second characteristic of Protectorate government at this time: its vindictive attitude to its opponents and its willingness to use extra-legal measures against them. The best example of this is the one aspect of the rule of the major-generals that was novel: the decision to fund the new militia by a discriminatory tax against anyone who had fought against parliament or had supported the royalist cause in any way since the outbreak of the Civil War in 1642. All these people who were worth at least £1,000 in lands were to pay 10 per cent of the rental income from their estates, and all those who possessed property but little landed estate were to pay £10 on every £1,500 of its value. In addition, royalists who had taken part in plots against the regime since the beginning of the Protectorate were to be imprisoned or sent into exile and have their estates confiscated by the state; while others who were suspected of being active royalists were to keep their estates but to suffer imprisonment or banishment. Punitive orders were issued forbidding ex-royalists from keeping arms, and from employing clergy suspected of royalist leanings. In December a proclamation was passed obliging all who were alleged to have had royalist pasts to enter bonds to be forfeited if they were convicted of conspiring against the regime. It is difficult to argue with S.R. Gardiner's judgement that 'every one of these orders frankly relinquished the domain of law'.[31]

In its public defence of what it was doing, the government did not deny that it was acting in extraordinary, possibly illegal ways. Its justification was that such measures were necessary to counter the aim of royalists, which 'was, and still is (though in the utter ruin and desolation of these Nations) to set up that Power and Interest which Almighty God hath so eminently appeared against' (document 9). There is no clearer statement of the regime's belief that, in order to punish royalists, the government must not be 'tied up to ordinary rules' than its declaration of 31 October, which sets out authoritarian, police-state-like intentions (document 11). Just how these were put into practice can be seen by the decision in October 1655 to establish a central registry in London to keep track of the movements of royalists. Under the control of a 'register', Thomas Dunn, the office was open daily on Mondays to Saturdays at 9–11 a.m. and 2–4 p.m., when all royalists visiting London were to report to it. 'Deputy-registers' at the major ports sent reports of suspicious people who arrived in the country to Dunn, and the major-generals were instructed also to send lists of royalists in their localities to enable the register to monitor their movements.

Historians have long debated whether John Lambert or Oliver Cromwell was the main driving force behind the establishment of this punitive system aimed at strengthening the security of the regime. Many historians have seen Lambert as its main architect and there is little doubt that he was fully committed to its establishment.[32] He was the chairman of the major conciliar committee that worked out the details of how the new militia should operate and what the roles of the major-generals should be. But it is misleading to single him out, or indeed anyone else, as the sole author of the scheme. As on many other occasions, it is more likely that councillors worked together on it, taking their lead from Cromwell, who, not for the first time in 1655–56, seems to have played a dynamic role. According to Thurloe, the Protector 'himself weighted every officer [of the new militia] with all possible care and exactness and spoke with most of them hymself'.[33] It was the Protector, too, who addressed them at a banquet in London in early August 1655, no doubt impressing on them the urgency of the security task facing them. But this is to say no more than that the Protector acted on behalf of and with the full support of Lambert and other councillors in getting across the government's message.

This message was not confined to security and punitive action against royalists. As the Council worked on successive drafts of the major-generals' formal instructions between August and October 1655, it became clear that they were also to be agents in advancing the cause of godly reformation. Hence the third characteristic of the Protectorate in the mid-1650s illustrated by the decision to appoint the major-generals: the commitment of its leaders to that cause and particularly their determination to advance it by an alliance with godly people like themselves in the localities. On this point it is perhaps worth reiterating that there probably was no conflict of emphasis within the Council. It is probably wrong to assume (as many have done) that it was Cromwell who pressed the cause of moral reformation and Lambert who saw security as being the prime aim of the major-generals. As has recently been persuasively argued by Professor Durston, 'Cromwell and his colleagues … saw security and reformation as indivisible twin goals and believed that neither would be achieved if pursued independently, for just as the godly reformation could not be brought about until the regime was secure, so real security would only be established when godly reforms had begun to take firm root'.[34] During the autumn of 1655 Cromwell and many of the councillors were driven to the conclusion that godly reformation needed to be given an even higher profile in the instructions given the major-generals as they set out on their missions into the ungodly, 'dark corners' of the land (document 12).

What caused this was news of an event overseas that shaped the policies of the Protectorate government even more strongly than the terrible reports from the alpine valleys of northern Italy earlier in the year. This was the failure of a combined naval and military expedition led by Admiral William Penn and General Robert Venables, known as the Western Design, that was a key part of the foreign policies of the government (as will be seen in chapter 6). Under the command of Penn and Venables a fleet of 30 ships and about 3,000 soldiers had set out in December 1654 to attack the heart of the Spanish Empire in the West Indies. On 25 April 1655 it suffered a humiliating defeat at San Domingo (on the island now known as Haiti) and the remnants of the force were forced to lick their wounds on the undefended island of Jamaica, from where Venables and Penn set off on the long journey home. It took three months before the news reached London, but when it did the impact was dramatic. The Protector was said to have shut himself away in a room for a whole day, convinced that the defeat was a sign of God's rebuke on him and the regime. God 'hath very sorely chastened us', he wrote to Venables's successor in Jamaica, Major-General Richard Fortescue. 'We have cause to be humbled for the reproof God gave us at San Domingo, upon the occasion of our sins, as well as others.' His letters to Penn's second-in-command in Jamaica, Admiral William Goodson, pointed out the same painful lesson. 'The Lord hath greatly humbled us at the sad loss sustained at Hispaniola', he wrote. 'We have provoked the Lord and it is good for us to know so, and to be abased for the same ... we should ... lay our mouths ... in the dust.'[35] It was a theme that was to find an echo in the words of many in the inner circle of Protectorate government in the latter part of 1655. Major-General Charles Worsley's comment is typical: 'The Lord help us to know what our sin is, and what his pleasure is, that we are so crossed and visited in Jamaica'.[36] The lesson to be learned from the experience that is implicit in these letters was made explicit in another of Cromwell's letters to Fortescue in the Caribbean: to regain God's blessing 'all manner of vice may be thoroughly discountenanced and severely punished; and that such a form of government may be exercised that virtue and godliness may receive due encouragement'.[37]

It is surely no coincidence that the last amendments made to the major-generals' instructions, issued on 9 October 1655, stressed the importance of putting into effect 'the laws against drunkenness, blaspheming and taking of the name of God in vain, by swearing and cursing, plays and interludes, and profaning the Lord's Day and such like wickedness and abominations', and suppressing unlicensed alehouses, gambling houses and brothels in London (document 12).

The major-generals were also not left in any doubt that in carrying out these tasks they had to work closely with the godly minorities in the localities. On 24 August 1655 the Council began to appoint commissioners for securing the peace of the Commonwealth, who were to work closely with the major-generals in the twin task of security and reformation. As has been made clear by Professor Durston's exhaustive study of these men, the one characteristic that they shared is a commitment to the same godly cause championed by the Protector, Council and major-generals.[38] Once again, recent research validates a conclusion of S.R. Gardiner over a century ago, this time that the major-generals established 'the rule – provisionally at least – of a Puritan oligarchy'.[39] The correspondence of the major-generals as they arrived in the localities reflects the joy they felt as they made contact with 'the good people', 'the best of people', 'the people of God', as they described their allies up and down the country. Their letters, too, are optimistic that they and their godly allies would bring about wide-ranging moral reformation. How much success this 'Puritan oligarchy' had in bringing about the hoped-for new Jerusalem is debatable (as will be seen in chapter 8). But, as can be seen by the evidence surveyed in this chapter, there can be no doubt that in the mid-1650s the Cromwellian Protectorate was strongly and sincerely committed to achieving it by the use of all means at its disposal.

Notes

1   The best starting points for understanding Puritanism are anything by P. Collinson, such as his *Godly People: Essays in English Protestantism and Puritanism* (London, 1983); Christopher Durston and Jaqueline Eales, eds, 'Introduction: the Puritan ethos, 1560–1700' in *idem*, eds, *The Culture of English Puritanism, 1560–1700* (Basingstoke, 1996) and John Spurr, *English Puritanism 1603–89* (Basingstoke, 1998).

2   P. Collinson, *The Elizabethan Puritan Movement* (London, 1967), pp. 26–7.

3   R.T. Kendall, *Calvin and English Calvinism to 1649* (Oxford, 1979).

4   Quoted in K. Wrightson, *English Society 1580–1680* (London, 1982), pp. 183–4.

5   W.C. Abbott, ed., *The Writings and Speeches of Oliver Cromwell* (4 vols, Cambridge, Mass., 1937–47), vol. 3, p. 511.

6   *Mercurius Politicus*, 15–22 February 1655, p. 5147.

7   D. Massarella, 'The politics of the army and the quest for settlement', in Ivan Roots, ed., *'Into Another Mould': Aspects of the Interregnum* (Exeter, 1998), p. 119. See also B. Taft, 'The humble petition of several colonels of the army: causes, character and results of military opposition to Cromwell's Protectorate', *Huntington Library Quarterly*, 42, 1978, which perhaps exaggerates the extent to which the three colonels' views were widely shared in the army.

8   The controversy began with a debate between C.H. Firth and R.D. Palgrave, 'Cromwell and the insurrection of 1655', *English Historical Review*, 3, 1888. My account in this and the following paragraph is based on Firth and A. Woolrych, *Penruddock's Rising* (Historical Association pamphlet, London, 1953) and Andrea E. Button, 'Penruddock's Rising, 1655', *Southern History*, 19, 1997.

9   Thomas Birch, ed., *A Collection of the State Papers of John Thurloe Esquire* (7 vols, London, 1742), vol. 3, p. 467.

10   Abbott, ed., *Writings and Speeches*, vol. 3, p. 671.

11   *Ibid.*, vol. 3, p. 745.

12   Christopher Durston, *Cromwell's Major-Generals: Godly Government during the English Revolution* (Manchester, 2001), pp. 19–20

13   Ronald Hutton, *The British Republic 1649–60* (Basingstoke, 1990), p. 67.

14   Abbott, ed., *Writings and Speeches,* vol. 1, p. 677.

15   B. Worden, 'Toleration and the Cromwellian Protectorate' in W.J. Shiels, ed., *Persecution and Toleration* (Studies in Church History 21, 1984), pp. 211–12, cited in A. Fletcher, 'Oliver Cromwell and the godly nation' in J. Morrill, ed., *Oliver Cromwell and the English Revolution* (Harlow, 1990), p. 211.

16   J.C. Davis, 'Against formality: one aspect of the English Revolution', *Transactions of the Royal Historical Society,* 6th series, 3, 1993. See also J.C. Davis, 'Cromwell's religion' in Morrill, ed., *Oliver Cromwell and the English Revolution,* p. 206.

17   Abbott, ed., *Writings and Speeches,* vol. 2, pp. 285, 303.

18   See J. Maltby, *Prayer Book and People in Elizabethan and Early Stuart England* (Cambridge, 1998) for this useful historical label.

19   David S. Katz, *Philo-Semitism and the Readmission of the Jews to England 1603–55* (Berkeley and Los Angeles, 1982) is the best book on this topic. See also Barbara Coulton, 'Cromwell and the "readmission" of the Jews in England, 1656', *Cromwelliana,* 2001.

20   Abbott, ed., *Writings and Speeches,* vol. 4, p. 52.

21   *Ibid.,* vol. 4, pp. 52, 53.

22   J.H. Round, 'Colchester during the Commonwealth', *English Historical Review,* 15, 1900; B.L.K. Henderson, 'The Commonwealth charters', *Transactions of the Royal Historical Society,* 3rd series, 6, 1912; William A.H. Schilling, 'The central government and the municipal corporations in England 1642–63' (unpublished PhD thesis, University of Vanderbilt, 1970).

23   P.D. Halliday, *Dismembering the Body Politic: Partisan Politics in England's Towns, 1650–1730* (Cambridge, 1998), p. 65.

24   Durston, *Cromwell's Major-Generals,* pp. 87–91.

25   *Calendar of State Papers, Domestic Series,* 1654, p. 46.

26   Quoted in Schilling, 'The central government and municipal corporations', pp. 105–6. See also Henderson, 'The Commonwealth charters', pp. 131–6, and N.L. Matthews, *William Sheppard: Cromwell's Law Reformer* (Cambridge, 1984), p. 52.

27   Quoted in Button, 'Penruddock's Rising', p. 105.

28   Earlier accounts by D.W. Rannie, 'Cromwell's major-generals', *English Historical Review,* 10, 1895, and Ivan Roots, 'Swordsmen and decimators: Cromwell's major-generals' in R.H. Parry, ed., *The English Civil War and After, 1642–58* (London, 1970) are now superseded by Christopher Durston's authoritative *Cromwell's Major-Generals: Godly Government.* I have drawn heavily on this book in what follows. See chapter 8 for the impact of the major-generals' rule.

29   John Morrill, 'Postlude: between war and peace, 1651–62' in J. Kenyon and J. Ohlmeyer, eds, *The Civil Wars: A Military History of England, Scotland and Ireland, 1638–60* (Oxford, 1998), p. 311.

30   For the 12 regional associations and the 16 active major-generals and their deputies, see Durston, *Cromwell's Major-Generals*, pp. 30–1.

31   S.R. Gardiner, *History of the Commonwealth and Protectorate, 1649–60* (4 vols, London, 1903), vol. 3, p. 323.

32   Gardiner, *Commonwealth and Protectorate*, vol. 3, p. 324, believed that Lambert had a key role in the establishment of the major-generals.

33   Birch, ed., *Thurloe State Papers*, vol. 5, p. 504.

34   Christopher Durston, '"Settling the hearts and quieting the minds of all good people": the major-generals and the puritan ministers of Interregnum England', *History*, 85, 2000, pp. 249–50. See also Durston, *Cromwell's Major-Generals*, p. 34.

35   Abbott, ed., *Writings and Speeches*, vol. 3, pp. 857–8.

36   Quoted in A. Fletcher, 'The religious motivation of Cromwell's major-generals' in D. Baker, ed., *Religious Motivation* (Studies in Church History 15, 1978), p. 261.

37   Abbott, ed., *Writings and Speeches*, vol. 3, p. 858.

38   Durston, *Cromwell's Major-Generals*, chapter 4. See also J. Sutton, 'Cromwell's commissioners for preserving the peace of the Commonwealth: a Staffordshire case study' in Ian Gentles, John Morrill and Blair Worden, eds, *Soldiers, Writers and Statesmen in the English Revolution* (Cambridge, 1996).

39   Gardiner, *Commonwealth and Protectorate*, vol. 4, p. 342.

4

Stresses within the Cromwellian Protectorate, June 1655 – June 1657

The lack of official conciliar records for the 1650s, other than order books which only list the decisions taken by the Council, makes the task of investigating the ways in which the Protectorate government worked fraught with uncertainty. Yet during the first two and a half years of its existence it is remarkable how few signs can be found of serious disagreements amongst the Protector, the councillors and the government's key advisers. As has been seen in previous chapters, during that period circumstances had worked to unite rather than divide those at the centre of the Protectorate government. From December 1653 to September 1654 they had all shared the exhilaration and excitement of at last themselves pushing ahead with the task of godly reformation, after years of urging others to do so. During the winter of 1654–55 the optimism that bound them together dwindled away. But, as was noted in the last chapter, during 1655 and the first part of 1656 it was replaced by a siege mentality that caused them to keep alive their common visionary aspirations and to sink any differences they might have had in order to pursue their goals.

However, from May/June 1656 onwards evidence of rifts between members of the Protectorate government becomes more abundant. As a result, most historians' accounts of the last part of the Cromwellian Protectorate are built around an image of 'the fracturing of the Cromwellian alliance' as a 'military' faction came to be increasingly at odds with 'civilian' opponents in the Council and at the Cromwellian court, a struggle in which the 'military' men were gradually forced to give way.[1] The outcome, it is often claimed, was to push the Protectorate in a more conservative direction, so that another image – 'the conservatism of the later Protectorate' – has also become generally accepted. There is, as will be seen, some validity in these images. Both before and during the long first session of the second Protectorate Parliament (September 1656 – June 1657) there were rifts amongst Cromwellian councillors and advisers on a scale that had not been apparent before. These divisions arguably represented a greater threat to the Protectorate than the crisis of 1655, since now the stability of the government was threatened from within rather than from enemies without. Nor can it be denied that one consequence of these internal tensions was the emergence of a 'new' Protectorate no longer based on a military constitution but one designed by parliament and more traditional in form.

The images of a 'fracturing Cromwellian alliance' and 'the conservatism of the later Protectorate' are not wholly without foundation. But, it will be argued in this chapter, this interpretation needs to be modified in certain crucial respects. The rifts that emerged were fluid and did not crystallise into hard, clear-cut factions that can be neatly categorised into 'military' and 'civilian' pigeon holes. More importantly, the seriousness of the rifts and their impact on the stability of the Protectorate and its development can be exaggerated. Behind a facade of 'dithering' and looking like a man 'trapped in indecision',[2] Oliver Cromwell reacted to the situation with some political skill. It will be seen that, by not aligning himself too closely with any of the competing groups within the government, he ensured that the divisions within the Protectorate did not undermine the stability of the regime. He also helped to engineer an outcome, the revised Protectorate constitution (the Humble Petition and Advice), which meant that the continuing quest for reformation did not have to be sacrificed in favour of a conservative settlement.

Return to rule with parliament

There is no reason to doubt the rumours, reported by the Venetian ambassador, royalist letter writers and others in May/ June 1656, that a major debate took place within the Protectorate Council at that time. Early in May 1656 all the major-generals had been called to London from the areas under their control to join in the Council's discussions of the continuing financial problems of the Protectorate. These had now reached crisis proportions due to the high costs of the Anglo-Spanish war and the failure of the decimation tax to provide sufficient money to fund the new militia.[3] According to the reports, various expedients to meet these problems were floated. Some councillors argued for increasing the amounts to be raised by monthly assessments; others for raising money by privy seal loans (like the forced loans of the 1620s); and some for increasing the rate at which the decimation tax was levied. Others proposed that a better way of raising money would be by calling another parliament rather than by relying on raising taxes that would be opposed since they relied solely on the executive power of Protector and Council. This last expedient was the one favoured by many major-generals, but it also received support from other Cromwellian advisers and councillors. It is difficult to read into these debates evidence of a conflict between 'military' and 'civilian' factions.[4] But what seemed to tip the balance of the debate in favour of calling another parliament, as far as most councillors were concerned, was the confident prediction of some major-generals that parliamentary elections would produce MPs much more friendly to the regime than those elected in 1654. If the Venetian ambassador can be believed, the debates were conducted with much bitterness. As the discussions proceeded, he wrote, there was 'no little ruffling of temper owing to sharp words passed between them upon points that they have never been able to agree about'. But eventually a majority of the Council (including a reluctant Protector) agreed, and writs for an 'extraordinary' parliament were issued in June.[5]

It soon became apparent that the confidence of the major-generals about the forthcoming elections was misplaced. Despite their optimistic predictions, most of the elections about which there is evidence were characterised by waves of hostility to the authoritarian measures of 1655 in general, and to the major-generals in particular.[6] Suddenly the optimistic tone disappeared from the major-generals' letters to their masters in London. 'I now begin to fear Suffolk', wrote Major-General Haynes in August 1656, 'finding so malignant a grand jury, who will have a great advantage to possess the country.'[7] Faced with the unexpected prospect of another hostile parliament, the Council took the decision, as it had done two years earlier, to purge it of those MPs who were considered most likely to be critical of the Protectorate. Again the sources are scanty, but what evidence there is suggests that Cromwell took a back seat in reaching and carrying out the decision. It also seems to have been one supported by both 'military' and 'civilian' councillors.[8] Even Roger Boyle, Lord Broghill, who was becoming influential in the inner Cromwellian circle after his support and service for the regime in Ireland and Scotland and who later worked against the army's influence in the government, supported the exclusions. On 22 September 1656 he was a teller with General John Lambert in a crucial parliamentary vote that defeated an attempt to make the exclusions null and void.[9]

The major difference between the exclusions of 1654 and 1656 is their scale. Only 12 MPs had been purged from the parliament of 1654 under articles 14 and 15 of the Instrument of Government, which gave the Council the right to exclude MPs who were proven to be guilty of specific 'offences', notably active support for the royalist cause since 1642, participation in the Irish Rebellion of 1641 or Catholic commitment. In 1656 the Council also used article 17 of the Instrument of Government, which specified only that MPs should be 'persons of known integrity, fearing God, and of good conversation'. This general clause was used (as Dr Egloff persuasively argues) as an excuse to debar many MPs who could not otherwise be shown to have actively opposed the Commonwealth and Protectorate.[10] An exact list of all those excluded does not survive, but most commentators agree that about 100 MPs were purged in 1656. In addition about 60 other MPs voluntarily withdrew from parliament in protest. Although some of these later returned, the purge of 1656 was much more sweeping than that at the start of the first Protectorate Parliament in 1654.

Yet the most notable aspect of the first few months of the second Protectorate Parliament is not the appearance of deep divisions between civilian and military Cromwellians but the surprising absence of the tensions between executive and legislature that had scarred the history of the first Protectorate Parliament. It is true that among the MPs who were excluded or who withdrew in protest were some of the Protectorate's most inveterate enemies, like the republican Commonwealthsmen Sir Henry Vane and Sir Arthur Heselrige, who later were to make the second session of this parliament such a fiasco. But it was far from inevitable that the rump of MPs who were left should have remained relatively quiescent without loudly voicing their opposition to the authoritarian measures of 1655 or the great breach of parliamentary privilege represented by the September purges. The exclusions did not go by without any opposition. On 18 September 1656 Sir George Booth presented a letter formally protesting at the exclusions, signed by 79 excluded MPs. This gave rise to five days of debate in which councillors and their allies met the charge that the exclusions were a breach of parliamentary privilege with justifications based on articles 14, 15 and 17 of the Instrument of Government.[11] Surprisingly this rearguard defence of the high-handed actions of the Council seems to have been successful. The most vociferous opposition came in pamphlets outside parliament, not from MPs (document 13). Parliamentary opposition soon petered out (on 22 September only 29 MPs voted against the exclusions) and the issue was not raised again until the end of the year, and then only briefly.

Moreover, subsequent research has not fundamentally altered Ivan Roots's conclusion reached 30 years ago that the long first session of the parliament was extremely productive.[12] In contrast to the barren legislative record of the first Protectorate Parliament, which did not pass a single statute, by the end of its first session in June 1657 the second Protectorate Parliament had presented 71 acts to the Protector for his assent. As early as November 1656 Oliver Cromwell, no doubt surprised, given his fears that the disappointing experiences of the previous winter in parliament might have been repeated, congratulated MPs that 'though you have sat but a little time ... you have made many good laws, the effect wherof the people of the Commonwealth will with comfort find hereafter'.[13] As the first session drew to a close in June, faced with all the acts he had been asked to agree to, he was reported as saying that 'if he should rise at 4 in the morning, he could not read them in a whole day'.[14]

What undoubtedly lay behind the Protector's delight at this achievement was the kind of legislation that was considered as much as its quantity. The many proposals for measures of social and moral reform discussed during the first session of the parliament are a reminder of the common ground between Protector, Council and many MPs on the need to reduce the numbers of alehouses, to legislate against profane swearing and drunkenness, and to put a stop to 'undecent fashions' among women. In addition to measures to put these moral reforms into effect, MPs also discussed law reforms, including Lambert's proposal for establishing a court of law and equity at York, a measure to relieve the plight of debtors in prison, and social reforms like those designed to set the poor to work and to regulate the wages of labourers and servants.[15]

Why was this parliamentary session so much more successful for Protector and Council than the previous parliament? The answer is not to be found in careful planning and behind-the-scenes manoeuvring by Protector or Council. In that respect at least H.R. Trevor-Roper's analysis of the political failings of the regime is valid.[16] Given the Protector's unwillingness to become involved in the parliamentary purge and his frequent assertions that he had no intention of interfering in the day-to-day business of parliament, his failure to give a lead to parliament is not surprising. He was, he said in April 1657, merely 'a good constable to keep the peace of the parish'.[17] That attitude in part at least explains Cromwell's lack of political leadership at this time. One can only conjecture why the Council remained similarly inactive. The most convincing explanation is that its members' unfounded confidence in the major-generals' ability to produce favourable election results had led them to believe that no political preparations for the parliamentary session were necessary.

There are two possible reasons why, notwithstanding Cromwell's lack of intervention, the session was not a total failure. First, the lesson that most MPs drew from what had happened in the first Protectorate Parliament was that all that would be achieved by continuing attacks on the government would be an early dissolution as in January 1655. This might explain their apparent willingness to co-operate with, rather than oppose, the government. But it is possible that many MPs had more positive reasons for acting as they did. Parts of Cromwell's opening speech to the parliament on 17 September 1656 may have encouraged support for the regime. It is probable that not everything that Cromwell said on that day was met with enthusiasm. His defence of the rule of the major-generals ('it hath been effectual for the preservation of your peace. It hath been more effectual towards the discountenancing of vice and settling religion, than anything done these fifty years') and his justification for the authoritarian measures of the regime in 1655 ('if anything should be done but what is according to law, the throat of a nation may be cut, till we send for some to make a law') must have grated on the ears of many who listened to the speech. But Cromwell's skilful explanation of the government's foreign policy was surely designed to tap the deep roots of anti-Catholic prejudices shared by most Englishmen at this time. 'Why, truly, your great enemy is the Spaniard', he said in a speech that, although often defying rules of grammar, had powerful oratorical force:

> He is. He is a natural enemy, he is naturally so. He is naturally so, throughout, as I said before, throughout all your enemies, through that enmity that is in him against all that is of God that is in you, or that may be in you, contrary to that that his blindness and darkness, led on by superstition and the implicitness of his faith in submitting to the See of Rome, acts him unto.

He also cleverly tarred royalists with the same brush of popery. 'Can we think that Papists and Cavaliers shake not hands in England?', he asked, in the next breath accusing them of being 'un-Christian' and 'un-English-like' (a phrase that Senator Joe McCarthy was to echo three centuries later in his accusation that Communist sympathisers in the United States were guilty of 'un-American activities'). Although MPs did not respond to this beguiling rhetoric immediately, and only granted subsidies for the war against Spain until January 1657, they did give the Protectorate's foreign policy their strong support. Nor were they likely to have found Cromwell's calls for further reformation disagreeable. Invoking Old Testament accounts of how the Israelites realised the need to reform themselves in order to secure God's help to keep them free of Egyptian bondage, Cromwell warned MPs against following 'a captain to lead us back into Egypt, if there be such a place – I mean metaphorically and allegorically so – that is to say, returning to all those things that we think we have been fighting against and destroying of all that good ... we have attained unto'. In a later part of the speech he pushed home the point in a purple passage that highlighted the deep importance of reformation:

> I am confident, that the liberty and prosperity of this nation depend upon reformation, to make it a shame to see men to be bold in sin and profaneness, and God will bless you. You will be a blessing

to the nation, and by this the more repairs of breaches than anything in the world. Truly these things do respect the souls of men,
and the spirit, which are the man. The mind is the man. If this be
kept pure, a man signifies somewhat; if not I would very fain to see
what difference there is betwixt him and a beast.[18]

As has been seen, this sentiment did not fall on deaf ears, and
MPs eagerly set about the task of reformation. It can too readily be
assumed by those who focus on the tensions between Protectorate and parliaments that there was no common ground between
government and MPs. Nothing could be further from the truth.

Conservative and radical Cromwellians and the making of the Humble Petition and Advice

Yet there is no denying that beneath the harmony and co-operation of the parliamentary session the two major issues that had
caused tensions between Protector, councillors and MPs in 1654–
55 were still there. Even a purge of parliament as massive as that
in 1656 could not produce an assembly in which the majority of
MPs were willing to accept either the continuing role and influence of the army in government or the religious liberty that
Cromwell and some of the councillors were willing to extend to
religious sects like the Baptists, other Independent groups and
even peaceable Quakers. As has been seen, these were the con-
tentious points that had led to the sudden end of the last parliamentary session. What made it even more likely than ever that
these issues would re-surface now is the fact that during the
autumn and winter of 1656–57 for the first time they also began to
cause divisions within the ranks of the Protectorate government
itself, between conservative and radical Cromwellian councillors
and advisers.

Recent research by Dr Patrick Little has provided confirmation
of the important role of Roger Boyle, Lord Broghill, in this process.[19] Broghill was a younger son of the first Earl of Cork and a
royalist in the Civil War in the 1640s, who had changed allegiance
in the 1650s and, as will be seen in chapter 7, became a major figure in the Cromwellian settlements in Ireland and Scotland. As a
result, by the mid-1650s his influence amongst Cromwell's advisers had risen considerably and this enabled him to form alliances
and friendships with more conservative elements within the

Cromwellian circle. As a member of the 'Old Protestant' group amongst the Irish landed elite, his commitment to Protestantism was not in any doubt.[20] But his religious position is best defined as 'Presbyterian' in that he had little sympathy for Independent sects like the Baptists, which he considered were a threat to the stability offered by a clearly defined national Church. These relatively conservative religious views harmonised with his desire to reduce the political power of the army and return to a more traditional form of government, even a monarchy, which he believed would provide a better guarantee of social and religious, as well as political, order than a military constitution. It is also likely that his preference for a civilian form of government was confirmed by the enmity that had developed between himself and General John Lambert during his time as commissioner in Scotland.

By the mid-1650s Broghill's political position was strengthened by his growing favour within the Cromwellian circle and his connections with the more conservative-minded Cromwellian councillors. He had 'long-standing' friendships with Edward Montague and Bulstrode Whitelocke, had worked with Sir Charles Wolseley, Philip Jones and John Claypole in the parliament of 1654, and was well-known to Thurloe, with whom he had worked in 1655 as Scottish commissioner. But the bulk of his political connections were with Scottish and Irish MPs. It has been calculated that between 9 and 15 Scottish MPs had been supported by Broghill in the 1656 elections. The number of Irish MPs with close links with Broghill and his Old Protestant allies was even higher, possibly 18. 'At its widest (and including MPs elected on allies' interests)', writes Dr Little, 'Broghill could call on the support of more than forty nine members – a tenth of all those elected.'[21]

It would be misleading to exaggerate the cohesiveness of the group that formed around Broghill (the label of 'conservative Cromwellians' adopted here is as likely to do that as is that of 'civilian Cromwellians'). As will be seen, members of this group did not act consistently on all issues. Nevertheless, they were much more keen than others, especially high-ranking army officers like Desborough, Fleetwood and Lambert and some of the major-generals, to see an end to the military constitution, embodied in the Instrument of Government, and during the winter of 1656–57 they worked to replace it with a constitution approved by parliament. But it is the contention of what follows that beneath the constitutional differences between conservative and radical Cromwellians on the respective virtues of a military or civilian constitution lay a more fundamental disagreement about the extent of religious change that was acceptable. Both groups saw themselves (and have been seen by historians) as advocates of 'reform'. But each viewed it differently. For 'conservative Cromwellians' like Broghill, 'reform' meant a return to traditional forms of government with guarantees of regular parliaments and limited religious liberty for Protestants within a strong national Church. For 'radical Cromwellians', like Fleetwood, the essence of 'reform' was not constitutional but religious. They, too, wanted a national Church but one that tolerated a much wider spectrum of Protestant views than 'civilian Cromwellians' and, more importantly, one that opened opportunities for people to achieve a godly reformation, a spiritual regeneration attained by loosening the controls on the expression of individual conscience.

In December 1656 and January 1657 two episodes brought these differences into the open: the case of James Nayler and the attempt to pass a Militia Bill to make permanent the decimation tax. As will be seen, these episodes also gave the initiative to the conservative Cromwellians and provided them with the political momentum to make public their proposal to replace the Instrument of Government with a constitution that restored the monarchy in the shape of King Oliver I.

The case of James Nayler

The case of James Nayler is an integral and significant part of the early history of the Quaker movement. Nayler was a leading member of the movement, which by the late 1650s may have been about 60,000-strong, a level of support bettered, among new religious sects, only by the Baptists. The essence of Quakerism as it developed in the period after the end of the Civil War was the belief that men and women should follow their 'inner light' – that is, what their consciences told them was right, since this was the voice of God. Quakers placed much less emphasis than other more orthodox Protestant groups on the Bible as a source of doctrine. They believed that 'the inner light', not the scriptural interpretations of church ministers, should guide their lives.

82

Nayler was one of a group of charismatic preachers (also including George Fox) to whom rank-and-file Quakers looked for leadership. In October 1656 he did something so extraordinary that many later commentators have been driven to dismiss it, as did Ivan Roots, as 'somewhat comical, strangely pathetic'.[22] In fact, to many Quakers Nayler's decision to re-enact Christ's entry into Jerusalem by riding into Bristol on a donkey with female followers strewing palms in his path was seen as a rational reflection of a central Quaker tenet that individuals should attempt to live the Christian experience to the full and that there was something of Christ in everyone.[23]

Only a handful of Nayler's contemporaries were able to see what he had done in that light. Nayler, by taking on the character of Christ (indeed by acting as though he were Christ), appeared to most people to be guilty of 'horrid blasphemy'. This was what the parliamentary committee which investigated the case between October and December 1656 charged him with. What gave venom to the charge was that to the vast majority of his fellow countrymen Quakers were considered to be dangerous and subversive people. Not only did they reject the authority of the Church and its ministers and the conventional framework of scriptural interpretation as laid down by the Church, but they also acted in ways which appeared to subvert the traditional social order as well. By refusing to take off their hats in the presence of their social 'superiors' and by habitually using the colloquial 'thou' rather than the formal 'you', they mounted an attack on the social hierarchy; by advocating the abolition of tithes, they were seen as attacking property rights; by refusing to swear oaths, they threatened the basis of legal procedure; and by allowing women preachers, they challenged the patriarchal social order.

Not surprisingly, therefore, the ten-day debate on the Nayler case in parliament produced outbursts of extreme and violent religious intolerance. Colonel Holland's tolerant speech was a rarity in a debate which occasionally plumbed the depths of religious bigotry. Major-General William Boteler even stated that he wished to see Nayler stoned to death, the penalty prescribed by Mosaic law for blasphemy. Yet others feared that a consequence of convicting and executing Naylor for 'horrid blasphemy' might be a precedent for further religious intolerance (document 14) and on 16 December 1656 a narrow majority of MPs voted by 96 to 82 against executing Nayler. Instead it was agreed that he should be pilloried and whipped twice, his tongue bored, and he should be imprisoned for life. No-one, with the possible exception of Colonel Holland, advocated that Nayler was innocent of any crime and should go free. Even Oliver Cromwell in his only public intervention in the case condemned what Nayler had done. In a letter to the Speaker of parliament on 25 December 1656 he wrote that 'having taken notice of a judgment lately given by yourselves against one James Nayler ... we detest and abhor the giving or occasioning the least countenance to persons of such opinions and practice, or who under the guilt of such crimes as are commonly imputed to the said person'.[24]

Yet it is clear that the Protector was far from untroubled by the Nayler case. The main point of his letter to the Speaker on 25 December was to ask what were the 'grounds and reasons' on which they had proceeded, raising (by implication) the question of whether the Instrument of Government allowed parliament to make judgements on religious matters, as it had done in the Nayler case. A couple of months later, in February 1657, he tackled that question by telling a meeting of army officers that 'the proceedings of this Parliament' showed that MPs 'stand in need of a check or balancing power (meaning the House of Lords or a House so constituted) for the case of James Naylor might happen to be your case'.[25] His audience needed no instruction on what he meant. The dangers of the Nayler case had been clearly spelled out by at least three speakers in the parliamentary debates of December 1656. 'I like it not, to leave it arbitrary to the judgment of after parliaments to determine what is blasphemy', said Luke Robinson on 12 December. On the following day Bulstrode Whitelocke made the same point: 'It will be of dangerous consequence for you to make a law for punishing of an offence by death, which was not so punishable before. One parliament may count one thing horrid blasphemy, another parliament another thing.' 'It is of dangerous consequence', declared William Sydenham on 15 December, 'to make a law under general terms and leave it to after ages to interpret your meaning.'[26] The fear that lay behind these comments was that many MPs might not draw a distinction between Nayler the Quaker and more moderate groups like Baptists and Independents.

Undoubtedly the major significance of the Nayler case in the history of the Cromwellian Protectorate was that, as well as polar-ising the supporters and opponents of religious toleration, it swelled the ranks of those who were willing to consider amend-ing (or even abandoning) the Instrument of Government.

The Militia Bill

Until the end of December 1656, however, constitutional change did not seem likely. On 28 October 'an Irish gentleman' (William Jephson, an ally of Broghill) had floated the idea of a return to a monarchical constitution in parliament, but had got little sup-port.[27] Rumours abounded of informal discussions taking place in political circles at this time. In November 1656 another Irish MP, Colonel John Bridge, reported a furious row he had had with Major-General James Berry in response to his suggestion that government return to be settled 'upon the old bottom'.[28] It is likely that Broghill and his allies were also meeting to consider constitutional changes that would reduce the power of the army, but, if so, they were kept secret.

Ironically, the opportunity to bring these discussions into the open came, not from conservative Cromwellians, but from a lead-ing radical Cromwellian, Major-General John Desborough. On 25 December 1656 (on the same day that Cromwell wrote to the Speaker raising the constitutional implications of the Nayler case) Desborough introduced a bill to make the decimation tax (and by implication the rule of the major-generals) permanent.[29] Why he decided to do this is a puzzle. The most plausible explanation is that he hoped, with the support of like-minded councillors, to push the bill through a House that was unusually small in num-bers as a result of the absence of many conservative-minded MPs who had left to spend Christmas at home, ignoring the official suppression of the festival. If that was Desborough's plan, it had only limited success. In the Christmas Day debate, Desborough received support from some councillors, Sir Gilbert Pickering, William Sydenham and John Lambert, and hard-line anti-Cava-lier MPs like Luke Robinson, whose speech echoed the Cromwellian rhetoric of the Protector's speech at the opening of parliament. But Desborough must have been surprised by the strength and coherence of the opposition to the bill from conservative Cromwellians, who used biblical arguments to buttress their claims that the decimation tax breached the 1652 Act of Oblivion that had offered pardons to all royalists who had not been active opponents of the republic since 1651 (document 14). Many royalists taxed by the major-generals came into that category. Although Desborough was allowed to proceed with the bill by a narrow majority of 88–63, when the bill was discussed again on 7 January and again later in the month it met very serious opposition, and it was finally quashed on 29 January 1657 by a decisive vote of 124–88.

By this stage at least there can be no doubt that the unity of the Cromwellian inner circle had fractured on the issue of whether or not the Instrument of Government, the foundation stone of the Protectorate since its establishment in 1653, should be abandoned. What was the Protector's attitude to this situation? Unfortunately, the surviving evidence is too partial and scanty to support a definitive answer.[30] The interpretation that is suggested here is that Cromwell made a conscious attempt to stand above both factions with the aim of eventually bringing them together again. This view is consistent with the way in which he had carefully distanced himself from the issues that had caused rifts to appear among his advisers since the summer of 1656: the decisions to call parliament, to exclude many MPs after the elections and to bring in a Militia Bill. It is likely that he was pulled towards making constitutional change by the Nayler case (as has been explained above) and no doubt by the informal talks he is known to have had at this time with Oliver St John and William Pierrpoint, and probably also with Broghill, Wolsely and other conservative Cromwellians.[31] Yet it is also highly probable that he was very reluctant to take the side of this faction and risk alienating the other, especially one member of it, John Lambert. Until this point, despite many rumours of jealousy between Cromwell and Lambert, based on the fact that Lambert was the only general who came near to rivalling Cromwell's popularity within the army, the two men had worked closely together in a combined effort to make a success of the Instrument of Government and the rule of the major-generals. Moreover, Cromwell shared the aspirations of Lambert and other radical Cromwellians for a much wider degree of religious liberty than that advocated by Broghill and the conservative Cromwellians.

When and why, then, did Cromwell decide to abandon the

major-generals and work for constitutional change? Before the end of February 1657 the only firm evidence that Cromwell had changed his mind is a speech delivered by Cromwell's son-in-law, John Claypole, on 7 January 1657 opposing the Militia Bill, which might have been made with the Protector's connivance. But 'might' is the key word in that sentence. Other evidence is even less sound, most of it being the reports of observers who wanted Cromwell to change his mind and who therefore seized on any-thing as 'evidence' that he had done so.[32] All that is certain is that he had made the decision by 27 February 1657, when he announced it at a meeting of army officers. 'It is time to come to a settlement', he told them, 'and lay aside arbitrary proceedings, so unacceptable to the nation.'[33] There are three possible reasons why he made that decision. The first has already been mentioned: the Nayler case had provided ample reasons for finding a consti-tutional safeguard against the religious intolerance of a single-chamber parliament. Second, Cromwell could not have missed the lesson to be drawn from the fact that parliament's grant of £400,000 for the Spanish war on 30 January 1657 was made on the day after the defeat of the Militia Bill: turning away from military rule might be rewarded by parliamentary co-operation. Third, and probably of most importance to Cromwell, though, is that four days before he addressed the army officers an alternative constitutional scheme to the Instrument of Government had made its appearance in parliament. What attracted Cromwell to it was the possibility that (suitably amended) it could be a means of re-uniting the divided Cromwellians.

The making of a 'new' Protectorate

On 23 February 1657 Sir Christopher Packe presented a paper in parliament 'tending to a settlement of the nation, and of liberty, and of prosperity'. Frustratingly for those in search of the origins of what was to be the basis of a new constitution for the Cromwellian Protectorate, Packe merely said that it had 'some-what come to his hand'.[34] However, most historians who have examined the episode are in agreement that the new constitution (called at this stage 'the Remonstrance') was the work of a group around Lord Broghill, consisting of Scottish and Irish MPs (notably William Jephson, John Bridge and Vincent Gookin) whose elections Broghill and his allies had supported in 1656, together with conservative Cromwellians like Sir Charles Wolseley, Philip Jones, William Pierrpoint, Edward Montague and Oliver St John, with whom Broghill also had close connections.[35] Significantly Packe's proposal was immediately opposed by Lambert, Sydenham, Desborough and Fleetwood. But they could not prevent a majority of 144–54 in favour of parliament considering the matter further. Much of February and March 1657 was spent doing just that, before the Remonstrance (now re-named the Humble Petition and Advice) was formally presented to the Protector on 31 March 1657.

During the next few weeks Cromwell made many favourable comments on the proposed constitution. On 8 April 1657 he praised it for providing 'the settlement of the chiefest things that can fall the hearts of man to desire'. Thirteen days later he was even more fulsome. He told a parliamentary committee: 'You have provided for the liberty of the people of God and of the nation, and I say, he sings sweetly that sings a song of reconciliation betwixt interests ... I think in this government you have made them to consist.'[36]

Why did he find the Humble Petition and Advice so attractive? As will soon be seen, not all its proposals were welcomed by him and his radical Cromwellian allies – notably the proposal that Cromwell should become King – but he may have been confident that these could be rejected. A more positive reason for his welcome for the Humble Petition and Advice was that none of its provisions conflicted with the constitutional 'fundamentals' he had outlined in September 1654.[37] Government was still to be by a single person and a parliament. Parliaments were to meet frequently (at least once every three years). Control of the army was shared by Protector and Council. It is true that the provisions regarding the fourth 'fundamental', liberty of conscience in religious matters, were a little more limited than those in the Instrument of Government. The clauses on religion in the Humble Petition and Advice were much more careful than those in the Instrument of Government to provide grounds to outlaw Unitarians and Quakers. But they, nevertheless, still secured protection for a wide variety of Protestant beliefs and made provision for a Confession of Faith to be agreed in the future 'according to the rule and warrant of the Scripture'. Thus the new constitution,

Cromwell believed, protected 'the liberties of men professing Godliness under a variety of forms amongst us'.[38] Above all, the new constitution proposed to erect a second chamber (called simply the 'Other House') that would, he hoped, provide protection against any further erosions of religious liberty that might follow in the wake of the Nayler case. Cromwell would have agreed with Thurloe's assessment that the Other House 'will be great security and bulwark to the honest interest'.[39]

During the prolonged negotiations on the constitutional proposals in the spring of 1657 it increasingly looked as if Cromwell would accept them, especially since parliament responded favourably and quickly to many of Cromwell's objections, including his criticism that the financial provision of £1,300,000 was inadequate. But the sticking point that could not be overcome was the issue of the kingship, which parliament had declared was an integral part of the new constitution. After much agonising, on 8 May 1657 Cromwell rejected the offer to become King Oliver I. A major personal reason for this decision was his providential world-view. As he saw it, the monarchy had been abolished in 1649 according to the will of God. Therefore to have restored it would have been to have flown in the face of God's judgement, bringing about the loss of God's support without which his visionary ambitions would, he believed, be demolished. On 13 April 1657 he made that providential reason against becoming King Oliver I very clear:

> Truly the providence of God has laid this title aside providentially … God has seemed providentially not only to strike at the family but at the name … God … hath not only dealt so with the person and the family, but he hath blasted the title … I would not seek to set up that that providence hath destroyed and laid in the dust, and I would not build Jericho again.[40]

But Cromwell's decision is also explicable by the political situation early in 1657, which threatened to tear the Protectorate apart from within. Explanations for Cromwell's refusal to become King need to take account of his relations with the now divided Cromwellians as well as his relations with God. What is suggested here is that an important reason why Cromwell refused the title is that he believed that to do otherwise would have destroyed for ever his chances of healing those divisions. King Oliver I would not have the bonds of trust with army officers and other radical Cromwellians that Lord Protector Cromwell still enjoyed. That was made clear by the fierce opposition to kingship expressed by army officers and the godly. Another important reason was that Cromwell may have also come to believe that by becoming King Oliver I he would have aligned himself so closely with Broghill and other conservative Cromwellians that he would have had no alternative but to accept their restricted, limited vision of reformation as a final settlement. When he rejected the offer of the crown on 8 May 1657 Cromwell had much evidence to hand of what that might mean. Early in 1657 a bill was going through parliament that would have introduced the use of a Presbyterian catechism. Equally of concern to him was the treatment of the Triers Ordinance in parliament. Although most of the Protectorate ordinances of 1654 were given unqualified approval by parliament on 28 April 1657, the Triers Ordinance, which was at the heart of the Cromwellian Church settlement, was amended by requiring that future commissioners for licensing ministers should be approved by parliament. Significantly one of the tellers in favour of this proposal in the parliamentary vote on it was Broghill. Cromwell may have seen this as an omen of what might ensue if he became King Oliver I.[41]

By rejecting the kingship that outcome was avoided. Parliament backed down from its insistence that the kingship was an integral part of the Humble Petition and Advice, and just over two weeks after Cromwell refused to become King it produced a revised version of the constitution that retained a Lord Protector as executive.[42] This was still not enough to gain Lambert's support. He refused to swear an oath of allegiance to Cromwell as required by the new constitution and withdrew (temporarily as it turned out) from the army and from politics. On 26 June 1657 Cromwell was re-invested as Protector. His ermine-lined robe and the offer to him of the sword of state and sceptre of gold were elements in a ceremony that was much more regal and splendid than the simple ceremony of 16 December 1653. These events have misled some historians into exaggerating the shift in the nature of the Protectorate in 1657. This is not a mistake made by Broghill, who followed his enemy, Lambert, by withdrawing (also temporarily) from the political scene in disgust at what had happened. He knew that there was little that was new about the 'new Protector-

ate'. The powers of Lord Protector Cromwell under the new constitution had not been eroded. Moreover, when the names of the
new Protectorate Council appointed by the Humble Petition and
Advice were announced, the only major change from the old
Council was the absence of Lambert. The divisions that had
appeared during the previous 12 months did not disappear, but
they had not succeeded in bringing about a fundamental alteration in the nature of the Cromwellian Protectorate.

Notes

1   Derek Hirst, 'The fracturing of the Cromwellian alliance: Leeds
and Adam Baynes', *English Historical Review*, 108, 1993; Carol S. Egloff,
'The search for a Cromwellian settlement: exclusion from the second
Protectorate Parliament, parts 1 and 2', *Parliamentary History*, 17, 1998.

2   Christopher Durston, 'The fall of the major-generals', *English
Historical Review*, 113, 1998, pp. 34, 37.

3   Peter Gaunt, '"The single person's confidants and dependants"?
Oliver Cromwell and his protectoral councillors', *Historical Journal*, 32,
1989, p. 557; S.R. Gardiner, *History of the Commonwealth and Protectorate*
(4 vols, London, 1903), vol. 4, pp. 253–5; Egloff, 'The search for a
Cromwellian settlement, part 1', pp. 184–6; Durston, 'The fall of the
major-generals', p. 19.

4   Egloff, 'The search for a Cromwellian settlement, part 1', pp. 184,
188, sees these debates as evidence of 'strains within the regime' that
reflected 'two separate world views' held by 'military Cromwellians'
and 'civilian Cromwellians'.

5   Quoted in Durston, 'The fall of the major-generals', p. 19. See
also Gaunt, '"The single person's confidants and dependants"?' p. 557,
for another report from the Venetian ambassador of Cromwell crying in
the Council and at one stage leaving peremptorily for Hampton Court.

6   Christopher Durston, *Cromwell's Major-Generals: Godly Government during the English Revolution* (Manchester, 2001), chapter 10: 'The
major-generals and the 1656 elections'.

7   Thomas Birch, ed., *A Collection of the State Papers of John Thurloe
Esquire* (7 vols, London, 1742), vol. 5, p. 230.

8   Gaunt, '"The single person's confidants and dependants"?',
p. 556; Egloff, 'The search for a Cromwellian settlement, part 1', pp. 190–
7. In my view Egloff exaggerates the role of the 'military grandees' in the
exclusions.

9   Patrick Little, 'The political career of Roger Boyle, Lord Broghill,
1638–60' (unpublished PhD thesis, University of London, 2000), pp. 222–
3.

10 Egloff, 'The search for a Cromwellian settlement, part 1', p. 188.

11 C.H. Firth, *The Last Years of the Protectorate* (2 vols, London, 1909), vol. 1, pp. 13–15.

12 Ivan Roots, 'Law-making and the second Protectorate Parliament' in H. Header and H.R. Loyn, eds, *British Constitution and Administration: Essays Presented to S.B. Chrimes* (Cardiff, 1974). The best recent assessment of the second Protectorate Parliament is Peter Gaunt, 'Oliver Cromwell and his Protectorate Parliaments: co-operation, conflict and control' in Ivan Roots, ed., *'Into Another Mould': Aspects of the Interregnum* (Exeter, 1998).

13 Ivan Roots, ed., *The Speeches of Oliver Cromwell* (London, 1998), p. 106.

14 J.T. Rutt, ed., *The Diary of Thomas Burton Esquire* (4 vols, London, 1828), vol. 2, p. 180, quoted in Roots, 'Law-making in the second Protectorate Parliament', p. 134.

15 Rutt, ed., *Diary of Thomas Burton*, vol. 1, has reports of many of these bills, e.g. on p. clxxxi the appointment of a committee to consider suppressing unlicensed alehouses, tobacco shops, etc.; Firth, *Last Years*, vol. 1, pp. 58–9.

16 H.R. Trevor-Roper, 'Oliver Cromwell and his parliaments' in R. Pares and A.J.P. Taylor, eds, *Essays Presented to Sir Lewis Namier* (London, 1956) and a revised version in his *Religion, Reformation and Social Change* (London, 1967). For a brief critique of Trevor-Roper's analysis, see Roger Howell, 'Cromwell and his parliaments: the Trevor-Roper thesis revisited' in R.C. Richardson, ed., *Images of Oliver Cromwell* (Manchester, 1993).

17 W.C. Abbott, ed., *The Writings and Speeches of Oliver Cromwell* (4 vols, Cambridge, Mass., 1937–47), vol. 4, p. 570.

18 Roots, ed., *Speeches of Oliver Cromwell*, pp. 79–106; the quotations are from pp. 100, 81, 84, 98.

19 Little, 'Political career of Roger Boyle, Lord Broghill'. The following paragraphs draw heavily on this excellent thesis.

20 See chapter 7 for the importance of this group in Irish and English history in the 1650s.

21 Little, 'Political career of Roger Boyle, Lord Broghill', pp. 224–6. See also P.J. Pinkney, 'The Scottish representation in the Cromwellian parliament of 1656', *Scottish Historical Review*, 66, 1967, and T. Barnard, 'Lord Broghill, Vincent Gookin and the Cork election of 1659', *English Historical Review*, 88, 1973.

22 Ivan Roots, *The Great Rebellion, 1642–60* (London, 1966), p. 205.

23 The best book on this fascinating episode is Leo Damrosch, *The Sorrows of the Quaker Jesus: James Nayler and the Puritan Crackdown on the Free Spirit* (Cambridge, Mass., 1990). See also T.A. Wilson and F.J. Merli,

'Naylor's case', *University of Birmingham Historical Journal*, 10, 1965–66.

24 Abbott, ed., *Writings and Speeches*, vol. 4, p. 366.

25 Roots, ed., *Speeches of Oliver Cromwell*, p. 112.

26 Rutt, ed., *Diary of Thomas Burton*, vol. 1, pp. 119, 130, 172.

27 Firth, *Last Years*, vol. 1, p. 64.

28 C.H. Firth, 'Cromwell and the crown', *English Historical Review*, 17, 1902, p. 43.

29 See Durston, 'The fall of the major-generals', for a full treatment of Desborough's decision and its consequences.

30 See *ibid.* for a careful assessment of the evidence, from which he comes to a slightly different interpretation from mine.

31 See, for example, Birch, ed., *Thurloe State Papers*, vol. 6, p. 37.

32 I think that Professor Durston's reasons for doubting that Claypole's speech is evidence that Cromwell had decided to abandon the major-generals at this stage are very persuasive. See Durston, 'The fall of the major-generals', p. 27.

33 Roots, ed., *Speeches of Oliver Cromwell*, p. 112.

34 Rutt, ed., *Diary of Thomas Burton*, vol. 1, p. 318.

35 The main secondary sources are Firth, *Last Years*, vol. 1, pp. 128ff.; Carol S. Egloff, 'Settlement and kingship: the army, the gentry, and the offer of the crown to Oliver Cromwell' (unpublished PhD thesis, Yale University, 1990), chapter 4; Little, 'Political Career of Roger Boyle, Lord Broghill', chapter 7; Durston, 'The fall of the major-generals', p. 34.

36 Roots, ed., *Speeches of Oliver Cromwell*, pp. 118, 152–3.

37 See chapter 2.

38 Roots, ed., *Speeches of Oliver Cromwell*, p. 116.

39 Birch, ed., *Thurloe State Papers*, vol. 4, p. 93.

40 Roots, ed., *Speeches of Oliver Cromwell*, pp. 136–7. See Barry Coward, *Oliver Cromwell* (Harlow, 1991), pp. 151ff. for a fuller discussion of this point.

41 Carol S. Egloff, 'Robert Beake and a letter concerning the Humble Petition and Advice, 28 March 1657', *Historical Research*, 68, 1995, p. 236. Cromwell vetoed the Catechism Bill on 9 June. Roots, 'Lawmaking', p. 136; Rutt, ed., *Diary of Thomas Burton*, vol. 2, p. 55.

42 See S.R. Gardiner, ed., *Constitutional Documents of the Puritan Revolution* (3rd edn, London, 1906), pp. 464–7, and J.P. Kenyon, ed., *The Stuart Constitution: Documents and Commentary* (2nd edn, Cambridge, 1986), pp. 324–30 for the text of the new constitution.

5

The end of the Cromwellian Protectorate, June 1657 – May 1659

Within two years of the re-installation of Oliver Cromwell as Lord Protector in June 1657, the Cromwellian Protectorate was over. Almost exactly a year after that, the Stuart monarchy was re-stored. This rapid turn-around of events has coloured historians' interpretations of the last phase of the Cromwellian Protectorate covered by this chapter. During its last months the Protectorate of Oliver Cromwell has often been portrayed as a regime that ran out of revolutionary steam. It is often said that the Protector, his energy sapped by old age, illness and the blow of his daughter's death, gave up the struggle to bring about reformation. Driven by the realisation that the new Protectorate constitution, the Humble Petition and Advice, was 'unworkable', Cromwell is said to have begun to listen more and more to conservative Cromwellians who urged him to call another parliament and accept the crown that some believed parliament would again offer him. Before that could happen, he died and his Protectorate ended in an atmosphere of deep gloom and disillusionment.

The history of the Protectorate of Richard Cromwell, who succeeded his father, has received similar treatment by historians who view the 1650s through the distorting lens of hindsight. Historical accounts of it have been almost universally negative. Richard, it is often assumed, was at best inexperienced in government, and at worst incompetent. The brevity of his rule was therefore unsurprising. With a man like Richard Cromwell at the helm, the Cromwellian Protectorate was bound to collapse.

This chapter is written in the belief that these negative interpretations of the end of the Cromwellian Protectorate stand in urgent need of modification. In what follows, the mounting problems facing the Protectorate between June 1657 and Oliver Cromwell's death in September 1658 will not be unduly minimised, but neither will the strength and continuing vigour of Oliver Cromwell's Protectorate during its last months. Similarly, the difficulties facing Richard Cromwell that brought about the rapid end of his Protectorate will not be glossed over, but neither will the successes that he had as Protector. These successes demand a more careful analysis of why the Cromwellian Protectorate ended in May 1659 than offered by those who assume that the outcome was an inevitable result of the failing powers of Oliver Cromwell or the personal inadequacies of Richard Cromwell.

The end of the Protectorate of Oliver Cromwell

It is not hard to see why the last 15 months of Oliver Cromwell's Protectorate have been portrayed in a very negative way. His regime faced an awesome catalogue of problems. Some of these had been apparent before June 1657. First and foremost amongst these were the escalating debts incurred by the regime's costly war against Spain and by the maintenance of large standing armies throughout the British Isles. On 21 April 1657 Cromwell estimated that, even given the £1,300,000 a year offered by the Humble Petition and Advice, the shortfall between government revenue and expenditure would be well over £500,000. The Protector prefaced that calculation by saying that he had 'little skill in Arithmetic as I have in the law', and on this occasion his typical self-deprecating comment may have been justified.[1] Moreover, there is little doubt that the financial situation was worsening rapidly. By the summer of 1658, according to C.H. Firth, the Protectorate's debts amounted to £1.5 million, and by the beginning of April 1659 a Commons committee put the debts at nearly £2.5 million, of which just short of £890,000 was made up of money owed to the army.[2] Whether the regime was on the verge of 'imminent bankruptcy'[3] during Oliver Cromwell's last months is a moot point, but there is no denying that the financial situation was grim.

Nor had the seriousness of the rifts within the regime or the intensity of opposition from outside diminished. Tensions

95

between conservative and radical Cromwellians continued to simmer beneath the surface of politics. A running theme in the correspondence between Henry Cromwell, Viscount Fauconberg and Lord Broghill for much of 1657–58 is their suspicions of Desborough, Fleetwood and other army generals. In February 1658 the Council was reported to be split on Desborough's and Fleetwood's proposal that a new decimation tax on royalist delinquents be introduced to help meet the regime's financial problems. When the proposal was defeated by moderate Cromwellians, Henry Cromwell told Thurloe: 'I am glad to heare, that as well non-legall as contra legall wayes of raising money are not hearken'd to ... Errors in raiseing money are the compendious wayes to cause a generall discontent.' His delight at the defeat of the proposal reflects the deep divisions among the inner circle of Cromwellians.[4]

Royalist intrigues, too, continued to present the regime with worrying problems. In January 1658 the Earl of Ormond arrived in England from Ireland intent on organising plots against the regime, and shortly afterwards another in a long series of royalist plots, this time one fronted by Sir Henry Slingsby, was uncovered by Thurloe's diligent counter-espionage system and the perpetrators were executed.[5]

Much more serious were the continuing signs of opposition within the Protectorate's main power base, the army. As has been seen, in July 1657 the only senior general who had the ability and personal charisma to act as a focus for this opposition, Lambert, had meekly obeyed Cromwell's order that he resign his army commission. Lucy Hutchinson's comment that he then spent his time tending his garden and working 'at the needle with his wife and maides' need not be taken literally. But her assessment that Lambert 'was watching an opertunity to serve againe his ambition' rings true in the light of his later activities.[6] Events were to prove that Lambert's withdrawal from politics was only temporary. Nor was Lambert alone in the army in opposing the revamped Protectorate. In February 1658 Major William Packer and five captains from Cromwell's own regiment openly voiced their discontent at what they felt was the Protectorate's deviation from the 'good old cause', a slogan that was to gain enormous support within the army a year later. All six were cashiered by Cromwell (document 15).[7]

What forced him to take this drastic action was the signs that the army malcontents had forged an alliance with the Commonwealthsmen, among whom Sir Arthur Heselrige, Sir Henry Vane and Edmund Ludlow were the most prominent. These were the most persistent and consistent of the Protectorate's enemies. Ever since its establishment the Commonwealthsmen had been united in their loathing of a regime that they believed had destroyed the sovereignty of parliament. In 1656 Vane published a tract, *A Healing Question*, which (in the guise of an appeal for unity among all opponents of the royalist cause) was intended to gain the support of those (including the army malcontents) who felt that Protectorate leaders had abandoned any visionary aspirations for the attainment of religious and political liberty that they had once held.[8] Cromwell and Council took steps to quash both the tract and its author, who was imprisoned, but it is likely that *A Healing Question* played a major role in the subsequent emergence of an alliance between Commonwealthsmen and army malcontents that was to prove fatally disastrous as far as the Cromwellian Protectorate was concerned.

Just how serious a threat this alliance could be became apparent when the parliament that had been prorogued in June 1657 met for its second session in January 1658. It is likely that the alliance was the main reason why the session lasted for only a few weeks. Even without the support they had in the army, the provisions of the new Protectorate constitution ensured that the Commonwealthsmen would be much more powerful opponents of the regime than ever before. Most obviously this came about because the new constitution took away the Council's power of excluding MPs from parliament, thus allowing the Commonwealthsmen and others prevented from taking their seats in 1656 to return to parliament. Yet equally important were two effects of erecting a second chamber. The first effect was to reduce the numbers of the regime's supporters in the Commons. During the last winter months of 1657 many of those invited to sit in the new chamber refused to do so. Notable among these were members of the old 'middle group' and Political Independents, like Oliver St John, who had been allies of Cromwell in the mid and late 1640s. The letter of one of these, Lord Saye and Sele, advising another, Lord Wharton, not to sit illustrates their objections, which neither

Protector nor Council could satisfy (document 16). As a consequence, Cromwell had to dilute the ranks of Protectorate supporters in the Commons by removing about 30 of them to serve in the Other House. Of equal importance, the erection of a second chamber gave the once-excluded MPs a glorious opportunity to depict the Protectorate, which had instituted a chamber that looked suspiciously like the old House of Lords, as a regime further sliding away from the principles of the 'good old cause', and themselves as the guardians of it.

On 25 January 1658 these events forced the Protector to make one of his rare direct interventions in parliamentary proceedings in a powerful speech pleading for an end to 'the calamities and divisions among us'.[9] He clearly still hoped that this appeal to moderate opinion in parliament against the tactics of the Commonwealthsmen might be successful in restoring the working relationship between Protector, Council and MPs that had characterised the first session of this parliament. There is little doubt that what forced him to change his mind was the evidence that the Commonwealthsmen were fomenting opposition to the regime not only in parliament but in the army as well. This came in the form of a republican petition promoted in the last days of January 1658 by radical elements in London, demanding the abolition of the Protectorate and the Other House and the restoration of a single-chamber parliament with all the powers possessed by the Rump Parliament of 1649–53. It also made a clear appeal for army support by its demands that religious liberty should be extended and that soldiers should only be cashiered by courts martial and not by Protectoral fiat. When it became known that this petition was to be presented to parliament on 4 February 1658, Cromwell decided to act. On that very day he took everyone by surprise, made an unscheduled visit to parliament and, after making an angry speech, dissolved parliament. There is little doubt that Cromwell felt he had to bring the second Protectorate Parliament to a sudden end in this way as the only means of overcoming the problem of an army–Commonwealthsmen alliance and thereby preserving army unity behind the regime.

Although that object was secured by this desperate measure, other problems remained. It is not surprising that the atmosphere amongst those at the centre of the Protectorate in the following months was very different from the atmosphere immediately after the Protectorate was established. Inevitably the exhilaration of those heady months had seeped away under the relentless pressure of mounting problems. But it is important that this point is not carried too far. There is another dimension to the last days of the Protectorate of Oliver Cromwell other than failure and disillusionment.

One of the most obvious areas of success in these later months is international affairs. By 1658 Britain under the Protectorate had achieved a position of Great Power status that it had never had before and was not to achieve again until the last decade of the seventeenth century. The capture of Dunkirk in June 1658 and the enormous damage that this did to Spanish power in Flanders is an indication of the way the Protectorate had succeeded in ensuring British security from foreign invasion by the time of Cromwell's death. This history will be more fully analysed in the next chapter. Moreover, the work of James Scott Wheeler and Mike Braddick has demonstrated how crucial were the 1640s and 1650s in the transformation of Britain into a 'fiscal-military state', one capable of raising enough money by tapping the true wealth of the country to sustain effective, active polices in the wider world, something that Britain had not been able to do before, although it was not achieved without great financial cost.[10] The achievements of British military and naval forces abroad in the later 1650s, underpinned by major changes in public finance, are in great contrast to the failures of overseas adventures by English monarchs from Henry VIII in the 1520s and 1540s to Charles I in the 1620s and late 1630s.

Far too much has also often been made of the scale and seriousness of internal threats facing the Protectorate of Oliver Cromwell in 1658. Despite the intrigues of Ormond (indeed perhaps *because* of them), the City of London's loyalty to the regime remained rock-solid. In a speech to the Lord Mayor, aldermen and common council of the City on 12 March 1658, Cromwell used the threat of instability posed by royalist intrigues to ensure that this was so. He painted a vivid picture of 'the imminent danger in which both the city and the whole nation was like to be involved by reason of the contrivements of Charles Stuart and his party both at home and abroad, who secretly have used the utmost of their endeavours to embroil the nation and this city – the principal place at which they aim – in a new war'.[11] A week later the City fathers responded with a warm address of loyalty and compliance in raising the City militia.[12]

The regime's success in dealing with army malcontents was even more significant. Royalists had never posed a major threat to the security of the Protectorate; army disaffection was potentially more serious. Yet *potentially* is the key word here. During the last year of the Protectorate of Oliver Cromwell *actual* signs of army discontent are few and far between. The dismissal of Lambert in July 1657 occasioned no protests at all from within the army. Similarly the cashiering of Packer and the five captains in February 1658 was followed by a period in which soldiers throughout England, Ireland and Scotland declared their loyalty to the regime. This was not achieved without considerable effort by Cromwell and other senior army officers. Before he dismissed Packer and his colleagues Cromwell stage-managed a gathering of about 200 officers in the Banqueting Hall in Whitehall for nearly two hours, using alcohol ('many bottles of wine were then drunk', reported one source) as well as oratory to secure from the officers a 'resolve to stand and fall, live and die, with my Lord Protector'.[13] The next month, Cromwell and Fleetwood spoke at similar meetings, all ending with presentations of addresses of loyalty to the Protector, signed by all present. On 27 March 1658 a declaration of loyalty from the whole English army was given to Cromwell and during the next three months newspapers, army newsletters and the correspondence of Thurloe and others tell of addresses of loyalty coming in from regiments in Scotland and Ireland, as well as in England.[14] 'I never observed a greater calme than at this time', wrote Thurloe to Sir William Lockhart, the Protectorate's ambassador in France, in March 1658. 'And as for the army, I do assure you, they are in a very good temper in all three nations.'[15] It may be that Thurloe's comment has an element of self-delusion about it; but the wealth of evidence of the army's loyalty throughout the British Isles at this time suggests that this was not the case.

Nor does the available evidence support a picture of a Protector who had not only lost his grip but had also given up the struggle to contain the tensions between radical and conservative Cromwellians, opting instead for a return to monarchy and a conservative settlement. Sources for this period are not plentiful and it *might* be that this is what happened. But the evidence for this picture is not strong. The only indication that Cromwell had resigned himself to accepting the crown if it were offered to him again when parliament next met is to be found in the letters of those who hoped that this would be the case. Fauconberg's often-quoted statement in his letter to Henry Cromwell on 20 April 1658 that the only uncertain thing about Cromwell's decision whether to become King was its timing ('Kingship is resolved on, but when uncertain'[16]) is a good example of this kind of wishful thinking. Nor does the composition of the committee of nine councillors (a mixture of conservative and radical Cromwellians), which was appointed to meet daily from June 1658 to discuss what might happen when another parliament met, suggest that Cromwell had abandoned his determination to balance the factions around him. The radical Cromwellians on the committee would have opposed very strongly any idea that Cromwell should make any major constitutional concessions in order to buy parliamentary financial and political support. These and other aspects of the last months of Cromwell's life support the contention that when the Protectorate of Oliver Cromwell ended the regime's visionary aspirations were still very much alive.[17]

The end of the Cromwellian Protectorate

To say that the task facing Richard Cromwell when he became Protector on his father's death in September 1658 was not an easy one is a gross understatement. Most of the difficulties experienced by his father remained to be tackled, and the problem of doing so was made many times more difficult by the circumstances in which Richard succeeded his father. Not only did he face the same implacable opposition to the Protectorate from the Commonwealthsmen as had his father, but the failure of Oliver Cromwell to groom his eldest son as his successor either by giving him a political education in government or by encouraging him to forge links with powerful elements in the army was a recipe for the growth of army mistrust to a level which threatened to bring about the collapse of the Protectorate. Yet a close analysis of the first six months of the Protectorate of Richard Cromwell from September 1658 to the end of March 1659 suggests that such an outcome was not inevitable.[18] During those six months Richard Cromwell was successful in containing both the opposition of the Commonwealthsmen and army discontent. One conclusion to be

drawn from this is that research into why the Cromwellian Protectorate suddenly came to an end after March 1659 needs to
focus less on Richard Cromwell's 'political inability' and more on
developments within the army that brought about a powerful
anti-Protectorate coalition of Commonwealthsmen and senior
and junior army officers. It is in these developments that the key
explanation for the collapse of the Cromwellian Protectorate in
May 1659 is to be found.

The first public announcement that Richard Cromwell was to
become the new Lord Protector was not made until after his
father's death on 3 September 1658. The process that led to that
announcement is shrouded in mystery. Especially uncertain are
the reasons why Oliver Cromwell failed to make arrangements
for the succession long before he died. Cromwell himself left no
clue as to his motives, leaving much room for speculation. One
obvious possibility is that his indecision on this issue, like Queen
Elizabeth I's when confronted with the urgency of naming a successor towards the end of her life, was rooted in a natural aversion
to confronting his own mortality. A more probable motive is that
(as in the kingship crisis of 1657) Cromwell was reluctant to be
seen by God as guilty of the sin of the selfish pursuit of ambition
for himself and his family. Given Cromwell's providential views,
this is an attractive hypothesis, but, in the absence of any hard
evidence, it remains no more than that. Equally uncertain is the
timing of Cromwell's decision to nominate his elder son as his
successor. Indeed such is the ambiguity and scarcity of the available sources that it is not even certain that Cromwell ever did so.
Earl Hause's claim that Cromwell in fact nominated Fleetwood as
his successor is difficult to disprove, but, as Austin Woolrych
argues, it is equally hard to accept. It is unlikely that Cromwell
towards the end of his life had a very high regard for Fleetwood's
political abilities and that he would have been willing to put the
task of ruling Britain and Ireland into the hands of a man whom
in February 1658 he called 'a milksop'.[19] Moreover, when Oliver
Cromwell died there is not one shred of evidence that anyone
ever mentioned the possibility that Fleetwood was the Protector's
choice. On the afternoon of 3 September 1658 immediately following Cromwell's death, at a meeting of the Council, attended
by 11 men representing both conservative and radical
Cromwellians, there was unanimous agreement that Richard

Cromwell should be proclaimed his father's successor. The likelihood is that this represented Oliver's wish made clear only in the last hours of his life.

Amidst these uncertainties about the way in which Richard Cromwell became Protector, though, there is one cast-iron certainty: its consequence was that the new Protector was singularly untrained for his new position. Before the end of 1657 he had been given no role of significance in the government of the Protectorate. Since his marriage in 1649 to Dorothy, daughter of Richard Major of Hursley near Winchester, he had lived the life of a country gentleman in Hampshire. Too much weight can be given to his father's comments in family letters that Richard was an idle wastrel. These comments are illustrative of Oliver's high standards of personal and public morality, together with a natural over-cautious parental concern; and it is thus a mistake to read them as objective assessments of Richard's personal qualities. Yet there is no denying that Richard Cromwell (unlike his younger brother, Henry) had held no major office until he was appointed to the Protectorate Council of State in December 1657, and even thereafter he appears to have been a peripheral figure in government circles.

His public visits to Bath and Bristol in June 1658, which were widely reported in newspapers,[20] raise the possibility that these were conscious attempts to establish Richard's public profile. But, if they were, they remain isolated examples. When Oliver Cromwell became Protector he had behind him a decade-long apprenticeship in the art of politics during and after the Civil War. This had transformed him into a very astute politician. In contrast, his son had not had this valuable political education. Nor, unlike his father, had he any strong connections with the army, and what contacts he had had in the world of politics were with conservative Cromwellians, like Sir Charles Wolseley, Edward Montague and Philip Sidney, Viscount Lisle. Radical Cromwellians, like Desborough, resented and mistrusted him.[21] Much may be uncertain about the process by which Richard Cromwell became Protector, but what is certain is that his transition from country gentleman to ruler of Britain and Ireland was much more rapid than had been his father's similar transformation. Consequently, it is difficult to disagree with Ronald Hutton's comment that 'never in English history has any person approached supreme power with such little practical preparation'.[22]

To anyone who has been prompted by this assessment to make the knee-jerk assumption that from Richard's accession the Cromwellian Protectorate went into a steep irreversible nose-dive, the next few paragraphs may come as a shock. Like some contemporaries, they may find, as Bulstrode Whitelocke reported after Richard Cromwell's audience with the French ambassador on 18 October 1658, that the new Protector 'did carry himself ... better than was expected'.[23] During the first six months of his Protectorate from September 1658 to the end of March 1659, he showed that he had enough political skills to have a fair amount of success in containing the two most dangerous sources of opposition to his Protectorate: the army and the Commonwealthsmen. Marvell's expectations of the young Protector in his poem *On the Death of Oliver Cromwell* may not have been totally groundless (document 17).

Richard's confidence in dealing with the army and Commonwealthsmen must have been boosted by the evidence of the popular support with which his accession was greeted. Addresses of loyalty to the new Protector flooded in from most parts of the country.[24] Contemporary observers also commented on the weakness of the regime's potential opponents. Four weeks into the new Protectorate, Bordeaux, the French ambassador, whose reports to Mazarin are very full and often perceptive, was very optimistic about the new regime's situation. Both the City of London and the army, he believed, were 'bound by their own interests to maintain the existing state of things, because of the advantages which they derive from it'. The Commonwealthsmen (Bordeaux called them 'Republicans'), he went on, were 'few' and 'without a Parliament, they will have some difficulty in making themselves heard'.[25] Judging by their correspondence, Richard's accession also further demoralised the royalists, prompting David Underdown to conclude that the Sealed Knot entered 'one of its periodic slides of confusion and indecision'. The royalist Earl of Clarendon later concluded that on Richard's accession 'the king's condition never appeared so hopeless, so desperate, for a more favourable conjuncture they could never expect than this, that had blasted all their hopes, and confirmed their utmost despair'.[26]

During the first weeks of his rule the new Protector showed many times that he was capable of capitalising on this advantageous situation. Because the sources are thin on the ground, only hints of this can be seen. One such case is the way the new Protector handled the religious question. He showed from the outset his determination that, under his leadership, the Cromwellian Protectorate would continue to maintain a national Church that was far broader than many others at that time dared to allow. This is why Richard Baxter, who worked energetically in the 1650s to put this Cromwellian ideal into practice, so enthusiastically welcomed Richard Cromwell's accession. Baxter's *Holy Commonwealth*, published in 1659, has been rightly called by William Lamont 'a love poem to Richard Cromwell'.[27] That Baxter was not mistaken in believing that the new Protector was committed to this comprehensive ideal can be seen in a remarkable speech Richard made on 14 October 1658 at the end of an 11-day conference of representatives from Independent churches that agreed on a 'Declaration of Faith and order owned and practised in the congregational churches in England'. Richard's speech shows that the new Protector was not immune from the sense of isolation that, it has been seen, sustained the visionary aspirations of his father and those around him at the centre of his government. His call for the maintenance of 'the foundacion of Syon' and his recognition that 'we are but a little handful, a little people' are the hallmarks of his father's speeches. Richard may have been literally justified in saying that 'I am not moulded to make speeches. I have infirmity, I want experience.' Yet his inexperience did not prevent him from hitting the notes that had gained his father so much support among the godly elements in the nation.[28]

This attribute was to stand him in good stead in dealing in the first few months of his Protectorate with many soldiers' deep mistrust of the new Protector and some of those around him. Just how serious a problem this was soon became obvious. On 18 September 1658 Richard was presented with an address, organised by Fleetwood and signed by over 200 army officers. While pledging their support for the Protectorate, the signatories made it clear that their support was conditional on the regime's pursuit of radical reform. Derek Massarella may be going too far in suggesting that the officers were claiming 'unambiguously that they were a separate estate, a new departure in English constitutional history', but he is right to pinpoint the importance of a document which showed how determined the army was that its views should not be sidelined in the new Protectorate.[29] Richard's reply to the address paid due attention to that fact and, accompanied as it was by moves to meet the army's demands for pay as well as for reform, it went some way towards mollifying his critics in the army. That it would not satisfy them fully, however, was obvious at the time. One of the sharpest critics of the army around the new Protector, Viscount Fauconberg, reported in code in a letter to Henry Cromwell that the address 'in the end I fear will prove a serpent'.[30] What gives authenticity to that comment is the fact that senior army officers like Fleetwood and Desborough were much more likely to be swayed by government concessions than were their fellow junior officers. Mistrust of the new Protector was much more deeply rooted among the latter and, ominously, this split in the army increased as many junior officers began to hold separate meetings in the army barracks in St James's Palace, while senior army officers met at Fleetwood's London home, Wallingford House.

Mistrust of the Protectorate among many junior officers was evidently growing fairly quickly. When Richard Cromwell appointed Edward Montague, a conservative Cromwellian who already was in charge of the navy, to the command of an army regiment, the grumbling of discontent among junior officers at their regular prayer meetings at St James's flared into a crisis. Early in October 1658 a group of junior officers threatened to draft a petition that would not only restate the demand that soldiers should only be cashiered after military courts martial but would also demand that Fleetwood replace the Protector as overall commander of the army. Richard Cromwell met this crisis with a judicious mixture of firmness and concessions. His speech to a meeting of angry army officers on 18 October 1658 bears comparison with his father's addresses to similar meetings of discontented army officers in the past. He took the sting out of the opposition by showing he adhered to many of the army's ideals and by promoting Fleetwood to Lieutenant General of the army. Shortly afterwards, too, he announced measures to meet the army's demands for their arrears of pay. But he was careful not to allow these concessions to weaken his control of the army (document 18). A few weeks later he held further conferences with army officers, culminating in another major intervention on 19 November 1658, following reports of quarrels and unrest at prayer meetings of junior officers. His speech on that occasion was again successful in defusing the opposition to the Protectorate.[31] It would be misleading to suggest that army suspicions of the Protectorate's conservative tendencies disappeared. They did not. Indeed the regal nature of the old Protector's funeral on 23 November 1658 was commented on unfavourably in both army and radical circles. Yet significantly there was no recurrence of threatening talk at meetings of army officers for at least the next few months. The correspondence of conservative Cromwellians during that period is peppered with loathing at the soldiers' political influence, a feeling that may have had more than a hint of jealousy at the way Richard Cromwell had managed by the end of 1658 to begin to overcome the gulf of mistrust between him and many in the army.[32]

By that time, however, the Protectorate of Richard Cromwell faced another major problem. At the beginning of December 1658 the government's financial needs forced the Council to call a new parliament, which was to meet in January 1659. As the French ambassador had noted a few months earlier, a parliamentary session was bound to give the Commonwealthsmen a platform from which they could launch attacks on the Protectorate. It soon became clear that they were well-prepared to do so, as they began holding daily meetings at Vane's house.[33] Events also played into their hands. The decision of the Council to revert to the pre-1653 electoral arrangements had the effect of increasing the overall number of MPs in the Commons and the proportion elected from borough seats, which made the task of parliamentary management by the government more difficult than it already was.[34] Furthermore, during the short session of the third Protectorate Parliament from January to April 1659 the Commons had no less than three Speakers whose record in controlling proceedings seems to have been less than firm.

There is little doubt that the Commonwealthsmen took full advantage of these favourable circumstances. The fruits of their planning meetings outside the House can be seen partly in their use of blatant filibustering tactics to frustrate their opponents in the debates in this parliament.[35] In one of these Sir Arthur Heselrige commented with heavy irony that 'I never spoke to the matter'.[36] Nothing could be further from the truth. He and his fellow Commonwealthsmen conducted a planned, frontal attack on a government bill introduced three days after the start of the session confirming Richard's title as Lord Protector. In speech after speech Commonwealthsmen, like Henry Neville, mounted an attack on the powers given to the Protector by the Humble Petition and Advice to control the army and veto legislation, and subjected the Other House to withering onslaughts.[37]

But it is important not to make the assumption that, vociferous though the Commonwealthsmen were, they were totally successful. The history of the first three months of the third Protectorate Parliament shows that they were not. Despite their speeches in parliament in favour of the army, their hopes of forging an alliance with army representatives in parliament met with dismal failure. Their petition linking their grievances with the army, on the lines of a similar petition planned to be introduced in Oliver Cromwell's parliament a year previously, met with a very hostile reception when it was presented to parliament on 18 February 1659. Realising that it aimed to reduce his powers considerably (it would, said the French ambassador, have reduced him to the status of the Doge of Venice), Richard Cromwell spoke at a meeting of army officers at Wallingford House and effectively blocked moves to gain their support for the petition. It is a measure of the Commonwealthsmen's failure in parliament that (as has been brilliantly shown by Austin Woolrych) they were forced in February 1659 to begin a pamphlet campaign outside parliament aimed at the army, which, though venomous in its attacks on the Protectorate, was not immediately successful. Nor did the Commonwealthsmen achieve their other parliamentary aims. In a series of votes in the Commons in February and March 1659 MPs not only accepted the principle of two Houses and voted to do business with the Other House (something they had refused to do in Oliver Cromwell's last parliament), but they also recognised Richard Cromwell's control of the armed and naval forces.[38] By the end of March 1659 the Protectorate of Richard Cromwell did not look like a regime with only a few weeks of life left.

Why, then, did the Protectorate collapse so suddenly? Two main reasons deserve emphasis. The first, which is not as important as the second, is that after the end of March the Commonwealthsmen's extra-parliamentary campaign to win support in the army was much more successful than it had been hitherto. This was so partly because their pamphlets became even more skilful in playing on the suspicions of those in the lower ranks of the army that their senior officers had become corrupt and were motivated solely by personal gain. They also continued to hammer home the refrain, originally sounded in Vane's *Healing Question*, that the 'good old cause' of religious liberty for which the army had fought before 1651 was being threatened by the machinations of those aiming to turn the Protectorate into a monarchy. In a series of effective pamphlets the guilty men were clearly identified as those who in 1653 had usurped the rule of the Long Parliament and brought about the end of 'the days of innocency and simplicity', to which the pamphlets advocated a return.[39] These sentiments, though not new, gained more support because contemporary events seemed to confirm that they were true. During February and March 1659 pro-monarchical speeches by MPs were frequent;[40] so too were proposals by MPs to reduce or even disband the army.[41] In March, too, MPs voted that the elections to parliament of two army Commonwealthsmen and former major-generals, Robert Lilburne and William Packer, were void. What also gave the Commonwealthsmen's pamphlet propaganda credibility was leaked stories of the Protector himself apparently taking the side of the opponents of another two of the junior officers' champions, Colonels Ashfield and Ingoldsby.

These events certainly helped the Commonwealthsmen in their efforts to raise the army's opposition to parliament and Protector to new heights. This situation, though, was not *by itself* enough to bring about the end of the third Protectorate Parliament and the Protectorate itself. What ensured that this happened is that the deterioration in relations between the junior ranks of the army and both Protector and parliament coincided with a major change in the attitudes of the senior army officers, Fleetwood and Desborough, to the developing crisis. The main argument of the rest of this chapter is that this change is the major reason why the Protectorate collapsed.

As has been seen, despite their concerns at the influence of conservative Cromwellians over the old and new Protectors, for more than two years Fleetwood and Desborough had never given anyone cause to doubt their allegiance to the Protectorate. From the end of March 1659 this was no longer the case. Although the negotiations took place in secret, it is likely that at about that time Fleetwood and Desborough began to put out feelers aimed at bringing about a close association with the Commonwealthsmen. Since their motives for doing this are naturally not recorded, all one can do is speculate what they were. Professor Woolrych suggests persuasively that Dr John Owen played an important role in weakening their commitment to the Protectorate by awakening their consciences to the dangers of pride and ambition. But it is likely, as Woolrych concedes, that more important in bringing about their attempted rapprochement with the Commonwealthsmen was a desire to counter Lambert's growing influence in the army and to try to control the increasing force of the army's discontent.[42]

If that was their aim, it is clear from what happened next that they failed miserably to attain it. During the next few weeks the Commonwealthsmen's influence in the army became stronger than ever. It is true that the provocative actions of MPs also helped to bring this about. During April 1659, as Woolrych aptly puts it, 'the Commons ... helped to dig their own grave' by taking action against the army and religious freedom.[43] The most blatant example of the former was the decision on 12 April to impeach Major-General Boteler for his maltreatment of royalists in 1656; and nothing could have been more calculated to fuel the anger of the army than the Commons' declaration of a public fast to seek God's pardon for not punishing 'blasphemies and errors' that many in the army subscribed to or at least believed were acceptable. While such displays of parliamentary opposition to the army and religious liberty were not new, now the senior army officers for the first time failed to act as a brake on the anger such action aroused in radical circles. Indeed in negotiating with the Commonwealthsmen and then in April resurrecting the General Council of Officers, Desborough and Fleetwood served to foment the army's anger.

The new role played by the army grandees explains why during the next few weeks the general Council of Officers became a powerful force that brought about the end not only of the third Protectorate Parliament but of the Cromwellian Protectorate as well. During the first meetings of the General Council of Officers the increased influence of the junior officers was reflected in the election of radicals like Colonel Ashfield to a committee to draft a petition to parliament. Desborough and Fleetwood tried to tone down the resulting petition, but it is difficult to avoid the conclusion that by this stage the senior army officers were powerless to prevent a collision between the army and both parliament and the Protectorate.

On 17 April Richard Cromwell made an attempt to prevent a split between the army and parliament at a meeting with officers, but without any support now from the grandees he was powerless. As events were to show, his next move was disastrous, but it is easy to see how in the circumstances he was seduced by the advice of conservative Cromwellians, like Broghill, that a preemptive strike against the army was the only chance to resolve the crisis. On 18 April the Commons voted to outlaw any further meetings of the General Council of Officers, and the Protector signalled his concurrence by announcing that that body was now dissolved. Not surprisingly, the bulk of the army reacted angrily. Fleetwood and Desborough belatedly avowed their loyalty to the Protector. But events had now spun out of their control. What finally cut the ground from under the feet of the senior officers was the debate on 21 April in the Commons on a motion to settle the army as a militia, which would have put the soldiers under parliamentary control. They now had no other option but to follow the calls of the Commonwealthsmen and junior officers for a dissolution of parliament. Richard at first refused to do this, but in the face of reports that only a few hundred soldiers had remained loyal to him and that others were disobeying the orders of the few officers who stood by him, he capitulated. Late on the night of 21 April he signed a document dissolving parliament, and next morning, after brief resistance, MPs likewise capitulated and departed for home.

As had happened six years before, military power had brought about the dissolution of a parliament. Paradoxically, though, this dissolution was to result in the recall of the very parliament that the army had sent packing in April 1653. This outcome illustrates how impotent were the army grandees after their decision to compromise their support for the Protector a few weeks earlier, for all the signs are that they did not want that outcome. During the next few days discussions of the senior army officers at Wallingford House centred on finding means to ensure that the Protectorate continued. But what actually happened illustrates that power during the last days of the Protectorate was wielded not by the grandees but by the Commonwealthsmen and their junior army officer allies meeting at St James's.

Against the background of a pamphlet campaign calling for the restoration of the Long Parliament, many of the officers cashiered by Oliver Cromwell were restored to their commands and many pro-Richard Cromwell officers were ejected. Significantly, among those who returned to their former army posts was John Lambert, and one of Richard's major conservative advisers, Broghill, left for Ireland. The decision of the General Council on 6 May to recall the Rump Parliament dissolved by the army in 1653 was, in these circumstances, inevitable. It was a decision that sounded the death knell of the Protectorate. When the Rump reassembled on 7 May, discussions continued about dealing with Richard Cromwell's debts and voting expenses incurred in his removal from the Protectorate palaces. But this amounted merely to tidying up loose ends. By this stage the country was governed by the General Council of Officers and the restored Rump. On 24 May Richard recognised the inevitable and signed a parliamentary paper resigning all his powers. The Cromwellian Protectorate was no more.

Notes

1   Ivan Roots, ed., *The Speeches of Oliver Cromwell* (London, 1998), p. 162. Figures in M. Ashley, *Financial and Commercial Policy under the Cromwellian Protectorate* (London, 1934), p. 96, indicate that the government debt was much greater than Cromwell believed. See J.S. Wheeler, *The Making of a World Power: War and Military Revolution in Seventeenth Century England* (Stroud, 1999), p. 209, for figures that detail the massive rise in military expenditure in the 1640s and 1650s, which made up nearly 85 per cent of the total expenditure of the state.

2   C.H. Firth, *The Last Years of the Protectorate* (2 vols, London, 1908), vol. 2, p. 265.

3   This is the judgement of Derek Hirst, 'Concord and discord in Richard Cromwell's parliament', *English Historical Review*, 107, 1988, p. 339.

4   Thomas Birch, ed., *A Collection of the State Papers of John Thurloe Esquire* (7 vols, London, 1742), vol. 6, p. 820.

5   Firth, *Last Years*, vol. 2, pp. 61ff.

6   Lucy Hutchinson, *Memoirs of the Life of Colonel Hutchinson* (ed. J. Sutherland, Oxford, 1973), p. 209.

7   W.C. Abbott, ed., *The Writings and Speeches of Oliver Cromwell*

(4 vols, Cambridge, Mass., 1937–47), vol. 4, pp. 740–1.

8 For a fuller and different interpretation of the purpose of *A Healing Question*, see Ruth E. Mayers, 'Real and practicable, not imaginary and notional: Sir Henry Vane, *A Healing Question*, and the problems of the Protectorate', *Albion*, 27, 1996.

9 Roots, ed., *Speeches of Oliver Cromwell*, p. 179.

10 Wheeler, *Making of a Great Power*, and M.J. Braddick, *The Nerves of State: Taxation and the Financing of the English State, 1558–1714* (Manchester, 1996).

11 Roots, ed., *Speeches of Oliver Cromwell*, p. 194.

12 Firth, *Last Years*, vol. 2, pp. 50–1.

13 Abbott, ed., *Writings and Speeches*, vol. 4, p. 737.

14 C.H. Firth, ed., *Selections from the Papers of William Clarke* (Camden Society, new series, vols 49, 54, 61, 62, 1891–1901), vol. 61, p. 144; Abbott, ed., *Writings and Speeches*, vol. 4, p. 769.

15 Birch, ed., *Thurloe State Papers*, vol. 6, p. 863.

16 *Ibid.*, vol. 7, p. 85.

17 This case is argued more fully in Barry Coward, *Oliver Cromwell* (Harlow, 1991), pp. 54–8. It receives support from the last official portrait of Oliver Cromwell by Edward Mansell. In it, writes L.L. Knoppers, 'we find no signs of regality, nor indeed of pomp. Cromwell's final portrait was the most puritan and plain style of all'. See *Constructing Cromwell: Ceremony, Portraits and Print 1645–61* (Cambridge, 2000), p. 130.

18 The main secondary sources for this period, on which the following paragraphs are largely based, are two biographies of the new Protector, Earl M. Hause, *Tumble-Down Dick: The Fall of the House of Cromwell* (New York, 1972) and R.W. Ramsey, *Richard Cromwell* (London, 1935); three works by A.H. Woolrych, 'The Good Old Cause and the fall of the Protectorate', *Cambridge Historical Journal*, 13(2), 1957, 'Last quests for settlement' in G.E. Aylmer, ed., *The Interregnum: The Quest for Settlement* (1972) and 'Historical introduction' in R.W. Ayers, ed., *The Complete Prose Works of John Milton*, vol. 7 (New Haven and London, 1980); and R. Hutton, *The Restoration: A Political and Religious History of England and Wales 1658–67* (Oxford, 1985).

19 Earl M. Hause, 'The nomination of Richard Cromwell', *The Historian*, 27, 1965; *idem, Tumble-Down Dick*, chapter 2; A.H. Woolrych, 'Milton and Cromwell' in M. Lieb and T. Shawcross, eds, *Achievements of the Left Hand* (Amherst, 1974), pp. 202–8; *idem*, 'Historical introduction', pp. 4–5. See also, Firth, *Last Years*, vol. 2, pp. 302–6.

20 For example, *Mercurius Politicus*, 1–8 July 1658.

21 In April 1658 Henry Cromwell wrote to Broghill that he was glad that his father 'will not let such as Disb [Desborough] affront my brother R.'. Birch, ed., *Thurloe State Papers*, vol. 7, pp. 56–7.

22 Hutton, *Restoration*, p. 18.

23 Echoing this theme, a newsletter reporting Richard's address at the opening of the third Protectorate Parliament in January 1658 said that it 'was beyond all expectations'. This and Whitelocke's comment are quoted in C.H. Firth, 'A speech of Richard Cromwell, 18 October 1658', *English Historical Review*, 23, 1908, pp. 734–5.

24 Hutton, *Restoration*, pp. 21–2.

25 M. Guizot, *The History of Richard Cromwell and the Restoration of Charles II* (2 vols, London, 1856), vol. 1, p. 234.

26 D. Underdown, *Royalist Conspiracies in England, 1649–60* (New Haven, 1960), p. 231; Edward Hyde, Earl of Clarendon, *History of the Rebellion* (ed. W.D. Macray, 6 vols, Oxford, 1888), vol. 6, pp. 98–9.

27 Richard Baxter, *A Holy Commonwealth* (ed. W. Lamont, Cambridge, 1994), p. ix.

28 Firth, 'A speech by Richard Cromwell', pp. 734–5.

29 D. Massarella, 'The politics of the army and the quest for settlement' in Ivan Roots, ed., *'Into Another Mould': Aspects of the Interregnum* (Exeter, 1998), p. 127.

30 Birch, ed., *Thurloe State Papers*, vol. 7, p. 406.

31 *Clarke Papers*, vol. 61, pp. 1068–70; Guizot, *History of Richard Cromwell*, vol. 1, pp. 202–4.

32 See, for example, Henry Cromwell to Fleetwood, 20 October 1658; Thurloe to Henry Cromwell, 2 November 1658; Fleetwood to Henry Cromwell, 9 November 1658; and Henry Cromwell to Thurloe, 17 November 1658; all in Birch, ed., *Thurloe State Papers*, vol. 7, pp. 454–5, 490–1, 498, 513–14.

33 C.H. Firth, ed., *Memoirs of Edmund Ludlow* (2 vols, Oxford, 1894), vol. 2, p. 50; Birch, ed., *Thurloe State Papers*, vol. 7, pp. 541, 550.

34 G. Davies, 'The election of Richard Cromwell's parliament, 1658–9', *English Historical Review*, 63, 1948; G. Nourse, 'Richard Cromwell's House of Commons', *Bulletin of John Rylands Library*, 60, 1977–78.

35 On this parliament see Ivan Roots, 'The tactics of the Commonwealthsmen in Richard Cromwell's parliament' in D.H. Pennington and K. Thomas, eds, *Puritanism and Revolution: Essays on Seventeenth Century History Presented to C. Hill* (Oxford, 1978); and Hirst, 'Concord and discord'.

36 J.T. Rutt, ed., *The Diary of Thomas Burton Esquire* (4 vols, London, 1828), vol. 4, p. 6, quoted in Hirst, 'Concord and discord', p. 342.

37 For example, Rutt, ed., *Diary of Thomas Burton Esquire* , vol. 3, pp. 34, 35, 132–4.

38 Woolrych, 'The Good Old Cause', pp. 138–44. The rest of this chapter relies a lot on this excellent article.

39 Quoted in Woolrych, 'The Good Old Cause', p. 140.

40 For example, speeches by 'Mr. Higgons' and 'Mr. Gewen' on 8 February 1659, Rutt, ed., *Diary of Thomas Burton*, vol. 3, pp. 125–8, 181.

41 For example, speeches by Sir Richard Temple on 5 March 1659 and 'Mr. Hungerford' on 7 March 1659, *ibid.*, vol. 4, pp. 40–1, 63–4.

42 Woolrych, 'The Good Old Cause', especially pp. 146–7.

43 *Ibid.*, p. 141.

Part II

The impact of the Protectorate

6

The Cromwellian Protectorate and the wider world

So far this book has focused on the nature of the Cromwellian Protectorate and on the aims and aspirations of those at its centre from its establishment in December 1653 until its collapse in the spring of 1659. In the next three chapters, although these matters will not be forgotten, the focus shifts to the impact made by the regime. Its impact on three areas will be examined: on Britain's place in the wider world of international affairs; on the place of Scotland and Ireland in the 'British' republic; and finally on the people of England and Wales.

In one sense, the first of these, which is the subject of this chapter, is the most straightforward of the three. Few would contest the conclusion that a major impact of the Cromwellian Protectorate on international affairs was to bring about a rise in Britain's status to a position in the world it had never enjoyed before. Certainly many contemporaries, friendly and hostile, English and foreign, spoke with a deafening intensity and unanimity on this point. Edmund Waller trumpeted it in verse in a poem written in the mid-1650s:

The seas's our own, and now all nations greet
With bending sail each vessel of our fleet;
Your power extends as far as winds can blow:
Or swelling sails upon the globe may go.
Heaven, that hath placed this island to give law,
To balance Europe, and her States to awe –
In this conjunction doth on Britain smile,
The greatest leader, and the greatest isle!

Hither the oppressed shall henceforth resort,
Justice to crave and succour at your Court;
And then His Highness, not for ours alone,
But for the world's Protector, shall be known.[1]

Foreigners also conceded England's great international power. On 17 June 1654 the Venetian ambassador in Spain reported to the Doge that 'the court of London has rendered itself conspicuous by the number of its negotiations with foreign powers. That crown has made itself the third power of Europe.'[2] So too did royalists. Sir Edward Hyde, Earl of Clarendon, writing after the Restoration, was no less effusive in his assessment of the foreign policy of the Protectorate:

> [Cromwell's] greatness at home was but a shadow of the glory he had abroad. It was hard to discover which feared him most, France, Spain, or the Low Countries, where his friendship was current upon the value he put upon it. And as they did all sacrifice their honour and interest at his pleasure, so is there nothing he could have demanded that either of them would have denied him.[3]

This view was put into sharper focus as England's reputation plummeted in the later seventeenth century. Sir William Lockhart, England's ambassador in Paris under both the Protectorate and Charles II, noted the decline in respect he was given by the French after 1660.[4]

That, however, is about as far as agreement on the foreign policy of the Protectorate goes. Much else about the aims and achievements of the regime in international affairs is highly controversial and has been so almost from the moment that the Protectorate collapsed until the present day.[5] As with many other aspects of the history of the Protectorate, opinion has tended to polarise: contemporaries and later historians have either vilified or praised its foreign policies. Not all contemporaries by any means were critical of them; nor have historians been universally hostile. Michael Roberts's work on Anglo-Swedish relations in the 1650s is especially laudatory. 'Cromwell's policy in the Baltic', he writes, 'was in point of fact right, and reasonably successful.'[6] However, by and large, most contemporary and later commentators have taken a more critical stance. The criticisms of the republican Slingsby Bethel, written in the 1660s, are particularly harsh (document 19). Another of Cromwell's enemies from the 1650s, the Commonwealthsman Edmund Ludlow, commenting like Bethel after the Restoration, also wrote an unqualified denunciation of Oliver Cromwell in foreign affairs.[7]

Few historians have been quite so forthright in their condemnation, although Ronald Hutton makes some choice, if extravagant, jibes. 'Had all English foreign policy been conducted with comparable foresight and common sense', Hutton comments sarcastically on the Protectorate's decision to fight the Spanish in the Caribbean in 1654, 'then England would probably not now exist.' His verdict on the campaign of the Protectorate's navy under Admiral Robert Blake in the Mediterranean in 1655 is no less censorious. It was, according to Hutton, 'a game of international smash and grab rather like the regimes controlling Germany and Italy during the late 1930s'.[8] Others, like Menna Prestwich, have been more restrained,[9] but nonetheless they have condemned the Protectorate for following outdated policies that looked back to the days of Elizabeth I and were no longer relevant in the world of the 1650s, which (it is alleged) saw religious passions cooling and secular, 'rational' motivation taking the place of 'irrational' religious enthusiasm. These kinds of critical assessments have led to Cromwellian foreign policy being discussed most frequently – indeed, one is tempted to write, solely – around one simple question: did the Cromwellian Protectorate sacrifice the country's true national interests in pursuit of outdated and irrational religious aspirations?

This chapter will not follow this trend. The closer one looks at this often-asked question, the more misconceived it seems to be. As will be seen, religious aspirations in international affairs in this period were not irrational and outdated.[10] Most statesmen in many European countries in the sixteenth and seventeenth centuries were concerned – albeit to varying degrees – to pursue religious ambitions in their dealings with other countries. Moreover, a second assumption implicit in this question is equally shaky: religious aspiration at this time did not inevitably conflict with the interests of nations. Considerations like these make it necessary to jettison the old question and to formulate others in order to open more fruitful approaches to the foreign policy of the Cromwellian Protectorate. Two, in particular, will be tackled in this chapter. Why did Britain in the 1650s embark on a novel activist role in Europe? And what were the consequences of that role for Britain and Europe? These questions will be used as a means of making intelligible the often-complicated relations between the Cromwellian Protectorate and the United Provinces, France, Spain, Sweden, and other European powers. The key to the answer to the first question (it will be suggested) lies in the intensity of the religious aspirations of those at the heart of the government of the Protectorate, which propelled them to embark on an activist role in Europe that was unprecedented in English history during the sixteenth and seventeenth centuries before 1689. As will be seen, this occasionally had disastrous consequences and it burdened the country with huge financial debts. But only rarely did the regime's religious aspirations push it to adopt foreign policies that can be unreservedly said to have harmed the country's strategic interests. On the contrary most commentators in the seventeenth century believed that the Protectorate's international policies significantly enhanced the country's interests and its prestige, making it for the first time in its history a major player in European affairs.

The activist role of the Protectorate in international affairs

The novelty of the Protectorate's activist and interventionist role in European affairs in the context of early modern English governments in general needs to be emphasised. The Anglo-Spanish naval war of the last decades of Elizabeth I's reign was hardly central to European affairs in the later sixteenth century. The pacifistic and arbitrating role of Elizabeth's successor, James VI and I, in European affairs may have accorded with the crown's straitened finances, but in international terms it was ineffectual. Charles I's intervention in the Thirty Years War, steadfastly avoided by his father, was ignominious and lasted for only a few years in the later 1620s, after which he led his country into a period of relative isolation from European affairs. After the Protectorate collapsed and the monarchy was restored, neither Charles II nor James II played a decisive role in international affairs and during their reigns their country was overshadowed by the might of France. In great contrast to all this, the Protectorate often took the initiative in European affairs. Reflecting Oliver Cromwell's motto on his personal coat of arms incorporated into the great seal of the Protectorate, *'pax overitur bello'* ('peace through war'), the government often did not shrink from using force to pursue its policies. Before looking at examples that support this assertion, it is worth asking why the Protectorate marked such a deviation from the normal trends of sixteenth- and seventeenth-century English foreign policy?

Two main reasons suggest themselves. The first is that the Protectorate inherited an activist foreign policy and the means to follow it from its immediate predecessors. Bernard Capp's excellent book on the Cromwellian navy shows clearly how that navy was built up by the Rump into a major European force. Traditionally, the wartime English navy had largely consisted of merchant ships hired from their owners and ships captured from the nation's enemies. From the early days of the republic the Rump, as well as relying on these means, also embarked on a huge ship-building programme. In March 1649 five new warships were commissioned, 20 new ships were built in 1650–51, and when the Dutch war began in 1652 30 more warships were ordered to be built. By 1653 the Rump had a massive navy of 180 ships, far greater than any of its main international rivals, France, Spain or the United Provinces. Capp also argues persuasively that this powerful navy enabled the Rump and Barebone's Parliaments to force a hostile international community to change its tune after its initial attempt to ostracise them as regicide regimes. Within a very short period France, Spain, the United Provinces and other European powers sent ambassadors to London and thereby recognised the republican regime. They were also compelled to acknowledge that it was a force to be reckoned with in European affairs, especially after it began to show its naval power in the Anglo-Dutch war that began in 1652.[11]

The second explanation why the Protectorate continued this activist role abroad is to be found in the religious aspirations that characterised the Protector, the Council and their supporters. It is not surprising that their zeal to defend Protestantism and to bring about a godly reformation did not disappear when they came to consider affairs outside England. In this chapter and in the documents at the end of the book, examples will be seen of this missionary aspiration in international affairs often voiced by spokesmen of the Protectorate (see, for example, Cromwell's reported speech in document 21). It would be wrong to read these, as some foreign ambassadors did, as the utterances of idealists who were out of their depths in the harsh world of diplomacy. It is true that neither Oliver Cromwell nor many of those around him had much experience in foreign affairs. Few of the members of the Protectorate Council in 1653 had direct diplomatic experience. Walter Strickland had been one of the parliamentary commissioners who had gone to the United Provinces in 1642 to try to persuade the Dutch not to support Charles I (which may be why he was chosen to accompany Oliver St John on a diplomatic mission to The Hague in 1651), and Lord Lisle had accompanied his father on an embassy to Paris in 1636. But others, like the Protector, had none. Moreover, few had lived abroad – the exceptions are Lawrence and Fiennes, who had lived in the United Provinces, and Rous, who had studied at Leiden University in 1597.[12] Not all of Slingsby Bethel's criticisms of the regime were well-founded, but it is difficult to disagree with his coy comment on Cromwell: 'I am apt to think he was not guilty of too much knowledge of them [foreign affairs]' (document 19). The same could easily have been said of most of those involved in shaping the foreign policy of the Protectorate.

In 1656 Christer Bonde, one of the Swedish ambassadors in London, was shocked to learn that, after the departure of Philip Meadowes to Portugal, few at the heart of Protectorate government were able to speak Latin, the main language of international diplomacy in this period. 'It is a scandal', Bonde wrote, 'they have no one who can write a decent line of Latin, but the blind Miltonius must translate anything they want done from English to Latin, and one can easily imagine how it goes', implying that this was recipe for disaster.[13] But he was wrong. The makers of foreign policy in the Protectorate were not political innocents. They had learned by hard experience to temper their idealistic enthusiasm with doses of pragmatism. As J.H. Elliott has written of statesmen like Olivares and Richelieu in early seventeenth-century France and Spain, 'they were forced to operate as best they could in a grey area of compromise, casuistry and equivocation, weighing political advantage against religious scruple and the dictates of conscience'.[14] Political craftiness and the pursuit of high ideals are not necessarily incompatible. As will be seen, religious concerns remained central to the foreign policy of the Protectorate, ensuring that the regime played a dynamic role in international affairs.

The Protectorate and the Dutch

In one respect at least, Bethel's analysis of the ending of the Dutch war by the Treaty of Westminster is correct: those at the centre of power were eager to make peace with the Dutch (document 19).[15] Peace negotiations with the Dutch had dragged on interminably under the Rump and Barebone's Parliaments. The situation was transformed after the establishment of the Protectorate and peace was rapidly concluded by April 1654. There is no doubt that Protector and Council were more eager to make peace with the Dutch than had been the republican regimes they replaced. But it would be a mistake to assume that they did not share some of the attitudes to the Dutch that had led to the outbreak of war in 1652.

As has long been recognised, commercial rivalry was a major ingredient in the hostility between the two nations. Dutch merchants had proved to be much more successful than the English in capturing the carrying trade in the Baltic and Mediterranean; and in the race for the valuable spice trades of east Asia, the Dutch East India Company had out-traded and out-fought its English rival. The Dutch victory in east Asia was symbolised by the forcible expulsion of English East Indian traders from Amboyna in the Spice Islands (modern Indonesia) in 1623, an incident that was known on the English side of the Channel as 'the Amboyna Massacre'. The Rump had appointed a committee to find a means of restricting Dutch trade, and the consequent Navigation Act of 1651, which decreed that all imports to England had to be in English ships or in ships of the country from where the imported good originated, was in part an attempt by the English to recapture some of the world's trade from the Dutch. Pincus's conclusion that the war was not the result of these commercial rivalries to any significant extent fails to carry conviction.[16]

But was this the main reason for the English hostility to the Dutch? It is easier to agree with Pincus's contention that it was not. Two other considerations drove a wedge between nations that ought to have been pulled together by their commitment to Protestantism and republicanism.[17] Both are to be explained by the influence within the United Provinces of the House of Orange, the family that had led the Dutch in their successful fight for freedom against Spanish rule in the later sixteenth and early seventeenth centuries. This had two adverse consequences for English attitudes to the Dutch. The first is grounded in the fact that the House of Orange was closely associated with the English republic's enemies, notably the Stuarts. Indeed Prince William of Orange, who died in 1650, had been married to Mary, daughter of Charles I of England. Even after William's death, the House of Orange and its supporters remained committed to the Stuart cause, posing the threat of a Dutch-backed Stuart invasion of England. The second consequence was an even more powerful solvent of potential Anglo-Dutch Protestant comradeship. Dutch support for the House of Orange drove some English republicans not only to fear the Dutch as a potential threat to English security but also to hate them as a nation that had reneged on the godly cause of Protestantism and republicanism and had gone over to the Antichristian forces of heresy and absolutism. The English (in Pincus's words) came 'to see the Dutch as fallen brethren, men who had been seduced by Mammon and monarchy'.[18]

What complicates this picture of English republicans being driven to loathe their Dutch fellow Protestants and republicans is that in the United Provinces, especially in the province of Holland and among merchants, the anti-Orangist party led by John de Witt gained a position of dominance in the government of the country after William of Orange's death in 1650. This accounts for the decision taken by the Rump at the end of 1650 to send Oliver St John and Walter Strickland to The Hague in an attempt to bring the two countries together. Indeed what St John and Strickland proposed when they arrived in January 1651 was nothing short of a union between the two countries. The English saw this as a means of permanently excluding the House of Orange from influence in the United Provinces. Not surprisingly, a nation that had only recently won its national sovereignty after a hard-won struggle was not willing to accept this. The effects on English republican opinion of this rejection, accompanied as it was by demonstrations of support within the United Provinces for the Orangist cause, was to confirm the English image of the Dutch as a nation that had turned its back on the case of Protestantism and liberty and had embraced the cause of absolutist universal monarchy that the House of Orange was seen to represent. The great merit of Pincus's analysis is to show that the passage of the Navigation Act in October 1651 and the outbreak of the Dutch war in June 1652 had these stronger causes than simple economic rivalry.

By the summer of 1653 it was clear that the English navy had won the war in the North Sea. In June 1653 the English navy under George Monck won a four-day battle off the Gabbard, and at the battle of the Texel on 31 July 1653 the English again won a major victory, in which the Dutch admiral, Martin Tromp, was killed. In mid-June 1653 de Witt sent commissioners led by Jerome Beverning to negotiate peace terms. There is little doubt that Cromwell and his allies, who were now at the helm of English affairs after the dissolution of the Rump, welcomed these moves towards peace. But it would be a mistake to believe (as did Bethel and some later historians) that they were in favour of peace at any price. Cromwell's reported comments to some members of the Dutch negotiating team in a conversation in St James's park on 14 July 1653 are often used to argue that they were. 'The interests of this nation and ours too consisted in the welfare of commerce and navigation', the Dutch ambassadors said that Cromwell told them. 'The world was wide enough for both.'[19] However, probably the most that can be read into this comment is that, like the members of the Rump who started the war with the Dutch and the radicals in Barebone's Parliament who were keen to continue it, commercial rivalry between the two nations was not the major concern. Like the supporters of the war, Cromwell and his allies were keen to secure guarantees that supporters of the House of Orange would be prevented from ever again regaining a dominant position in the United Provinces.

Unlike many radicals inside and outside Barebone's Parliament, however, Cromwell and his allies were willing to accept that the Dutch (like the Scots in 1648) were a people who could be persuaded to return to paths of godliness by means short of being brought to their knees by war. Consequently, when the Protectorate was established many of the harsh proposals that had been pressed on the Dutch in the peace talks in late 1653 were dropped. The Dutch were no longer asked to recognise English ownership of the North Sea and to lease fishing rights there for 21 years; nor were they pressed to promise to limit their navy to 40–60 warships. The peace talks moved fairly rapidly to a successful conclusion by the Treaty of Westminster, which was signed in April 1654. The terms were more lenient on the Dutch than those that would have been made if it had been concluded before the establishment of the Protectorate. Yet the treaty undoubtedly met the two aims for which the English had fought the war.

Since protection of England's commerce had been of lesser importance, the Protectorate did not insist that the Dutch make major economic concessions. Significantly, the calculation of the compensation owed by the Dutch in reparations was left to independent arbitration. Yet England's commercial interests were not totally ignored. From this point of view what was not dealt with by the treaty was as significant as what was. A notable omission from it was the Navigation Act, which remained in force. This was spotted very quickly by James Waynwright, the London agent of an English merchant-cum-government agent in Hamburg, Richard Bradshaw. 'You may take note', wrote Waynwright to Bradshaw on 5 May 1654, 'notwithstanding the articles [of peace], the act for trade and shipping stands good to all intents and purposes.'[20] Moreover, as a direct consequence of the treaty, peace brought many benefits to English merchants whose trade had suffered badly throughout the world, but especially in the Baltic.[21] There, English ships had been seized by both the Dutch and the Danes, who had allied during the war to prevent English merchants from entering the Baltic through the Sound separating Sweden and Denmark. Peace ensured that that co-operation ended and paved the way for the re-establishment of English trade on equal terms with other nations. This was later confirmed by separate commercial treaties made between England and Sweden (April 1654) and England and Denmark (September 1654).

Much more stringent terms were imposed on the Dutch to ensure that the major political aim of the war (as defined by the Rump, Barebone's Parliament and the Protectorate) was achieved. Not only were the Dutch forced to promise not to aid any enemies of the English, but they also agreed to order their ships to strike the flags and lower their topsails when passing English ships, thus explicitly recognising the Protectorate as the legitimate regime in England. An even greater concession was secured from the Dutch in a secret agreement, in which representatives of the province of Holland promised never again to appoint any member of the House of Orange to the position of *Stadholder*, the effective head of state in the United Provinces. When assessed against the aims for which the English had fought the Dutch war, the Treaty of Westminster was a very satisfactory outcome of the republic's first major intervention in foreign affairs.

The Protectorate and the Baltic

To a large extent the Protectorate's policies regarding the Baltic reinforce the two main conclusions reached in this chapter so far: first, that religious aspirations were a powerful force behind its foreign policies in general; and, second, that it is not always correct to assume that these aspirations led the regime to take decisions that neglected the country's interests. On the contrary, the consequences of its foreign policies were more often than not to protect these interests and to enhance the country's international standing.

Early in 1655 Charles X of Sweden sent to London two ambassadors, Peter Julius Coyet (in March) and Christer Bonde (in July), not only to ratify the commercial treaty between England and Sweden made in the previous year, but also to negotiate a closer alliance. He hoped that this would provide English help for his northern war against Poland. Shortly after this, Sweden became embroiled in a war with Denmark also and so Charles X became even more desperate that his ambassadors secure an English alliance. Very full reports to Charles X from both ambassadors on these negotiations survive.[22] These make clear that Coyet and Bonde were convinced that the English government, taking a lead from the Protector, was very keen indeed on the idea of allying with Sweden as the centrepiece of a great Protestant crusade that would strike at two of the main centres of the European Catholic cause in Europe, Vienna and Rome (document 20). How valid is this perspective?

As has been seen in chapter 4, members of the Protectorate government reacted firmly to the domestic crisis they faced in 1655 with a determination to take on their enemies and to pursue, not abandon, the cause of godly reformation. It is not surprising, therefore, that this feeling should also have coloured their attitudes to contemporary foreign affairs. This may account for their willingness to view Charles X as another Gustavus Adolphus, an earlier Swedish king whom many English Protestants in the later 1620s and early 1630s had seen leading a Protestant military crusade against Catholic tyranny in Germany in the Thirty Years War. There is no reason to doubt the sincerity of these aspirations, especially since (as will be seen shortly) similar ideas lay behind the decision taken in 1654 by Protector and Council to send a joint army-naval expeditionary force (the Western Design) to strike at the heart of Spanish Catholicism in the Caribbean.

However, what is less certain is that the Protector and Council ever believed (as the Swedish ambassadors seem to think that they did) that a Protestant crusade in continental Europe was attainable. The history of the Protectorate's negotiations with the Swedes suggests a more mundane conclusion: that the main *immediate* aim of the regime's Baltic policies was to ensure that no power (Denmark, the United Provinces or Sweden) should dominate the Baltic and so prevent it being open to English merchants, as had happened during the Anglo-Dutch war. Despite the offers made by the Swedes of concessions to English merchants in the Baltic, the English government consistently refused to enter a Swedish offensive alliance. Only limited numbers of Scottish and English soldiers were allowed to join the Swedish army in its successful campaigns against Poland, and the only concrete outcome of the negotiations between the two countries in London was a second commercial treaty signed in July 1656. The hopes of the Swedish ambassadors that, by playing on Cromwell's dreams of a pan-Protestant crusade in Europe, they would draw the Protectorate into an offensive alliance with Sweden, produced enthusiastic rhetoric and tears from the Protector. But that is all. The English government restricted the help it gave the Swedes to a mediating role between it and its enemies. The part played by the Protectorate diplomat Philip Meadowes in bringing about the Treaty of Roskilde in February 1658 is the best example of this policy in operation. This treaty between Sweden and Denmark prevented Denmark from restricting access to the Baltic, which suited the English very well. Moreover, both Oliver and Richard Cromwell showed that they were prepared to go even further in protecting English interest in the Baltic, threatening to send fleets there to counter Dutch moves that jeopardised those interests. In March 1659, when another crisis erupted in the Baltic, an English fleet under Edward Montague was sent there by Richard Cromwell with firm instructions to tackle any power that threatened English interests there.

The Protectorate and France and Spain

The day-to-day history of relations between the Protectorate and France and Spain (and indeed all European powers) is complex, fluctuating and occasionally contradictory.[23] Yet running through that history is a clear and consistent theme: the continuation of the pro-active role that had characterised English foreign policy since the establishment of the republic in 1649. The Protectorate, like the Rump and Barebone's Parliaments before it, only rarely seemed content, as had Tudor and Stuart regimes before and after it, to react to events as they unfolded. More often than not it showed a willingness and eagerness to take the initiative in European affairs.

A good illustration of this pro-active theme is the method used in 1656 to persuade the Portuguese to ratify the commercial treaty they had made with England in 1654. For this there was a precedent. In 1650 the Rump had ordered the English navy under Blake to provide a show of power off the Portuguese coast to force John IV of Portugal to abandon his support for the Stuarts. Similarly in the spring of 1656, when John IV was reluctant to ratify his promise made in 1654 to allow English merchants freedom of trade with Portugal and the right to practise their Protestant faith, Blake was again ordered to sail off the coast near Lisbon. Heavy-handed the tactics might have been, but they were successful. In May 1656 John IV duly agreed to the English demands.[24]

The same forwardness in international affairs can be seen in the Protectorate's dealings with France and Spain, Europe's two leading powers, which had been at war with each other since 1635. Very soon after the establishment of the Protectorate the ambassadors of both nations in London, Alonso de Cardenas of Spain, and Paul de Baas and Antoine de Bordeaux of France, began to work hard to secure an alliance with England. In these parallel negotiations that lasted throughout the spring and summer of 1654 Protector and Council took a leading role. On 4 April 1654 the Council appointed two sets of commissioners to treat with the French and Spanish ambassadors, and during the next three months or so the government's agents made no secret of their efforts to persuade both countries to outbid each other in their quest for an English alliance. Nor were they unsuccessful. Between March and June 1654, on the direct prompting of representatives of the Protectorate, the Spanish gradually raised their offers from £120,000 to £300,000 for an English alliance against France, only to learn that the Council had approached the French ambassadors proposing that their country pay £400,000 for English assistance in a French war against Spain (see document 23).[25]

Protector and Council were less united on the question of which of the two powers they should favour. Sources of debates within the Council on this issue are very thin on the ground. But the report that has survived of a debate on 20 July 1654 reveals a divided Council, with Lambert arguing against the Protector's preference for a war in the Caribbean against Spain, on the grounds that it would be ruinously expensive (document 21). There is little doubt that some councillors preferred a French alliance, others a Spanish alliance. In the end Cromwell's wishes prevailed. It is typical of the foreign policy of the Protectorate that few argued for the kind of peacekeeping-by-arbitration role in Europe that James VI and I had taken on in the early decades of the century. Within three months of the ending of the Anglo-Dutch war, the Protectorate had embarked on another war with Spain in the West Indies.

Why? The answer most often given to that question is that naval war in the Caribbean provided a means to employ the navy that was now standing idle after the end of the Dutch war. It is also often said that naval war against Spain was decided on in the expectation that it would pay for itself by the capture in the Caribbean of Spanish shipping, silver and other prizes. Neither of these arguments should be discounted; both were made by Cromwell in the foreign policy debates in the Council on 20 July 1654 (document 21). But it is doubtful whether these were the most important considerations behind the decision to go to war with Spain.

The main reason was that Cromwell and some of those around him had a vision of the world in which Catholic Spain was the leader of the forces of Antichrist intent on subverting Protestantism in Europe. Cromwell's speeches to parliament reflected a deep loathing of Spain. This was not surprising in a man whose formative years were those in which the epic struggles of Elizabethan seamen in the Spanish Main were very recent. Moreover, during the 1620s and 1630s, both inside and outside parliament,

Puritan MPs associated with Cromwell, like John Pym, John Elliot and the second Earl of Warwick, had planned to mount privateering crusades against Spanish power in the Caribbean.[26] These views were rooted in the past, but it is surely misleading to call them outdated, unfashionable relics of past modes of thought. On the contrary, they were widely voiced in the mid-1650s. Not everyone held them with the intensity of some of those who shaped the foreign policies of the Protectorate, but many at the time would have found the apocalyptic case for a war against Spain in the Caribbean 'modern', 'rational' and persuasive.

But was it realistic? The case that the war could be limited to the Caribbean and that it would pay for itself by the capture of Spanish ships, silver and other possessions was a weak one, as events were to prove. But there is a much more persuasive case that counters another charge made against the Protectorate's decision to throw its weight against Spain. Critics like Slingsby Bethel argued that England thereby destroyed the European 'balance of power', as France was by this stage the rising power in Europe. Yet few had the foresight to see that France would in the later seventeenth and eighteenth centuries become England's major rival in Europe. In the mid-1650s the fact that France's close proximity across the English Channel made it a much more threatening launching pad for a Stuart invasion of England than the distant shores of Spain was a powerful argument for friendship with France against Spain. Only the benefit of hindsight gives any credence to the charge that the Protectorate's foreign policies destroyed a European balance of power to the subsequent advantage of France.

Nor did the religious zeal that thrust the regime into a war with Spain lead it to do so without first carefully exploring the alternative strategy of war against France. Central to this option was the proposal to co-operate with Spanish troops in aiding the French Huguenots in their struggle against Louis XIV. This was pressed on the English government by the Prince of Condé, a leader of the Frondes rebellion against the French monarchy, and his agent in London, Barrière, in and after April 1653. Even after the fall of one of the main provincial centres of rebellion in the princely Frondes, Bordeaux, to Louis XIV's forces on 20 July 1653, the feasibility of the plan continued to be investigated. At least two undercover missions were sent from England to France with the aim of assessing the strength of support within the Huguenot community for it. In November 1653 Joachim Hane brought back reports on Huguenot opinion in Le Havre and La Rochelle in northern France. In the early days of the Protectorate another agent, Jean-Baptiste Stouppe, a Swiss-born Protestant who worked as a church minister in London, was sent by the Council to use his religious and kinship connections to test Huguenot opinion in south-west and southern France. After travelling to Bordeaux and the Cévennes, the heartland of French Protestant survivalism, and escaping the attempts of Louis XIV's minister, Mazarin, to arrest him, he returned to England on 12 July 1654. He reported that he had found little favour among French Protestants for an Anglo-Spanish backed uprising against Louis XIV. Protector and Council received that report only days before the crucial meeting of the Council on 20 July when Cromwell spoke so passionately in favour of sending an expeditionary force to attack Spanish colonies in the Caribbean. It is highly likely that it was Stouppe's report that finally persuaded a majority in the Council to back this fateful decision.[27]

The decision had three main consequences. The first cannot be accounted anything other than disastrous. The defects of the Western Design that set out in December 1654 under the command of General Robert Venables and Admiral William Penn are well known. It was badly supplied, the soldiers under Venables's command were chosen indiscriminately, and the dual leadership of Venables and Penn led to squabbling and indecision.[28] Although reinforcements were recruited when the expeditionary forces reached Barbados, the attempt to capture the Spanish colony of San Domingo in April 1655 was an ignominious failure. Nor was the subsequent capture of the (largely) undefended island of Jamaica seen as adequate compensation, since at the time it was of little value. This was an assessment subsequently confirmed by the commanders appointed to govern it (document 22). Although their stay there was brief, the fact that Venables and Penn were imprisoned in the Tower of London on their arrival home is a reflection of the damaging impact of the defeat at San Domingo on the Protectorate government.

A second consequence of the decision to embark on war with Spain in the West Indies was to bring about an Anglo-Spanish war in Europe. Here the effects were not as disastrous as in the Caribbean. The war with Spain at sea revealed the superiority of the Protectorate's navy under Blake. Its successes ought not to be exaggerated, nor its huge financial costs minimised. But the navy had major successes in campaigns in the Atlantic, notably the capture of the Plate Fleet, together with its cargo of silver (of which it is estimated nearly £250,000 eventually reached London),[29] by an English fleet commanded by Sir Richard Stayner on 8 September 1656, and on 20 April 1657 the capture off Santa Cruz in the Canary Islands by Blake and Stayner of another Plate Fleet, this time minus its cargo of silver. In August 1657 Blake returned home, dying *en route*, and received a hero's funeral in Westminster Abbey.

The third consequence of the decision to embark on war with Spain in the Caribbean was to push England into an alliance with France. That this was not inevitable is shown by the many outstanding sources of tension between the two countries. In 1654 English ships had supported English settlers in seizing French possessions in Acadia (Newfoundland). From 1653 the two countries were in a state of undeclared war at sea and in October 1654 Blake's fleet forestalled a French attack on Naples with a naked display of naval power. Above all, the massacre in April 1655 of Vaudois Protestants in the alpine valleys of northern Italy by a close ally of the French, the Duke of Savoy, served to keep Anglo-French relations very cool. The impact of this event on the domestic history of the Protectorate was seen in chapter 4. Its effects on international history were to stir up a flurry of diplomatic activity, as English agents, including Samuel Morland, John Pell and George Downing, set off on diplomatic missions to Protestant states in Europe and to France to pressurise Mazarin and Louis XIV into forcing the Duke of Savoy to make restitution for the massacres. By early August 1655, under French pressure, the Duke gave in, easing the way to better Anglo-French relations. On 24 October both countries signed a defensive alliance promising not to aid each other's enemies. But an offensive Anglo-French treaty was not completed until March 1657 after long negotiations between the Protectorate's ambassador in Paris, Sir William Lockhart, and Mazarin.

Even before then England and France had begun to co-operate in campaigns on land in Flanders. In November 1656 Lockhart agreed to send 3,000 English troops to attack two towns in the

Spanish Netherlands, Dunkirk and Gravelines, with the promise that, when captured, they would be handed over to the English. In September 1657 an English fleet gave support while French troops captured another Flemish town, Mardyck. By the spring of 1658 Anglo-French forces had taken most of west Flanders, and these victories climaxed on 24 June 1658 with the successful Anglo-French attack on Dunkirk, which was then handed over to the English.

The impact of the Protectorate's adventurous foreign policy on the domestic history of the regime has been seen in earlier chapters: notably the enormous addition it made to the Protectorate's financial problems, and the loss of confidence that the defeat of the Western Design inflicted on many at the heart of the government on the eve of the major-generals experiment. Looked at from a wider perspective, though, the Protectorate's foreign policies had made England (if only temporarily) a major European power, a foretaste of what it was to become again, and for a much longer period, from the early eighteenth century to the middle of the twentieth.

Notes

1 Quoted in S.R. Gardiner, *History of the Commonwealth and Protectorate 1649–56* (4 vols, London, 1903), vol. 4, pp. 193–4.

2 *Calendar of State Papers Venetian*, 1654–55, p. 224.

3 Sir Edward Hyde, Earl of Clarendon, *History of the Rebellion* (6 vols, Oxford, 1888), vol. 6, p. 94.

4 G.M.D. Howat, *Stuart and Cromwellian Foreign Policy* (London, 1974), p. 94.

5 See the bibliographical essay.

6 M. Roberts, 'Cromwell and the Baltic', *English Historical Review*, 76, 1961, p. 405.

7 C.H. Firth, ed., *Memoirs of Edmund Ludlow* (2 vols, Oxford, 1894), vol. 2, pp. 2–3.

8 Ronald Hutton, *The British Republic 1649–60* (Basingstoke, 1990), pp. 109–10.

9 M. Prestwich, 'Diplomacy and trade in the Protectorate', *Journal of Modern History*, 22, 1950, *passim*.

10 R. Crabtree, 'The idea of a Protestant foreign policy' in Ivan Roots, ed., *Cromwell: A Profile* (London, 1973) is the best support for this assertion.

11   B. Capp, *Cromwell's Navy: The Fleet and the English Revolution 1648–60* (Oxford, 1989), pp. 4–5 and *passim*.

12   T. Venning, *Cromwellian Foreign Policy* (Basingstoke, 1995), pp. 20–1.

13   M. Roberts, ed., *Swedish Diplomats at Cromwell's Court 1655–56: The Missions of Peter Julius Coyet and Christer Bonde* (Camden Society, 4th series, vol. 36, 1998), p. 282.

14   J.H. Elliott, *Richelieu and Olivares* (Cambridge, 1984), p. 128.

15   Bethel, however, throughout makes an assumption shared by many others who have written on the Protectorate foreign policy: that it was the foreign policy of Oliver Cromwell. This could be a mistake that misses the important role played by the Council in the making of policy during the Protectorate.

16   S. Pincus, *Protestantism and Patriotism: Ideology and the Making of Foreign Policy, 1650–68* (Cambridge, 1996), *passim* and especially pp. 78–9 and chapter 6.

17   This and the next paragraph is based on Pincus's brilliant analysis of the causes of the first Anglo-Dutch war in *ibid.*, chapters 2–6.

18   *Ibid.*, p. 75.

19   W.C. Abbott, ed., *The Writings and Speeches of Oliver Cromwell* (4 vols, Cambridge, Mass., 1937–47), vol. 3, p. 73.

20   S.M. Ffarington, ed., *The Farington Papers* (Chetham Society, 1st series, vol. 39, 1856), p. 175, quoted in Capp, *Cromwell's Navy*, p. 85.

21   See Capp, *Cromwell's Navy*, p. 85, and Pincus, *Protestantism and Patriotism*, pp. 171–9, for good analyses of the economic damage to English merchants inflicted by the war in all parts of the world.

22   Roberts, ed., *Swedish Diplomats at Cromwell's Court*, *passim*.

23   There is no better proof of this assertion than T. Venning's account of these relations in his *Cromwellian Foreign Policy*, *passim*.

24   Gardiner, *History of the Commonwealth and Protectorate*, vol. 4, pp. 237–40, and Capp, *Cromwell's Navy*, pp. 68 and 97–8. The fullest treatment of Anglo-Portuguese relations in the 1650s is E. Prestage, *The Diplomatic Relations of Portugal and England, 1640–60* (Watford, 1925).

25   Gardiner, *History of the Commonwealth and Protectorate*, vol. 3, chapter 34; Capp, *Cromwell's Navy*, pp. 86–7.

26   See K. Kupperman, 'Errand to the Indies: Puritan colonisation from Providence Island through the Western Design', *William and Mary Quarterly*, 3rd series, 45, 1988 for the antecedents of the Western Design in Puritan plans of the 1620s and 1630s.

27   Gardiner, *History of the Commonwealth and Protectorate*, vol. 3, pp. 5, 111–12, 115, 157–60; C.H. Firth, ed., *Selections from the Papers of William Clarke* (Camden Society, new series, vols 49, 54, 61, 62, 1891–1901), vol. 61, p. 207. For Hane's mission, see C.H. Firth, ed., *The Journal of*

Joachim Hane (Oxford, 1896). The best modern account of Stouppe's mission and its significance is in an (as yet) unpublished lecture by Giorgio Vola, 'The travels in France of Cromwell's secret agent, the Reverend Jean-Baptiste Stouppe', delivered at the Huguenot Society meeting held on 17 January 2001.

28   S.A.G. Taylor, *The Western Design* (Kingston, Jamaica, 1965); Gardiner, *History of the Commonwealth and Protectorate*, vol. 3, chapter 43; Capp, *Cromwell's Navy*, pp. 87–91.

29   Capp, *Cromwell's Navy*, p. 98.

7

The Cromwellian Protectorate and Scotland and Ireland

Different attitudes to Scotland and Ireland

The ways in which the Cromwellian Protectorate set about the awesome and novel task of ruling the whole of the British Isles have been briefly described in chapter 2. This chapter looks at that topic in greater depth and also tackles the important question of the impact on Scotland and Ireland of rule by the Protectorate. The most obvious starting point for this discussion is to emphasise again the different attitudes of those at the centre of power in the Protectorate to both these countries. These attitudes were almost identical to those of the members of the Rump Parliament who, before the establishment of the Protectorate, drafted the two documents that were meant to provide the blueprint for republican rule of Scotland and Ireland, the Declaration Concerning the Settlement of Scotland produced at the end of 1651 and the Act for the Settlement of Ireland passed by the Rump in August 1652 (documents 24 and 25). Both reflect the aim of the conquering English republicans to punish those Scots and Irish people who had resisted English armies in the recent past, but (as has been seen) the punitive clauses of the Declaration Concerning Scotland were as nothing compared to the draconian punishments that the Act of 1652 decreed against Irish people found guilty of rebellion. Moreover, probably as a result of Oliver Cromwell's influence,[1] the Rump decided against annexing Scotland. The Declaration proposed to offer the defeated Scots a political union of the two countries, and provisions were made for elected Scottish representatives to meet to discuss these proposals in 1652. (These were the negotiations for a union that was eventually brought into being by an ordinance of Protector and Council in 1654.[2]) Although it may not have been a point that would have been appreciated either by these delegates who met to approve a union that reduced the independence of Scottish government, law and the Kirk, or by Scots who lived through the Cromwellian Union (document 26), it is nevertheless true that the Declaration Concerning the Settlement of Scotland reflected the much less vengeful, more conciliatory attitudes of the English towards the Scots than towards the people of Ireland.

These differences are explicable almost entirely by the fact that Scotland and Ireland had taken completely different routes since the Reformation. Whereas the Reformation had made rapid strides in Scotland since the mid-sixteenth century, in Ireland it had put down only very shallow roots. The result was to make the Irish polity a complex mixture of ethnic, religious and social groups. The main supporters of Protestantism in Ireland were Presbyterians, who came largely from Scotland and settled in Ulster in the early seventeenth century, and Old Protestants, the descendants of English settlers who had acquired land in Ireland in the late sixteenth and early seventeeth centuries (before 1649 they are often called 'New English'; after 1649 they are better labelled 'Old Protestants' to distinguish them from the Protestant settlers who came to Ireland after the Cromwellian conquest).[3] These Protestant groups were an embattled minority surrounded by a largely Catholic Irish population, among whom 'the Gaelic Irish' (descendants of native Irish families) and 'the Old English' (descendants of pre-Reformation English settlers) were the most prominent groups. By the early seventeenth century Catholicism not only remained the religion of the vast majority of the Irish population, but it was also being revivified by priests trained in the Catholic Counter-Reformation tradition.

The rule of Thomas Wentworth (from 1640 Earl of Strafford) in Ireland in the 1630s had succeeded in uniting Protestants and Catholics (New and Old English, as well as Gaelic Irish) against Charles I's government. But in 1641 the outbreak of the Irish Rebellion, led by members of the Old English and Gaelic Irish landed elites and supported by spontaneous militant activity by Catholic tenant farmers, brought out into the open massive

Catholic–Protestant divisions in Ireland. Equally as important, the Irish Rebellion served to confirm the conviction among many English Protestants that Irish Catholics were the Antichrist incarnate. Therefore, for some militant English Protestants, like Oliver Cromwell, 1641 was a defining moment, after which, they believed, God required the punishment of the Irish. This is part of the explanation for the harshness of the Act for the Settlement of Ireland, which (S.R. Gardiner calculated) would have led to the judicial execution of about 80,000 Irishmen if it had been fully implemented.[4] As will be seen, in the eyes of many Protestants in England, Irish Catholics were not even worthy of conversion.

The Scots, on the other hand, were Protestants and deserved very different treatment. As has been seen, Oliver Cromwell's military campaigns against them in 1650–51 were marked by a reluctance to fight them and a preference instead for negotiations in order to convince the Scots to abandon their intolerant Presbyterianism.[5] These different English attitudes to the Scots and Irish are fundamental to an understanding of the history of the two nations in the 1650s. They account for the fact that (as will be seen at the end of this chapter) the Cromwellian Protectorate had a much greater and more long-lasting effect on Ireland than on Scotland.

Similar attitudes to Scotland and Ireland: conquest and reformation

Yet too much can be made of these differences. In what follows stress will be put on the similarities between the histories of Scotland and Ireland under the Protectorate. First and foremost among these is the fact that the English rulers wanted to achieve similar things in both countries: to crush all opposition to English rule and then to follow conquest by a radical programme of reformation. By the time the Protectorate was established in 1653 the first of these aims had been largely achieved, albeit at a huge ongoing financial cost. The English army was in effective control of Ireland and most of Scotland apart from the Highlands, where a rebellion led by William Cunningham, Earl of Glencairn and John Middleton that had begun in January 1653 had gained support among many of the major Highland clans. This was suppressed by the commanders-in-chief of the English army in

Scotland, Robert Lilburne and (from May 1654) George Monck, but only after a long and ruthless campaign against the rebels. 'Rigor and ruyne' was how one Scotsman, Archibald Johnston of Wariston, ruefully described Monck's campaign of devastation to prevent the rebels living off the Scottish countryside.[6] Even after the rebellion ended in 1655 Monck felt it necessary to build new fortifications in the Highlands. Not surprisingly, the suppression of the revolt and the maintenance of English control in Scotland and Ireland were only achieved at enormous expense. Efforts to reduce the size of the armies of occupation met with some success. The English army in Scotland was reduced from 18,000 in 1654 to 10,555 in 1657, and the size of the English army in Ireland fell even more steeply, from about 35,000 in 1649 to about 9,000 in 1657.[7] Yet the cost of maintaining England's military control fell much less dramatically. Between January 1649 and November 1656 the annual cost of the English army in Ireland was about £400,000. Despite the reductions in the army's size the equivalent figure in 1658 was £336,000. In 1659 the English army occupying Scotland cost well over £270,000 a year. The result was to keep taxation levels in Scotland and Ireland very high (document 26). Even so it was necessary to draw on England to subsidise the armies. In 1659 £148,000 (over one half) of the annual cost of the English army in Scotland came out of the English assessment tax.[8] This was the high price that was paid by the English for their effective conquest of the rest of the British Isles.

As will be seen, reformation was much harder to achieve than conquest. Yet it is important not to underestimate the strength and sincerity of the desire of the leaders of the Protectorate to bring about change in Ireland and Scotland. Ever since the later sixteenth century English voices had urged that conquest of Ireland should be followed by reformation, and Nicholas Canny has recently shown how many of the features of Cromwellian policy in Ireland, including the transplantation and resettlement policies, had been envisaged by some in England well before the 1650s.[9] Yet never before the 1650s had there been such a vigorous attempt by those at the heart of English government to bring about reformation in both Ireland and Scotland.

As has been seen in chapter 2, the keynote of the envisaged reformation in both countries was anglicisation. Having broken the power of the Scottish and Irish landed and clerical elites, the explicit intention was to promote an English (and Cromwellian) version of Protestantism by a campaign of evangelisation and education, to export English customs and law, and to bring Scottish and Irish government into line with that in England. There were many motives behind this desire to make Scotland and Ireland more like England. Some believed that reformation in Scotland and Ireland was necessary in order to safeguard the cause of reformation in England by weakening its enemies abroad. Others saw reformation in Scotland and Ireland (especially the latter) as an opportunity to try out wide-ranging radical reforms that might be later applied to England. But it is difficult to avoid the conclusion that the most powerful motive that drove the English to try to anglicise Scotland and Ireland was a firm belief that English religion, law, customs and government were infinitely superior to those anywhere else in the British Isles.

From that assumption it was only a small step to believing that it was their God-given mission to bring English light into the darkness of Scotland and Ireland. There is no better illustration of this belief than the words of Colonel John Jones, an English parliamentary commissioner in Ireland from 1650 to 1654. The English, he wrote, had been led by God 'into a strange land and to act in as strange a work, a work that neither we nor our forefathers knew or heard of: the framing or forming of a commonwealth out of a rude mass'. Others used similar metaphors to make the same point (Thomas Harrison, Henry Cromwell's chaplain from 1655 to 1659, talked of Ireland as 'clay upon the wheele, ready to receive what forme authority shall please to give it'; John Cook, the Chief Justice of Munster, compared Ireland to 'a white paper', as did Oliver Cromwell).[10] Scotland was seen in the same light, as a country that could not but benefit from anglicisation. The people of Scotland, trumpeted the parliamentary Declaration Concerning Scotland in 1651, would under English rule be given the benefits of English tenurial agreements that would 'enable them, their Heirs and Posterity, to live with a more comfortable subsistence then formerly, and like a free People, delivered (through Gods goodnesse) from their former slaveries, vassalage and oppressions'.

The Protector and his English Council clearly shared these sentiments; they put them into practice in the three ordinances of 1654 seen in chapter 2. They were also held by others outside the

143

Protectorate Council; in the autumn of 1654, a newsletter reported a debate in the parliamentary committee for Irish affairs that concluded with a vote 'that Ireland should be hereafter called West England'.[11] I have found no better illustration of the anglocentric nature of aspirations that lay behind the Protectorate's policies for both Scotland and Ireland in the 1650s.

The extent to which and the ways in which these aspirations were pursued in the 1650s depended in part, of course, on those who were appointed as the regime's governors in Scotland and Ireland. There are striking similarities in the types of people appointed to those positions on both sides of the Irish Sea and in the changes in the ways both countries were governed. In the early years of the Protectorate both countries were ruled by a military commander-in-chief, Charles Fleetwood in Ireland and Robert Lilburne in Scotland, and a group of parliamentary commissioners, most of whom were (or were closely associated with) radical Independents. In the early months of the Protectorate the only major changes that took place in this pattern of government were the appointment of Fleetwood as Lord Deputy of Ireland, an office which had been abolished by the Rump in 1652, and Lilburne's replacement in May 1654 as commander of the English army in Scotland by Monck.

In the summer of 1655, however, major changes occurred in the government of both countries. In May 1655 the English Council announced that Scotland was to be ruled by a new Council with Roger Boyle, Lord Broghill as its president. Broghill was (as has been seen) a man of more moderate religious and political views than Lilburne, and his arrival in Edinburgh along with his Council in September 1655 signalled a new phase in the history of Scotland under the Protectorate. At roughly the same time, in July 1655, Henry Cromwell, Oliver's eldest son, arrived in Dublin as general of the Irish army and member of the Irish Council. He had been appointed to these positions in December 1654, but his father had failed to give his son his full backing. The result was an uneasy period in which power in Ireland was divided between Henry Cromwell and Fleetwood. This situation was only partially resolved in September 1655 when Fleetwood left Ireland for good, since he remained as Lord Deputy *in name* until September 1657. Yet from the middle of 1655 Henry Cromwell held *de facto* power in Ireland, a situation that (as in Scotland) marked a shift in power to a man with more moderate religious and political views than his predecessor.

This change in leadership is usually linked with a trend in Protectorate policies in Scotland and Ireland towards moderation and conservatism and a move away from the full implications of the regime's original intentions in both countries. This is broadly true, but there is some danger in exaggerating the sharpness of the change and its coincidence with the appointments of Broghill and Henry Cromwell. As will be seen in the following discussion of two of the most important aspects of Cromwellian policies in Scotland and Ireland, the trend towards more moderate and less vengeful English rule of both countries preceded their appointments and was only accelerated in 1655.

Punitive policies against the Irish and Scots

The Act for the Settlement of Ireland envisaged that Irish people would be punished on a horrific scale. Roughly 10 per cent of the Irish population would have been executed if the act had been fully carried out. Many army radicals close to Fleetwood also intended that Irish Catholic tenants as well as their Catholic landlords should be forcibly removed from their property and resettled in Connaught in the west of Ireland (document 27). Connaught was chosen largely for strategic reasons, so that the Catholic population could be corralled in an enclosed ghetto isolated from other parts of Ireland by a line of Protestant garrisons along the line of the river Shannon. Although these harsh policies were not put fully into practice, during Fleetwood's rule of Ireland until 1655 much was done, apparently with the full support of the Protector and the English Council. Henry Cromwell's advice, sent from Dublin when he was on a brief visit there in March 1654, to replace Fleetwood and begin a policy of broadening the basis of support for the Protectorate, was ignored. Fleetwood and the Irish Council began vigorously to carry out the transplantation policy.

The principles behind this policy were not new. Catholic landowners in Munster in the 1580s and 1590s and in Ulster during the reign of James I in the early seventeenth century had been uprooted and transplanted. In 1642 the English parliament had passed an act confiscating 2.5 million acres in all four provinces of

Ireland to be granted to 1533 'adventurers' who had pledged financial and military support to quash the Irish Rebellion. After 1649 the Rump and Barebone's Parliaments passed acts extending this principle by promising that soldiers in the large English army in Ireland should also be paid by grants of confiscated Irish land.[12] Yet, encouraged by a Protectorate ordinance of June 1654,[13] Fleetwood and the Irish Council developed these earlier plans on a scale that had never been seen before.

In December 1654 William Petty, whose main claim to fame hitherto had been as a medical theoretician and practitioner, was commissioned by Fleetwood and the Irish Council to measure and survey all the forfeited estates. The resultant 'Down' survey, which was completed in 1659, greatly facilitated both the clearance of Catholic landowners from their estates and the forcible emigration and transportation of Irish soldiers and others. Using Petty's figures, it has been estimated that 34,000 Irish soldiers chose to enlist in armies in France and Spain rather than face Cromwellian vengeance. It has also been calculated that about 12,000 other Irish people were rounded up and transported to work on sugar plantations in the West Indies.[14] Plans to transplant royalist Protestant landowners and Scottish Presbyterian settlers were dropped (in September 1654 they were allowed to pay money fines as composition for their delinquency). Those that suffered most from transplantation were the Catholic landed elite (document 28). The only detailed local study of their loss is a 'computerised profile of landholding in west Ulster' by Kevin McKenny. This shows that only 5 of the 58 Gaelic Irish landowners of 1641 in that region retained their estates, that 41,290 acres were confiscated, and that the estates were largely granted (initially at least) to about 600 adventurers and 1,200 soldiers.[15] Much of the land was then re-sold to existing Protestant planters, the Old Protestants, a result which had major economic, social and political implications for the long-term development of Ireland, as will be seen. This pattern seems to have been repeated throughout Ireland, so that the Catholic share of Irish land fell from 59 per cent in 1641 to only 22 per cent by 1660, when the bulk of landed estates owned by Catholics was in Connaught.[16]

One can only imagine the thousands of tragic individual tales that lay behind these stark statistics of people who were subjected to forcible emigration, transportation or dispossession of their homes and estates in the 1650s. Yet, as devastating as were the effects of the punitive policies against the Irish, they were not as great as they might have been if the legislation authorising them had been put fully into effect. The High Court of Justice set up by the 1652 Act for the Settlement of Ireland decreed that 'at most hundreds, not thousands' were to be executed,[17] and by the end of 1654 it had stopped sitting. Moreover, it soon became obvious that the transplantation policy could not be fully implemented. Petty's survey, remarkable though it was, severely overestimated the amount of land in Connaught on which dispossessed land-owners could be resettled, and so even the policy of transplanting Catholic landowners slowed down. Equally as important is the fact that there were not enough English Protestant settlers willing to migrate to Ireland to replace dispossessed Irish tenants and farm labourers. Even English soldiers were reluctant to settle on the land they had been granted.

As a result, the Lord Deputy of Ireland and his Council were forced to turn away from army radicals, like Richard Lawrence, a Baptist army officer, who urged a policy of wholesale ethnic cleansing of all Irish Catholics (document 27). Instead the views of Old Protestants who urged a more limited policy of transplanta-tion began to have some effect. Especially influential was a pam-phlet by an Old Protestant, Vincent Gookin, called *The Great Case of Transplantation Discussed*, published in June 1655. This argued strongly against a policy of wholesale transplantation on the grounds that Irish men and women were needed to work farms on the confiscated estates, and that there was not enough land in Connaught to accommodate all Irish people. Gookin also claimed that the mass of Irish people would be less resistant to a campaign of Protestant evangelisation if they were isolated from the Catho-lic landed elite.[18] The first two of these arguments certainly had a great deal of validity. Even before Henry Cromwell arrived in Ire-land, the government's policy had begun to turn away from wholesale ethnic cleansing; after his arrival the arguments of Gookin became even more influential because of Henry Cromwell's increasingly close association with the Old Protes-tants. Excessively harsh punitive policies were abandoned.[19] The mass of the Irish population was not affected. The main victims were the Catholic landed elite.

In Scotland, as in Ireland, the Protectorate inherited and maintained a policy aimed at punishing the native population for their armed opposition to the English in the late 1640s and early 1650s. One reason why Glencairn's Rising became a serious threat to English rule in Scotland was that the rebels gained powerful support from nobles and gentry in the Lowlands as well as the Highlands who were stung into rebellion by the English policies begun in 1651 of confiscating the lands of all the great landowners of Scotland and of enforcing the laws relating to debt very strictly. Both policies were designed to break the power of the Scottish landed elite as decisively as the transplantation policy was intended to destroy the landed elite in Ireland.

Even before the establishment of the Protectorate, however, Robert Lilburne, the commander of the English army in Scotland, began making concessions to some of his enemies in the Highlands in order to weaken their support for Glencairn's Rising. In December 1653 Lilburne and his officers urged the Scottish Council to moderate its policies even further. They drew up a formal statement recommending that the laws on debt should be put into effect less stringently and that all sequestrations and forfeitures of estates should be cancelled.[20] In the early months of the Protectorate this advice was partially accepted, as can be seen by the issuing of two ordinances, one passed on 16 May 1654 for the relief of debtors, and the other on 12 April 1654, the ordinance of pardon and grace. The latter did not cancel the policy of sequestration and forfeiture of estates, but only 24 named persons were to have their estates confiscated and another 73 were allowed to pay fines for the return of their estates. While this still represented a major attack on the wealth and power of the principal nobility and gentry of Scotland, the ordinance signalled a significant moderation of the original policy. A few months after the passage of the ordinance of pardon and grace the English Council relaxed its harsh policies even further. In response to a petition of 7 July 1654 from Scottish nobles affected by the ordinance, the Council ordered that if the 73 named in the ordinance paid one-third of their fines, a committee of judges and the commissioners for sequestration would hear pleas of mitigation. This procedure was authorised by another ordinance of 19 August 1654. Frances Dow has shown that by April 1655 the English Council had agreed that all but 8 of the 73 should pay reduced fines. As she says, this was 'a major concession to an important section of the

Scottish community ... A recognition that the political and economic interests of the gentry and nobility had to be considered if the government of Scotland was to run smoothly was the lesson learned by Lilburne and Monck from 1651 to 1655.'[21] It was one that was not lost on Lord Broghill either.

Religious reforms

This trend in Protectorate policy in both Scotland and Ireland towards moderation and pragmatism can be seen even more clearly in the religious policies of the regime, especially under Henry Cromwell in Ireland and Lord Broghill in Scotland.

Radicalism and idealism were allowed full rein in Ireland in the early years of the Protectorate when Fleetwood was in control there. The most dramatic illustration of this is the rapid growth in the number of Baptists and other radical religious sects in Ireland in the early 1650s, especially amongst the English army of occupation. By 1655 the military governors of 12 garrisons were said to be Baptists, and with powerful support in high places the numbers of Baptist soldiers grew rapidly.[22] One result was to provoke tensions within the Protestant community in Ireland, as Scottish Presbyterians, Independents and Old Protestants resented the patronage given by Fleetwood to the Baptists. When Henry Cromwell made his brief visit to Dublin in March 1654 he commented on the way that Fleetwood's attitude was producing religious and political instability, but (as has been seen) the Protector ignored his son's warning.

It was, therefore, not until Henry Cromwell arrived in Ireland as commander-in-chief of the army in July 1655 and (after Fleetwood's departure in September 1655) *de facto* Lord Deputy that a marked change took place in the direction of the Protectorate's religious policies in Ireland. It is difficult to exaggerate Henry Cromwell's dislike of Baptists. His reports to London are peppered with statements like the one he made in a letter to Thurloe in December 1655. He was determined, he wrote, to 'be careful to keep them [Baptists] from power whoe, if they hade it in their power, would express little tenderness to those that would not submitt to their way'.[23] To counteract the Baptists, Henry Cromwell initially formed links with other Protestant groups, principally the Dublin Independents and their leader, Dr

Samuel Winter, and then with the Scottish Presbyterians in Ulster. In November 1655 he brought to a successful conclusion efforts to get Presbyterians to accept government salaries. In this Sir John Clotworthy, an Anglo-Irish Presbyterian, played a crucial role, as he was to do in a similar situation in Scotland. But the linch-pin of Henry Cromwell's religious policies was the links he forged with Old Protestants, like Lord Broghill, who were by and large former supporters of the episcopalian Church of Ireland. Increasingly, Henry Cromwell moved closer to Dr Edward Wroth, a former clergyman in the Church of Ireland and since 1646 Dean of Cork. In 1657 Wroth established the Cork Association of Ministers in order to control access to the ministry and to combat the influence of radical sects. As will be seen in the next chapter, Richard Baxter and others established similar associations in England in the 1650s, but Wroth's vision was much more restricted than Baxter's. As Toby Barnard writes, 'uniformity, not toleration, was his [Wroth's] overriding concern'.[24]

There could be no greater contrast than between Fleetwood's patronage of Baptists and Henry Cromwell's appointment of a Presbyterian as his chaplain, his invitations to ministers known for their conservative religious views to come to Ireland, and his offer of a government salary to Bishop Griffiths Williams.[25] The question of whether such policies inhibited the Protectorate's aspirations for the Protestantisation of Ireland will be considered shortly. What is certain is that Henry Cromwell's increasingly conservative religious policies cemented his relationship with the Old Protestants and brought religious and political stability to Ireland.

In the early years of the Protectorate Scotland was also riven by serious factional divisions within the dominant Protestant (Presbyterian) Church, the most serious of which was that between Protestors and Resolutioners.[26] (Protestors were a minority within the Kirk who in the period after the battle of Dunbar [September 1650] presented a remonstrance repudiating any intention of fighting for Charles II or helping to restore him to the English throne. The leaders of the Protestors were Patrick Gillespie, James Guthrie and Archibald Johnston of Wariston, who called for a purge of the former Engagers from Church and state. Resolutioners represented the vast majority in the Kirk. Led by Robert Douglas, James Wood and the Edinburgh clergy, they opted for a more conciliatory policy towards royalists and the King, for whom they continued to say public prayers.)

Both groups were extremely hostile to the kind of state intervention in religious affairs that English Presbyterians and many English Independents accepted. The issue that divided them was their attitude to Charles II. The refusal of the Resolutioners to abandon the practice of saying public prayers for Charles II was one reason why in the early years of the Protectorate Lilburne and Monck (like Fleetwood in Ireland) allied closely with the more radical and less popular Protestors. Moreover, mirroring the situation in Ireland, this was a policy that received the support of the Protector and the English Council. After discussions with Gillespie and others in London in March and May 1654, the Protector and Council on 8 August 1654 issued an ordinance, popularly known as 'Gillespie's Charter'. Its main provision was the appointment of clerical and lay commissioners who, like the triers in England, were to approve the appointment of all church ministers to their livings. Of the 57 Scottish triers the vast majority were Protestors associated with Gillespie. Not surprisingly, this met with strong opposition from the Resolutioners, but it was also opposed by a faction within the Protestors led by Guthrie and Wariston, who were less inclined to accept the principle of state intervention in Church affairs than Gillespie and others. As a result Gillespie's Charter remained a dead letter.

When Broghill arrived in Scotland as Lord President in September 1655, therefore, he was faced with a not dissimilar state of religious and political instability to that facing Henry Cromwell in Ireland. His response was (like Cromwell's in Ireland) to try to broaden the basis of support for the Protectorate by forging links with the dominant Protestant faction in the country. Patrick Little has recently conclusively demonstrated that Broghill did not come to Scotland (as has usually hitherto been assumed) with no connections in or experience of the country. He had close family ties with powerful Scottish noblemen, and months before he went to Scotland he had been in touch with Scottish Resolutioners.[27] The role of Sir John Clotworthy in facilitating these contacts (as he had done in bringing together Henry Cromwell and Scottish Presbyterians in Ireland) emphasises the 'British' nature of politics in the 1650s. All this explains why in early October 1655, within weeks of arriving in Scotland, Broghill had secured the agreement of all the Resolutioner ministers in Edinburgh not to say public prayers for the King. By the end of 1655 many other Resolutioners had made similar agreements.

Dr Little has also challenged the usual historical interpretation of what happened next.[28] Following Julia Buckroyd and Frances Dow, most historians have believed that, after his initial success with the Resolutioners, Broghill turned to the Protestors to try to unite the two factions. His failure, it is argued, prompted Broghill to create a 'centre party' composed of moderates from both parties. Only when this expedient in turn failed in the late summer of 1656 did Broghill again approach the Resolutioners to become the main prop of the Protectorate's religious policies in Scotland. Dr Little's contention is that Broghill's consistent policy even before he went to Scotland was to work for this alliance. Broghill's approach to the Protestors in the autumn of 1655 and his announcement that he intended to put Gillespie's Charter into operation for the first time are seen by Little primarily as a means of discrediting Monck, who was closely associated with the Guthrie faction among the Protestors. Furthermore, Little argues, the rumours of the creation of a 'centre party' were merely a smokescreen behind which Broghill conducted his campaign against Monck and Guthrie and forged closer links with the Resolutioners.

Despite these differences of opinion, what is clear is that by the end of July 1656 Broghill had made a very close alliance with leading Resolutioners. This is the significance of additional instructions that were sent to Edinburgh on 31 July 1656, in which the Protector and the Council at Whitehall agreed to pay the salaries of Kirk ministers, a scheme to be administered by the Scottish Council in liaison with lay presbyteries. Like Henry Cromwell in Ireland, Broghill in Scotland had made an alliance with the dominant Protestant faction in the country the keystone of Protectorate rule. The outcome was to rescue both countries from the instability that was the result of over a decade of bruising military violence and political and religious turmoil.

The limited achievement of reform in Scotland and Ireland

But was stability in Scotland and Ireland achieved at the expense of the regime's reforming aspirations? There is little doubt that, when one looks at the campaigns of evangelisation in both countries designed to promote the kind of Protestant settlement hoped for by Oliver Cromwell and those around him, the answer is 'yes'. In both countries the campaign was a complete flop. This is less surprising in Scotland than in Ireland. In Scotland the Presbyterian Kirk had a settled parochial structure in which the power of the Kirk and its ministers remained strong. Very few Presbyterians, whether Protestors or Resolutioners, were willing to see the growth of Independency or the introduction of state control in religious affairs, especially when they were imposed by a foreign government. As a result very few Independent congregations appeared in Scotland in the 1650s. In Ireland, on the other hand, conditions seemed to offer the campaign of English Protestant evangelisation a better prospect of success. After a long period of warfare, violence and persecution, Catholic priests and laity were much less well organised to resist than the powerful Presbyterian Scottish Kirk. Yet the failure of the English to promote anglicised Protestantism was as marked in Ireland as in Scotland.

The Church of Ireland had been dismantled in the late 1640s, and the record of all English governors in Ireland from the 1640s to 1660 in filling that gap was very poor. It proved extremely difficult to persuade well-qualified ministers to go to Ireland and those who went knew nothing of Irish conditions and spoke little or no Irish. Consequently, their main success was among English soldiers or Protestants who had just come to settle in Ireland. They had very little impact on those Protestants who had come to Ireland before 1649 or on the mass of the Catholic population of Ireland. Extraordinarily, as Toby Barnard discovered, Trinity College Dublin trained no Irish-speaking clergy between 1641 and 1660, and the one preacher who was sent by the government in Dublin to preach among the resettled Irish in Connaught stayed there for only a few months. Only one religious book was published in Irish in the 1650s, a translation of William Perkins's *The Christian Directory*. In 1653 the only set of a fount of Irish type disappeared and was never replaced. It is true that the story is not one of total failure. Some progress was made in reorganising parishes, ministers received government salaries, and Catholic sources after the Restoration claimed that priests had to reconvert some Catholics who had embraced Protestantism in the 1650s.[29]

Yet there is no doubt that the 1650s witnessed no reversal of the long-term trend from the Reformation onwards of the failure of

Protestantism to make inroads into Irish Catholic support. A principal reason may have been that Protestant ministers in Ireland expended their energies on quarrelling and disputing with fellow Protestants rather than on evangelisation among the Catholic population. But it may be that a more important explanation is that some Protestants felt that the Irish were beyond conversion by persuasion and that able Protestant ministers turned their attention to other 'dark corners' of the world than Ireland. This failure was not unique to the government of the 1650s, but the Cromwellian Protectorate undoubtedly played its part in bringing about the extraordinary situation that 'Ireland is the only country in Europe where the Counter Reformation succeeded against the will of the head of state'.[30]

The campaign to bring the 'benefits' of English law and government to Scotland and Ireland had slightly more success. Though some historians may have been guilty of exaggerating its extent,[31] there is no doubt that English rule of Scotland and Ireland in the 1650s marked a return to a settled system of government and justice after the turmoil of the 1640s and early 1650s, when the normal rhythms of the law and government had been badly disrupted. Moreover, even a Scottish historian whose judgement is generally hostile to the record of Protectorate rule of his country concedes that 'it would ... be going too far to say English rule brought no benefits in the administration of justice in Scotland. It seems very likely that the English judges were more impartial than their predecessors, less influenced by vested interests and the power of great men.'[32] What helped matters was that, especially under Broghill, although attempts continued to be made to introduce English law and English-type JPs, Scottish judges were appointed to sit alongside Englishmen. In Ireland, too, the judicial system began to work again after the anarchy of the previous decade or so. Yet in both countries very little progress was made towards the kind of anglicisation of law and government that had once been envisaged. Oliver Cromwell's hopes expressed in 1649 for the erection of a completely new system of justice in Ireland were not realised.[33] At the heart of the judicial system in Ireland in the late 1650s were the traditional Four Courts in Dublin.

The Protectorate's British legacy

The dominant theme of the Cromwellian Protectorate's rule of Scotland and Ireland is achievements falling very short of aspirations. As the cost in men and money of holding down both occupied countries remained high, there is a lot to be said for Derek Hirst's contention that 'the British problem was to prove as damned an inheritance for the Republic as it had been for Charles I, whom it had done so much to destroy'.[34] Moreover, when the Protectorate collapsed and monarchy was restored in Britain and Ireland in 1660, much of what had been achieved in Scotland was swept away. The Act Recissory passed by the restored Scottish parliament in March 1660 revoked all legislation since 1633. Scottish nobles and gentry regained the power and influence they had lost in the 1650s, and once again (as had been the case between 1603 and the start of the English occupation of Scotland) the only constitutional link between the two countries was their shared Stuart monarch. The one major long-term impact of Cromwellian rule on Scotland was to make the idea of union with England a very unpopular prospect among most Scottish people. The union of the two countries in 1707 came about in spite of, certainly not because of, the Cromwellian union less than 50 years earlier.

The long-term impact of Cromwellian rule on Ireland was much more decisive and significant. In great contrast to England and Scotland, where most of the land taken from the republic's enemies was restored to its former owners in the 1660s, most of the property taken from Catholics during the Cromwellian campaign of confiscation and transplantation was never returned. The Irish parliament that met in 1661 did appoint commissioners who sat as a Court of Claim, to which Catholics could submit claims for the recovery of their estates on the grounds that they had not been involved in the rebellions of the 1640s. Some of these claims were allowed and Catholics recovered about 850,000 acres from the soldiers and adventurers to whom they had been granted. But this made only a tiny dent in the massive amount of land lost by Catholics as a result of the Cromwellian land settlement. As has been seen, the share of land held by Catholics in Ireland fell from 59 per cent in 1640 to just over 20 per cent in 1660, and the main gainers were Old Protestants, who proved very successful in buying property from soldiers and adventurers. McKenny's case study of West Ulster confirms this picture. In that region, of the 41,290 acres that were lost by Catholic landowners in the 1650s, 91 per cent came into the hands of Protestant settlers who had gone to Ireland before 1641.[35]

The Catholic elite also lost much political power and social influence as well as wealth. Catholics had been ejected from the government of most Irish towns in the 1650s,[36] and this situation was not reversed in 1660. The scale of the loss of political power by Catholics in Ireland is illustrated by the fact that only one Catholic sat in the Irish parliament of 1661. Yet what the Cromwellian Protectorate did not change was the attachment of the bulk of the population of Ireland to Catholicism. The restored Church of Ireland had the support of the Protestant landed elite, but it had as little success as the Cromwellian Protectorate in reversing the triumphal trend of the Catholic Counter-Reformation in Ireland.

Notes

1   F.D. Dow, *Cromwellian Scotland 1651–60* (Edinburgh, 1979), pp. 30–1.
2   See chapter 2.
3   The best introduction to this important group is T.C. Barnard, 'Planters and policy in Cromwellian Ireland', *Past and Present*, 61, 1973.
4   S.R. Gardiner, 'The transplantation to Connaught', *English Historical Review*, 14, 1899, pp. 703–4. Gardiner's comment on this number, that it was 'hardly, if at all, to be paralleled in the annals of civilised nations', unfortunately cannot be made by a historian writing at the beginning of the twenty-first century.
5   See chapter 2.
6   Quoted in Dow, *Cromwellian Scotland*, p. 123.
7   D. Stevenson, 'Cromwell, Scotland and Ireland', in J. Morrill, ed., *Oliver Cromwell and the English Revolution* (Harlow, 1990), p. 177.
8   T.C. Barnard, *Cromwellian Ireland: English Government and Reform in Ireland 1649–60* (Oxford, 1975), p. 26; Dow, *Cromwellian Scotland*, p. 219.
9   N. Canny, *Making Ireland British 1550–1650* (Oxford, 2000), *passim* and pp. 551–3.
10   Quoted in Barnard, *Cromwellian Ireland*, p. 14. See chapter 2 for Cromwell's statement.
11   Cited in a footnote in the foreword to the paperback edition of

Barnard's *Cromwellian Ireland* (Oxford, 2000), p. xxi.

12   K.S. Bottigheimer, *English Money and Irish Land* (Oxford, 1971); Canny, *Making Ireland British, passim.*

13   See chapter 2.

14   Patrick J. Corish, 'The Cromwellian regime 1650–60' in. T.W. Moody, F.X. Martin and F.J. Byrne, eds, *A New History of Early Modern Ireland* (Oxford, 1976), pp. 360–4. For the harsh treatment many Irish immigrants received in the West Indies, see H.M. Beckles, 'A "riotous and unruly lot": Irish indentured servants and freemen in the English West Indies, 1644–1731', *William and Mary Quarterly,* 3rd series, 47, 1990.

15   Kevin McKenny, 'The seventeenth-century land settlement in Ireland: towards a statistical interpretation' in Jane H. Ohlmeyer, ed., *Ireland from Independence to Occupation 1641–60* (Cambridge, 1995).

16   Barnard, 'Planters and policies', p. 32.

17   Corish, 'Cromwellian regime', p. 360.

18   British Library, E234/6.

19   Barnard, 'Planters and policies', *passim.* For the important role of the Old Protestants see also Patrick Little, 'The first unionists? Irish Protestant attitudes to union with England 1653–59', *Irish Historical Studies,* 23, 2000.

20   Dow, *Cromwellian Scotland,* p. 113.

21   *Ibid.,* pp. 157–9.

22   Barnard, *Cromwellian Ireland,* pp. 98–106. See also Phil Kilroy, 'Radical religion in Ireland 1641–60' in Ohlmeyer, ed., *Ireland from Independence to Occupation.*

23   Quoted in Barnard, *Cromwellian Ireland,* p. 107.

24   *Ibid.,* p. 121.

25   *Ibid.,* pp. 124, 130–1.

26   Julia Buckroyd, 'Lord Broghill and the Scottish Church, 1655–56', *Journal of Ecclesiastical History,* 27, 1976, and Dow, *Cromwellian Scotland,* chapter 9 and *passim,* are good studies of the religious situation in Scotland in the 1650s.

27   Patrick Little, 'The political career of Roger Boyle, Lord Broghill, 1636–60' (unpublished PhD thesis, University of London, 1999), pp. 153–5.

28   *Ibid.,* pp. 155–73.

29   Barnard, *Cromwellian Ireland,* pp. 174, 176, 179–80.

30   H. Hammerstein, 'Aspects of the continental education of Irish students in the reign of Elizabeth I', in T.D. Williams, ed., *Historical Studies: VIII* (Dublin, 1971), quoted in Barnard, *Cromwellian Ireland,* p. 182.

31   For example, H.R. Trevor-Roper, 'Scotland and the Puritan Revolution' in his *Religion, the Reformation and Social Change* (2nd edn, London, 1972).

32   Stevenson, 'Cromwell, Scotland and Ireland', p. 176.

33   See p. 36.

34   Derek Hirst, 'The English Republic and the meaning of Britain', *Journal of Modern History*, 66, 1995, p. 543.

35   McKenny, 'Seventeenth-century land settlement', pp. 198–9.

36   Barnard, *Cromwellian Ireland*, chapter 4.

8

The Cromwellian Protectorate and England and Wales

How did the Cromwellian Protectorate affect the lives of men and women in England and Wales in the 1650s? It would be foolish to claim that this chapter gives a full or definitive answer to such a wide-ranging question. Answering it is made especially difficult by the nature of the relatively few primary sources that have survived for the decade and by the fact that most of those who have written about it until recently have assumed that the collapse of the Protectorate and the restoration of monarchy were inevitable. Most of those who lived during the Protectorate and who wrote after its demise were, unsurprisingly, reluctant to acknowledge that they had accepted, let alone supported, the republic. Richard Baxter's vilification of the Protectorate in his later writings hides the fact that during the 1650s he had been far from unsympathetic to the aspirations of both Protectors, Oliver and Richard.[1] It is also possible that some people destroyed evidence of their activities in the 1650s that might have been interpreted by the restored monarchy as collaboration with the regicide regime. Moreover, the history of the Protectorate's rule of England and Wales is easily distorted by the knowledge of what happened in 1659–60. Because the Stuart monarchy was restored in 1660, it is often wrongly assumed that the 1650s was a decade of growing royalist opposition to, and seething discontent with, the Protectorate. The result has sometimes been to give a perverted picture of the Protectorate, minimising the extent to which the regime was accepted in England and Wales and exaggerating its failures.

The main aim of this chapter is to go some way towards correcting that distortion. It begins by illustrating that the Protectorate was never universally accepted in England and Wales and that at times (as during the regime of the major-generals) its popularity plummeted. It will also be seen that the Protectorate fell quite a long way short of achieving what many of its leaders and supporters had hoped for. But the chapter also gives emphasis to what the regime did achieve in England and Wales. It shows that, although the Protectorate can hardly ever be said to have been popular, it was accepted by the vast majority of people in England and Wales until it collapsed in the late spring of 1659. There is much evidence that the Protectorate's impact on both countries was not totally negative. During the Cromwellian Protectorate changes were effected that, although they were not exactly those that been envisaged by the regime's architects and supporters, were extremely significant at the time and (as will be explained in the conclusion of this book) in the future.

Opposition

One does not have to look very far to find evidence of opposition to the Protectorate in England and Wales during the 1650s. Some individuals made no secret of their loathing of the regime and what it stood for. As has been seen already, quite often these were men, like Thomas Harrison and the three colonels, who had been closely associated with Oliver Cromwell before 1653 but who now could not be restrained from denouncing him and the Protectorate for (as they saw it) reneging on the principles of the 'good old cause' for which they had once fought.[2] The most outspoken of these was Edmund Ludlow, who had been appointed by the Rump as a parliamentary commissioner and lieutenant-general in Ireland, but refused to sign a document formally acknowledging the power of the Protectorate. Later, recounting a conversation that he had with Henry Cromwell, who had been sent to Ireland in March 1654 as an emissary of the new regime and who urged Ludlow to reconsider his decision, Ludlow said that he could not serve a regime that ruled by military power alone:

> All things ought for the future to run in their proper and genuine channel; for as the extraordinary remedy is not to be used till the ordinary fail to work its proper effect, so ought it to be continued

no longer than the necessity of using it subsists; whereas this that they call a government had no other means to preserve itself but such as were violent, which not being natural could not be lasting.[3]

Examples of similar negative attitudes to the Protectorate can be found throughout the English provinces and Wales. They come from all parts of the country and from all parts of the religious and political spectrum. As has been seen, few royalists took their opposition to the point of rebellion. Like the royalist poets Edmund Waller, Abraham Cowley and Henry Vaughan, who emphasised the virtue of 'pastoral retreat', and other royalist writers like Isaac Walton who in *The Compleat Angler* idealised the delights of 'rustic withdrawal', most of them kept their heads down.[4] William Dugdale was one of these who immersed himself in writing annual almanacs, as well as in historical research for his book *The Antiquities of Warwickshire*, which was published in 1656. Yet even he spiced his works with comments satirising the Protectorate. His almanac for 1657 poked fun at the religious radicalism of the regime, which he pilloried as 'Sir John Presbyter' whose coat of arms represented the 'families of Amsterdam ... in a field of toleration ... House of Geneva ... in a field of separation, marginal notes on the bible false quoted ... Country of New England [which] bears for her arms a prick-eared preacher perched upon a pulpit, proper, holding forth to the people a schismatical Directory', and Scotland with 'the field of rebellion, charged with a stool of repentance'.[5]

Sir John Hobart, a Norfolk royalist, made his loathing of the Protectorate much more explicit. Although a supporter of limited episcopacy and a man of 'constitutional royalist' views, he had played no active part in politics in the 1640s. But after the army's purge of parliament in December 1648 and the execution of the King in January 1649, he became an open opponent of all the regimes of the 1650s, especially the Protectorate, which he consistently portrayed, both in his private papers and in speeches in the third Protectorate Parliament, as tyrannical military governments. In a typical passage from his manuscript papers he denounced the Instrument of Government as a 'mere juggle and the worst of tyrannies under the pretended name of a commonwealth ... What provision is made in it for the safety and freedom of men's persons let full prisons, Jamaica, and other dismal places of banishment declare.'[6] This point of view was not very far away from those lawyers and judges who in 1655 questioned whether the government was legally entitled to levy taxes without parliamentary approval.[7]

It was a viewpoint also voiced from other points of the political spectrum than that occupied by conservative royalists and lawyers. The millenarian Fifth Monarchist Vavasour Powell made the same charge of military tyranny against the Protectorate in a pamphlet, *A Word for God*, published in 1655. According to Powell, since the Protectorate was led by a man who had seized power for his own self-advancement, not surprisingly it neglected 'the advancement of Christ's kingdom, the extirpation of Popery, the privileges of Parliament, and the liberty of the subject'.[8] Powell's charges were not left undefended,[9] but they were often repeated in the 1650s. From yet another point on the political spectrum, the Commonwealthsman-republican Herbert Morley put similar views. Although he kept his key position as an important local governor in Sussex, he became an implacable opponent of the government after the military dissolution of the Rump. In the words of the best historian of mid-seventeenth-century Sussex, 'by grasping power and ruling with the support of the army ... [Cromwell] alienated a man who saw parliamentary government as the essence of all that he had fought for'.[10] In the days before public opinion polls it is impossible to know how many people in England and Wales shared these views. But it is highly likely that many (probably the majority of people) disliked the regime's close associations with the army.

In addition to a generalised dislike of military rule, the origins of this unpopularity can be located in three particular fears about the effects of the Protectorate on life in the localities. All of them were exaggerated fears but none was completely groundless.

The first was a fear that was especially strong among the landed and urban elites who had traditionally held positions of authority in the localities. For many of these people the Protectorate came to be seen as a regime that threatened their political and social hegemony by accelerating a shift in the balance of power towards men lower down the social scale. As will be seen, studies of the 1650s have shown that local power was never wrested completely out of the hands of the gentry and wealthy merchants. But it is clear that many more lesser gentry and merchants held local government offices in the 1650s than ever before. This shift in power away from the upper ends of the landed and mercantile elites had begun before the establishment of the Protectorate. No parliamentary county committee in the 1640s ever corresponded to the caricature of the Isle of Wight committee portrayed by Sir John Oglander as a group of low-born men from outside the traditional governing class, 'Ringwood of Newport, the pedlar; Maynard, the apothecary; Matthews, the baker; Wavell and Legge, farmers, and poor Baxter of Hurst Castle'.[11] But in most counties that have been studied, during the 1640s lesser gentry who had never before been JPs or deputy lieutenants appeared on the county committees. In the early 1650s county committees disappeared and more traditional local government offices, principally peace, militia and assessments commissions, became more prominent. But what frightened members of the traditional governing class was the drastic purges of these commissions (principally of JPs) carried out by the Rump and Barebone's Parliaments in the early 1650s. These were especially severe in Wales. Stephen Roberts suggests that the composition of the Commission for the Propagation of the Gospel in Wales 'represented a shift in the balance of lay power in Glamorgan during the 1650s aimed … at and dependent on the Welsh "middling sort"', and Philip Jenkins describes the dominance in that county (even after the Commission for the Propagation had been disbanded in 1653) by a group of lesser gentry led by Philip Jones of Langyfelach as marking 'a real transfer of power'.[12]

There were no similar large-scale purges of local government during the Protectorate, and, as will be seen, some men from traditional ruling families returned to or retained their offices on the bench or as commissioners for the militia and assessments. But the government continued to rely a great deal on men from outside the elite groups. In Warwickshire during the 1640s and 1650s 'the actual government of the county was undertaken mainly by comparatively minor gentry'. Between 1645 and 1660 only 4 of the 42 men appointed as JPs during that period had been commissioners of the peace before the Civil War began in 1642. Moreover 18 of them were below gentry status.[13] Similarly in Cheshire of the 30 men who were 'in some fashion active as Justices between 1645 and 1659 … only nine of these belonged to families represented on the Bench between 1603 and 1642'.[14] Herefordshire and

Gloucestershire are two other counties that show this same pattern of 'a minor social revolution in government'.[15]

To an extent this reliance for local government on men from slightly lower down the social scale than before came about because the Protectorate had no alternative after the purges of royalist sympathisers and the refusal of many conservatives to serve. But, as will be seen later in this chapter, it was a situation that was not unwelcome to some of those at the centre of power in the Protectorate and it is possible that they did their best to promote it. There is evidence that in some cases Protector and Council favoured the appointment of men in county and town government who shared their godly aspirations irrespective of their social standing. In these circumstances the fears of 'county' families that during the Protectorate their slender hold on local power was being even further eroded were not without foundation.

The second fear that gripped many of the propertied classes was that it seemed as though the Protectorate threatened to make permanent the high levels of taxation that had been established during the civil wars of the 1640s.[16] Then new taxes had been devised, principally monthly assessments (a land tax that set quotas to be raised county by county that took account of the distribution of regional wealth in the country) and the excise (a purchase tax on most everyday consumables). Together with customs dues, these made up the bulk of the government's revenue and by the 1650s huge sums were being raised. Between 1650 and 1659 £3,777,864 was raised from customs, £3,720,910 from the excise and £6,676,578 from assessments (the annual average figures for each are £419,762, £413,434 and £741,842).[17] The scale of these taxes can only be appreciated by comparing them with what had gone before. Mike Braddick's calculations of the total government revenue raised during the reigns of Elizabeth I, James I, Charles I (before 1640), and during the Commonwealth and Protectorate show the massive rise that had taken place:

1558–1603	£18,360,000
1604–25	£12,544,000
1626–40	£11,996,000
1649–60	£18,919,000

When these figures are translated into annual average figures the growth in the financial demands made by the government, especially after 1640, are even more startling:

1558–1603	£408,000
1604–25	£557,333
1626–40	£856,857
1649–60	£1,891,900

Not only had government revenue increased by over 120 per cent between the 1630s and the 1650s, but the percentage raised by the assessment tax had increased from 14 per cent to over 90 per cent.[18]

Not surprisingly, this sudden transformation in the tax burden was a major grievance and a cause of tension between the regime and the MPs in the Protectorate Parliaments, which had resulted in some reduction in the size of the monthly assessments.[19] But, as the above figures show, the tax burden remained extremely high throughout the 1650s. As will be seen in the conclusion to this book, it only fell slightly even after the Restoration and rose to even greater heights by the end of the century. There is no denying that there was a great deal of substance behind the fears that the Protectorate marked a step towards permanent high taxation in England and Wales.

The third fear that lay behind opposition to the Protectorate was extreme anxiety that the regime was encouraging religious radicalism, which it was believed would unleash social and political disorder. Though not 'tolerant' by modern standards, the Cromwellian Church settlement allowed a degree of religious diversity that many feared threatened to subvert the control of the Church by legally appointed ministers and their gentry patrons. It will also be seen that public discussion of religious issues flourished during the Protectorate. To conservative opinion these developments were thought to presage the kind of attacks on the social and political order that many assumed were the inevitable consequences of any relaxation of religious uniformity. Whether these fears were well-founded is debatable, but what gave them a great deal of credence was the activities of one religious group that flourished during the Protectorate: the Quakers.

The rapidity of the rise of the Quakers, their success in gaining adherents especially among the 'middling' and 'lower sorts' in society, and the reasons why they were loathed by 'respectable' people have been seen in chapter 4 in connection with the case of James Nayler in the second Protectorate Parliament in December 1656. The hostility vented at Nayler in that parliament was but the tip of the iceberg of conservative condemnation of the Quakers in the provinces during the 1650s. Many of their actions and words seemed to support the conclusion of Edward Butler, MP for Poole, in the debate on Nayler. Quaker 'principles and practices', he declared, 'are diametrically opposite both to magistracy and ministry; such principles as will level the foundation of government into a bag of confusion'.[20] Orthodox Puritan ministers, like Ralph Josselin of Earls Colne in Essex, were jeered at in the streets by Quakers as 'your deluder' and 'false prophet'.[21] In Bristol, where Quakerism was very strong and received some protection from the army garrison commander there, Colonel Adrian Scrope, complaints of Quakers violently interrupting services in what they derogatorily called 'steeple houses' were common.[22] Quaker enthusiasm and militancy were matched by the ferocity of the responses of many local officials. 'In the mid-1650s', writes the best historian of the Quakers in the 1650s, 'there was a concerted drive in several counties to limit the expansion of the movement.' The authorities in Devon and Cornwall, for example, set up watches on highways and bridges 'for the preventing of this great contagion, that infects almost every corner of this Nation'.[23] Cases of Quakers being arrested and then whipped and imprisoned as vagrants were common (document 29). It is quite clear, though, that Quakers were not alone in suffering from this kind of hostility. So too did the Protectorate's reputation.

The argument of the rest of this section is that the most important effect of the rule of the major-generals in the localities of England and Wales, which was established by Protector and Council in 1655,[24] was to intensify greatly all these fears and thus ensure the continuing opposition encountered by the Protectorate throughout its existence. However, in the light of some recent historical writing which has sought to play down the negative impact that the major-generals had on opinion in the country, it is essential to concede that this argument can be carried too far. H.M. Reece's doctoral thesis, though still unpublished, has been enormously influential and persuasive in showing that the novelty of the intrusion of the army in local affairs, represented by the rule of the major-generals, can easily be exaggerated. Both before and after the major-generals experiment, there was a significant military presence in many parts of England and Wales.[25] Nor, as others have shown, can the major-generals be seen unreservedly as agents of centralisation aimed at usurping the political power of the governors of provincial England and Wales.[26] When they arrived in the localities they did not replace the JPs and sheriffs in counties, the mayors and aldermen in towns, or any other existing officers of local government, but aimed to work in co-operation with them. It is also very important to stress that one of the reasons for the establishment of the rule of the major-generals was to ease the burden of taxation, by reducing the size of the expensive standing army and replacing it with a cheaper local militia paid for by the regime's royalist enemies. Nor did all the major-generals pursue policies that promoted radical religious sectarianism. Indeed there can have been few local governors who pursued repressive campaigns against Quakers with such vigour and brutality as Major-General Boteler, who in May 1656 sent in the Northamptonshire militia to disperse an 800-strong Quaker meeting near Northampton.[27]

However, all this ought not to tempt historians to conclude that the impact of the major-generals on opinion in England and Wales was 'very slight'.[28] The actions of the major-generals confirmed the widespread belief that the Protectorate would undermine the political power of the gentry, ruin their economic fortunes by perpetuating high taxation, and unleash sectarianism that would turn their ordered social world upside down. It may have been intended that the relationship between major-generals and local governors would be co-operative, but in reality it was often not. The letters from many of the major-generals that survive in Secretary Thurloe's archive are littered with expressions of the mistrust they felt for many of the local justices. Major-General James Berry's charge against the JPs in Monmouth in February 1656 is typical: 'I am much troubled with these market townes, every where vice abounding and magistrates fast asleep'.[29] Chris Durston's recent study of the major-generals concludes that they 'presided over an ambitious attempt to remodel the county magistracy'.[30] This is confirmed by his discovery that the demands of the major-generals for the replacement of 'wicked' and 'lazy' justices by 'well-affected' men met with a great deal of success.

During the period when the major-generals were in the localities the numbers of men added to and removed from local commissions of the peace rose greatly and remained high also during the year after the major-generals left.[31]

Nor were gentry anxieties allayed by the failure of the major-generals to reduce the levels of local taxation. It had been hoped that the major-generals would be able to do so by establishing local militias paid for by a decimation tax levied on those identified as having aided the royalist cause in the present or in the past. Unfortunately, this policy went badly wrong and the consequences on local opinion were often disastrous. It needs to be emphasised that there is very little evidence that there was any opposition to the security measures put into effect by the major-generals that were aimed at discovering and quashing royalist conspiracies. As has been seen in chapter 3, these seem to modern eyes to be extremely heavy-handed, authoritarian measures. But there are only a few signs that they caused offence at the time (apart, that is, from royalists who were directly affected by them) in the way that modern historians with liberal views hostile to a police state might assume.

What did cause contemporary concern about the major-generals' security measures was that they were underpinned by the decimation tax, assessed and collected by local commissioners who were appointed to assist the major-generals. Lists of all the royalists subjected to the new tax do not survive, but it may be that the total was between 1,000 and 2,000.[32] The tax had a dual impact on opinion in the country that was far more serious than such a small figure might suggest. First, since the commissioners investigated and revealed the activities of people in the conflicts of the 1640s, they reopened bitter local divisions and delayed the process of 'healing and settling' that was an essential precondition of the reconciliation of the nation to the Protectorate. Second, and probably of more importance, the major-generals and their local commissioners did not have the time or administrative resources to impose the tax as fully or as effectively as they would have liked. It is also highly likely that they were hindered in its assessment and collection by the fairly frequent interventions of Protector and Council on behalf of individual royalists who petitioned to be exempted from the tax. Chris Durston estimates that about one-quarter of the royalists who it is known ought to have paid the tax petitioned to be exempted.[33] It is not known how many of these petitions were successful, but it is significant that complaints at the Protector's and Council's favourable treatment of royalists are a constant theme in the major-generals' correspondence with Thurloe. As a result it is difficult to disagree with Durston's gloomy conclusion that the decimation tax yielded an amount far below that which was needed to fund the new militia.[34] A direct consequence was that the rule of the major-generals did not enable a significant reduction to be made in the general level of the tax burden as had been hoped. Instead the major-generals helped to confirm an image of the Protectorate as a military, high tax regime.

It was, though, probably another aspect of the major-generals' activities that caused more opposition than anything else. Not all the major-generals followed their moral reform instructions with the energy of Charles Worsley in Lancashire and Cheshire or Sir John Barkstead in and around London. But everywhere the major-generals made contacts with people who shared their aspirations for godly reformation and promoted some of them to the commissions for securing the peace of the commonwealth. It will be seen in the next section that they made very little headway in achieving this particular goal. The point that needs emphasis here is that the major-generals' *attempt* to do this is enough to explain why they were so hated in the country by the summer of 1656. This hostility was such that (as has been seen in chapter 3) they failed to ensure the return of men favourable to the Protectorate in the elections to the second Protectorate Parliament and were subjected to an outburst of hostility in the parliamentary debates on the Militia Bill that would have made permanent the decimation tax and the major-generals. The parliamentary speeches in that debate (document 14) reflect the immense hostility aimed at the major-generals. They also encapsulate many of the reasons why the Protectorate itself failed to gain enthusiastic and wide support in England and Wales.

Failure

Given the level of opposition faced by the Protectorate, it is not surprising that many of the aspirations for revolutionary change hoped for by Oliver Cromwell and those around him made very little impact. Of these one of the most important was the attempt to bring about changes in the festive calendar (ceremonies connected with rites of passage and popular pastimes, which provided the framework for everyday life) with the aim of promoting a moral reformation in people's thoughts and behaviour. This was a broad aspiration that the Protectorate inherited from the parliamentarian regimes of the 1640s and early 1650s. By the time of the establishment of the Protectorate a legislative framework had been erected designed to bring about what Chris Durston aptly calls 'a cultural revolution'.[35]

In the 1640s the Long Parliament had passed legislation outlawing maypoles as 'a Heathen vanity, generally abused to superstition and wickedness'. Its Directory of Public Worship, which in 1645 replaced the Book of Common Prayer, denounced popular celebrations 'vulgarly called holy days, having no Warrant in the Word of God'; and in June 1647 a parliamentary ordinance outlawed the celebration of Christmas, Easter and Whitsuntide. These festivals were to be replaced by a new secular holiday to be held on the second Tuesday of every month, by regular fast days, and by the strict observance of Sunday as a day devoted entirely to prayer and religious exercises. The Directory of Public Worship also stripped the old Book of Common Prayer rites of baptism, marriage and death of what were considered to be 'popish' practices, and instead set out instructions for much simpler services with minimal ceremony. Making the sign of the cross at the baptism ceremony was abolished. The marriage service dispensed with the exchange of rings and the husband's promise to worship his wife with his body. Barebone's Parliament took this reform even further by an act outlawing church weddings altogether, replacing them with civil ceremonies performed by JPs. The burial of the dead, according to the Directory of Public Worship, was to take place 'without any ceremony' and did not even require a minister to be present. By 1653 moral reformation, too, had received similar legislative attention, notably by the Rump, which had passed two acts in 1650. One condemned anyone found guilty of swearing and cursing to fines and whipping, and another enacted the draconian penalty of death for those convicted of adultery and three months' imprisonment for fornication.

As has been seen in earlier chapters, the leaders of the Protectorate gave the aspirations behind this legislation their full support. Protector and Council passed ordinances in 1654 outlawing cock-fighting and horse-race meetings. The moral reformation clauses in the instructions to the major-generals reflected the regime's support for this attempted cultural revolution. Moreover, the occasional days of thanksgiving and humiliation that Protector and Council ordered to be held in the 1650s were designed to maintain official impetus for the campaign.[36]

What impact did the campaign have on life in England and Wales? It was not completely unsuccessful. In most communities in England and Wales there were pockets of people who shared this zeal for reformation and who seized the opportunity to put it into effect. When he was Mayor of Coventry in 1655–56 Robert Beake energetically carried out a full-scale campaign against sabbath-breakers and unlicensed alehouses. In March 1656 he even sent soldiers into the countryside surrounding Coventry to arrest those travelling on Sundays. The activities of other godly magistrates rarely reached the heights of Beake's zeal, but the work of Edmund Hopwood in south-east Lancashire and Captain John Pickering in the West Riding of Yorkshire in securing convictions of alehouse keepers, drunks, swearers and sabbath-breakers shows what could be achieved (document 29).[37] When a godly magistrate found an ally in the local minister the effect could be equally dramatic. In King's Norton in Worcestershire, Richard Gravis JP and the local minister, Thomas Hall, succeeded in closing down many alehouses.[38] Moreover, in many towns where godly elites had already gained control, their ongoing programmes of reformation were aided by the support of the government at Westminster.[39]

Since all the major-generals (with the possible exception of Charles Howard)[40] were, to varying degrees, driven by godly zeal, local campaigns like Beake's were given a significant impetus in 1655–56. Without any doubt this was most true in the areas controlled by Major-Generals Worsley and Barkstead. Worsley's efforts in Lancashire against alehouses – in January 1656 he and his commissioners agreed to close 200 alehouses in the hundred of Blackburn and a greater number in Salford – are well-known, causing some contemporaries and historians to put down his death at the early age of 34 to the stress he subjected himself to. Barkstead's campaign for godly reformation in and around

London was scarcely less zealous, as he set about attempting (with some success) to sweep prostitution off the capital's streets, suppress cock-fighting and bear-baiting by closing the beargarden in Bankside, and outlaw horse-racing on Hackney Marsh.[41]

Despite the efforts of godly governors like these, it is difficult to avoid the general conclusion that any progress towards the hoped-for cultural revolution was very patchy and limited. It is true that, in coming to that conclusion, one needs to guard against excessive reliance on pessimistic assessments of godly magistrates and ministers, who were prone to see the world in terms of an unending struggle against the mass ranks of the ungodly and therefore to exaggerate their lack of success. Yet other evidence suggests that they were right. Indeed such is the consensus of historians on this point that only very brief treatment of the catalogue of failures is necessary here.[42]

In all parts of the provinces that have been studied the old festive calendar proved to be very resilient. Despite official disapproval, Christmas continued to be celebrated. Prosecution rates of moral offences remained low in the 1650s and (according to Anthony Fletcher) were exceeded in the 1660s and later.[43] The reasons for these failures are clear. There were simply not enough godly ministers and magistrates committed to the campaign of moral reformation to make it anything other than a patchy success. Most JPs, constables and other local officials at best paid lip-service to the campaign or at worst ignored it altogether. Moreover, popular allegiance to the religious calendar of the Book of Common Prayer was strong, and there is abundant widespread evidence of staunch refusal to abandon traditional lifestyles that a minority condemned as 'ungodly' (document 30). Two examples from Warwickshire and Somerset must suffice to emphasise the strength of popular resistance to the attempted cultural revolution and its assault on traditional festivals like Christmas and Easter. At the Easter quarter sessions at Warwick in 1655 'idle and vain persons' from Henley-in-Arden were accused of erecting 'may-poles and may-bushes, and for using of morris dances and other heathenish and unlawful customs, the observation whereof tendeth to draw together a great concourse of loose people and consequently to hazard the public peace'. Christmas celebrations, too, continued to be held, as Matthew Eyre of Frome in Somerset found to his cost when he was beaten up on Boxing Day 1657 by a group of mummers who had been 'drinking, playing cards and fiddling all day in disguised habits'.[44]

Acceptance

The impact of the Protectorate on England and Wales was not only characterised by opposition and failure. The speed with which many people were reconciled to the new government may have been slowed down by the fears and anxieties seen above, but the process of its acceptance was not halted. What was there about the Protectorate that ensured that reconciliation to the regime was at least as strong a theme as opposition to it?

The first aspect that worked in this direction, certainly for the propertied classes, was that, although their grip on local power was loosened, the men who replaced them were still by and large gentlemen. Moreover, despite this worrying shift in the social balance of power, local government operated effectively in maintaining order. Over 25 years ago in a study of Cheshire in the 1650s John Morrill concluded that 'whatever caused a widespread gentry rebellion in Cheshire in the summer of 1659, it was hardly a craving for the firm and responsible local government supposed to have existed twenty years before, which had been lost'.[45] Since that was written surprisingly little work has been done on the impact of the Cromwellian Protectorate on local government in England and Wales. But what has been done suggests that Morrill's conclusion can be applied more generally. Even Andrew Coleby, in a study of Hampshire after 1649 which is generally critical of the achievements of the county's local governors in the 1650s, concedes that JPs there were 'up to the task' of administering the county. Others have been much less grudging in their assessments. In Gloucestershire, writes A.R. Warmington, 'although the power of the gentry was not entirely broken, it was demonstrated that county government could continue without a Tracy or a Stephens [major county magnate families] at the heart of it. The ruling clique carried out jobs meant for more substantial men than they were.'[46]

The work of A.L. Beier and Ann Hughes on Warwickshire, which provides one of the fullest recent assessments of the work of local governors in the 1650s, shows the efficiency with which

Warwickshire JPs and other local officials responded to the distress left by the severe economic depression that hit the country in the late 1640s and early 1650s. Beier found that Warwickshire JPs in the 1650s undertook three times the amount of business relating to poor relief than had their predecessors in the 1630s, and Hughes's more comprehensive investigation suggests a high level of efficiency by JPs in and out of quarter sessions.[47] As Stephen Roberts found in Devon and Morrill in Cheshire, Warwickshire JPs during the Protectorate also showed a willingness to respond inventively to the problems they faced, for example by striving for greater equity in the assessment of local taxation.[48] 'The lower social status and the religious zeal of local governors [in Warwickshire] after 1645', concludes Hughes, 'along with the fact that they came to prominence as a result of the struggle of broad social groups against the king meant that they were more aware of the problems of middling and poorer elements in society and were not solely concerned with social hierarchy and social control.'[49] More work needs to be done on other localities to test whether that conclusion can be applied more generally. But what is fairly certain is that local governors everywhere, in responding well to the problems of poverty, ensured that social distress did not escalate into riots. The 1650s saw hardly any outbreaks of enclosure and grain riots.[50] Alongside their success in clamping down on royalist conspiracies and rebellions, local governors ensured that stability was restored to the country's economic and social life after the upheavals of the previous decade.

What must have also helped the process of acceptance of the regime by conservative opinion is that the Protectorate brought about no major revolution in landownership. This must have been reassuring to many landowners, because for many of them there would have been times during the decade before the establishment of the Protectorate when it seemed likely that such a revolution would occur. Indeed, so badly did the economic fortunes of large landowners seem to have been hit during the 1640s and early 1650s that some historians once believed that these contemporary fears were justified. It is not difficult to see why historians of the stature of C.H. Firth thought that this was the case.[51] During the Civil War not only did rent roll incomes fall drastically as a result of the direct effects of warfare, but also both sides subjected the estates of their enemies to confiscation and large composition fines. Royalist landowners suffered even more, since in 1651 and 1652 three acts were passed by the Rump Parliament confiscating the estates of 780 and authorising their sale by Trustees of the Commonwealth, and during the Protectorate many landowners with royalist connections had to pay the punitive decimation tax.

However, damaging as these measures were, it is now clear that they did not bring about a permanent redistribution of property. Landowners' rental incomes quickly recovered after the end of the Civil War,[52] the impact of composition fines on landed estates amounted at the most to the equivalent of two years' annual income, the decimation tax only lasted a year, and the percentage of the landowning classes of England and Wales that was badly affected by the confiscation of estates was very small. Regional studies and investigations of individual landed families undertaken during the second half of the twentieth century showed that most landowners survived the crisis, and that even those who lost estates by confiscation and enforced sales did not suffer permanent damage. By careful estate management and in some cases with the aid of sympathetic help from Protector and Council, they were able to keep their losses to a minimum and often to recover lost estates.[53] Even Charles Stanley, eighth Earl of Derby, whose father had been executed for royalism in 1651, some of whose estates had been confiscated and sold by the Trustees of the Commonwealth, and who had sold estates in order to pay parliamentary-imposed fines, managed to recover many lost estates before 1660. The Stanleys' economic fortunes suffered, but there are no good reasons to believe the complaints of Earl Charles in 1662 that he had to live 'sparingly a country life upon that little fortune is left me'. The Stanleys' economic fortunes survived the 1640s and 1650s relatively unscathed.[54] Numerous studies confirm that this was generally the case.

The Protectorate's success in Scotland, Ireland and in international affairs also helped to reconcile many people to the regime, largely because it gave them a guarantee against invasion from north of the border or across the seas. This security was only achieved at a great financial cost, which (as has been seen) caused not a little resentment. But one wonders if some came to think that it was a price worth paying. What gives some credence to this suggestion is Mike Braddick's findings about the exceptionally

175

low arrears in the collection of the assessment tax in the 1650s in many English counties. In Cheshire, Braddick found that 'for a total of thirty-nine months during the 1650s the collector for the county collected nearly £16,000 with an arrear of only five per cent'. Similar high yields were recorded in most of eastern England, Kent and Sussex, a level of success and lack of sustained resistance that Braddick explains by the fact that the taxes 'were assessed by local people under the direction of commissions composed of substantial local men'.[55] It might also be valid to add the possibility that some of these local men realised that the taxes were an essential precondition of the stability and security the country enjoyed under the Protectorate in international affairs as well as home.

By the late 1650s there are signs that life was returning to normal after the upheavals of Civil War and its aftermath. Taxation levels fell slightly. The rule of the major-generals was very brief: most arrived in the counties only in November 1655 and none returned to the localities after the meeting of parliament in the late summer of 1656. Many local studies show that more great gentry families than ever began to be represented again on the Bench from 1657 onwards and that the rifts in gentry society that had appeared during and after the war were closing rapidly.[56] Further evidence is provided by seemingly trivial events in 1657 like the gatherings of ex-parliamentarians and ex-royalists around the dinner table of the Cheshire gentleman Thomas Mainwaring, and at the funeral at Warwick of Francis, third Lord Brooke.[57]

In the light of these kinds of development, historians have become wary of pre-dating the point at which the majority of people began to give substantial support for the restoration of the Stuarts. They have found very few signs of this before the end of the Protectorate. Well-informed royalists at the time felt the same. The Cornish royalist Joseph Jane was not alone in his pessimistic assessment of the royalist cause in the summer of 1658, when he wrote that 'God must give new hearts before He gives new blessings, for in our condition it is mere presumption to hope'.[58] Even after the Protectorate ended, as the pathetic support that Sir George Booth's rebellion received in August 1659 was to show, it was a long time before there were any signs of enthusiasm for the restoration of the monarchy.

Change

Slowly, then, as it became evident that the regime would not prevent life in the localities from returning to something like pre-war normality, the Protectorate began to win the battle to secure the acceptance of the people of England and Wales. It would be misleading, though, to leave this analysis of the impact of the Protectorate at that. As well as a return to normality, the Protectorate brought about important changes, at least in the short term, to the political and religious life of England and Wales.[59]

Since the Protectorate was a regime run largely by men who desperately wanted to put into effect the kind of godly reform of society that Puritans had been advocating since the later sixteenth century, it is not surprising that (as has been seen) men with similar aspirations should come to the fore in local government in the 1650s, taking advantage of the favourable circumstances to attempt to bring about a godly reformation in their localities. That attempt failed, but it will be argued here that an unintended and unforeseen consequence of the activities of these godly rulers of England and Wales, supported by their allies at the centre of government, was to contribute to a crucial change in the political culture of the country, which became characterised to a much greater extent than ever before by deep ideological divisions.

This is a process which can be seen most clearly in the 1650s in the history of some provincial towns, in which struggles for political control had already emerged between godly partisans of the parliamentarian cause and their conservative opponents. The Long Parliament and the Rump Parliament in the late 1640s and early 1650s had passed acts that barred royalists from exercising power in towns and had thrown their weight behind godly elites. During the 1650s Protector and Council signalled their intention to continue to provide official support for their godly allies in urban government.[60] The extent of that commitment and of its success has been understated in the past.[61] The Protectorate was much more pro-active in its support of those it considered to be 'well-affected' to the regime in England and Wales than it was in Scotland and Ireland. The conciliar committee for municipal charters discussed in chapter 3 did not last long enough to effect a wholesale remodelling of municipal charters in the interests of the Protectorate's local supporters, but it did have some successes, notably in Colchester. There a new Cromwellian charter in 1656 proved to be decisive, at least for as long as the Protectorate lasted, in giving the upper hand to a radical godly group led by Henry Barrington in its long-running struggle with its moderate opponents.[62]

The major-generals proved to be very effective agents in this respect. Major-General Edward Whalley's interference in the affairs of Lincoln towards the end of 1655, which involved dismissing the ex-royalist mayor and forcing on the town his own nominee as town clerk, was condemned by the town corporation as 'an usurped, illegal pretended power'. But that he was probably unrepentant is seen by his subsequent exultant report to Thurloe after he had helped some godly constables in Coventry by getting rid of an alderman who had obstructed their drive against unlicensed alehouses. This, he wrote, 'hath strucke the worser sort with force and amazement; but exceedingly rejoyces the hearts of the godly'. There is little doubt that this view was shared by other major-generals, like Thomas Kelsey, Tobias Bridge and John Desborough, as they ousted the opponents of godly reformation from (respectively) Kingston in Surrey, High Wycombe in Buckinghamshire and many towns in the West Country.[63]

In other towns, too, godly elites entrenched themselves in power. Ian Roy's study of Worcester, Oxford and Gloucester is especially significant in showing this process and pointing to one of its major consequences:

> The town halls had seized the opportunities … to co-operate with the republican regimes in order to further their own interests. Anxious to forward a godly reformation and to extend their own power they had proved zealous and efficient … Inevitably they produced a reaction … The government of corporations had become a matter of political controversy.[64]

Godly elites in many towns were temporarily triumphant, but they did not succeed in exterminating all opposition. P.D. Halliday, building on Ian Roy's pioneering work, writes that they had created 'a world that played a different kind of politics, one that permitted, or even encouraged, the exclusion from government of some with the proper social credentials because their political loyalties or religious sympathies made them suspect'.[65] It may be that, when more work has been done on the provinces during the Protectorate, it will be possible to build on that insight by showing more generally that the political culture of the country was becoming more deeply riven by ideologically based controversy than ever before.

There are many indications that this process was accompanied by another significant change in the country's political culture: an increase in the numbers of people involved in government and in debates about political issues. There is a danger of exaggerating the novelty of this development in the 1650s. There is now a large body of work by historians which has demonstrated the extent to which political debates in the early seventeenth century were not restricted to a narrow elite at the upper end of society.[66] Moreover, some historians recently have shown that popular participation in public life was considerable by the mid-seventeenth century.[67] At the very least, though, the Protectorate saw a significant increase in popular participation in government and in political debate. 'It seems likely', writes John Morrill, 'that the bureaucracy of local government – the hordes of assessors, collectors, commissioners, over and above the traditional officers of the civil parish (the constables, overseers and churchwardens) – spread responsibility more widely than ever before, especially among those groups on the margin of literacy.'[68] Ann Hughes takes this point even further by suggesting that, in discussing complex legal matters like indemnity cases, more people than ever before came to discuss 'questions of legality and necessity, justice and tyranny'.

Insufficient work has been done on the local government of English and Welsh counties to make certain that she is right in claiming that this was part of 'the increasing politicisation of provincial England'.[69] But there is much to be said for this view. Opportunities for the expression of political and religious ideas in print, which had flourished in the 1640s, were not seriously limited in the 1650s. Those at the centre of government during the Protectorate seem to have been less concerned than the monarchical regimes they replaced to control the press. Royalist and popular satires of Cromwell and the regime were published alongside heroic images.[70] Pamphlets, treatises, poems and ballads flooded from the printing presses on an infinite variety of subjects, making political news and debates ever more accessible to more people than ever before. In addition, coffee houses, which are seen by some historians as one of the key elements in the development of 'a public sphere' of wider public debate, were established in London and elsewhere in the 1650s.[71]

Popular political awareness was also increased by the way that the Cromwellian Church settlement helped to make religion a major topic of public debate. Again, one must be careful not to minimise earlier developments. Peter Lake and David Como, for example, have brilliantly demonstrated the existence in early Stuart London of 'an underworld' of popular religious debates.[72] Others who have worked on the 1640s have shown the ways in which religious debates became more public, less prone to official control and censorship, and more widely reported.[73] The Cromwellian Protectorate saw the continuation of that process. Lively public religious debates in print and face-to-face public disputations were common. It might be thought that the issues at the centre of these debates – on the nature of the predestinarian theology, the validity of infant baptism, and so on – are ones that would hardly capture the popular imagination. Such a thought would be wrong, judging by the large audience that flocked in January 1655 to the parish church in Chesterfield to listen to a public debate on the rights and wrongs of an educated ordained ministry between James Nayler, the Quaker, and Immanuel Bourne, rector of Ashover in Derbyshire, and other examples of religious debates that attracted large and sometimes vociferous audiences.[74]

In what other ways did the Cromwellian Church settlement bring about changes in England and Wales? In what follows it is suggested that the settlement had a major impact on life in England and Wales. This argument for change, though, needs to be qualified. The Cromwellian Church settlement did not change the fact that the English Church had been subjected to secular authority since at least the Reformation. As has been seen in chapter 2, ordinances of Protector and Council in 1654 had established commissions of triers and ejectors. These were very active in implementing the new Church settlement, especially after the arrival of the major-generals in the localities. The most recent study of their work shows that 'the Triers Committee, in its full five years of existence, passed judgement on well over 3,500 ministerial nominees' and that the local ejectors were 'active in nearly two-thirds of English counties between 1654 and 1659'. In addition, Oliver Cromwell's participation in this lay control of the Church was considerable. 'He made', according to one estimate, 'approximately 40 percent of all the presentations on which the Triers deliberated.'[75] Nor did the Cromwellian Church settlement seek to subvert the notion that there should only be one national Church. Blair Worden's path-breaking article has shattered for ever the idea that the Protectorate aimed to bring about modern notions of 'religious toleration', consisting of freedom of religious thought and practice outside the discipline of the national Church.[76] As has been seen, both the Instrument of Government and the Humble Petition and Advice banned groups like Socinians, Quakers and Anglicans, as well as Catholics. At times of crises which seemed to threaten the Protectorate's continued existence, these groups were repressed, sometimes with military force. Occasionally Anglicans were dealt with as severely as Quakers (document 31).

Yet emphasis on repression and uniformity in the Cromwellian Church settlement can obscure the extent to which the 1650s was a period of relative religious freedom in England and Wales. Even the regime's religious enemies were not subjected to a systematic campaign of repression. Protector and Council tried only occasionally to stem the tide of hostility against Quakers and Socinians. Only two Catholic priests were executed during the Protectorate. Moreover, except at times of political crisis, Anglicans were often left in relative peace to worship according to the outlawed Book of Common Prayer, and were able to live 'in some degree of uneasy relationship with the Cromwellian Establishment'.[77]

However, the most significant feature of religious life in England and Wales during the Protectorate is the flourishing of many different types of Protestantism, groups that *later* crystallised into separate religious denominations outside the national Church. It needs to be emphasised strongly that this did not happen to a great extent during the 1650s. Only the Baptists in England and Wales developed regional and national institutions that promoted exclusive 'closed communions'.[78] Much more typical of religious life in England and Wales in the 1650s was the appearance of diverse religious congregations, many of which cannot be crammed into the tight confines of denominational labels like 'Presbyterian' and 'Independent'.[79] What these congregations had in common – a commitment to one national Church – was more important than their differences on points of theology and liturgy. Moreover, their commitment to one national Church was strengthened by the Protectorate's success in providing money to ensure that church ministers received adequate salaries. From 1654 this was done with some success by the Trustees for the Maintenance of Ministers, which replaced the Committee for Plundered Ministers.[80] Adam Martindale, who was the minister at Rostherne in Cheshire, was no doubt not the only one to look back to the 1650s as days of prosperity and efficiency in his pastoral work:

> I now enjoyed great liberty to work and had work enough to do preaching twice every Lord's day to a great congregation ... preaching of many funerals and baptizings, besides no few occasional sermons at the chapels in the parish. I had my part also, in maintaining my [preaching] exercise in Staffordshire yearly, two in Lancashire and four in Cheshire, besides the great running one of many speakers in those eastern parts and the lecture in Chester.[81]

Yet, even ministers like Martindale were uneasy about what the relative religious freedom allowed by the Protectorate might lead to. Hence the promotion by groups of church ministers in the 1650s up and down the country of 'associations' designed to establish a stronger form of unity and discipline than that exercised by triers, ejectors and individual initiatives by Protector and Council. Richard Baxter's Worcestershire Association was just one such body that attempted to unite 'Presbyterians' and 'Independents' (document 32). The breadth of religious views encompassed by these associations was much wider than similar organisations in Ireland. But their aim was the same: to maintain one national Church.

These associations were not a total failure. They reflect the vitality and diversity of religious life in England and Wales under the Protectorate. Yet in the last resort they failed to hold securely most mainstream Protestant opinion within one national Church. The edifice creaked and began to split apart at the seams. Perhaps that outcome was inevitable. Post-Reformation English Protestantism had never been united but had always been rent by divisions between groups with different visions of what the national Church should be. During the Protectorate, which was a regime that tolerated more public debate about religion and a greater practice of forms of Protestantism than ever before, these divisions, although not yet hardening into 'denominational' rifts, nevertheless grew. The consequence was that during the Protectorate life in England and Wales became characterised by deep religious, as well as political, divisions.

Notes

1 Richard Baxter, *A Holy Commonwealth* (ed. W. Lamont, Cambridge, 1994), p. xi.

2 See chapter 2.

3 C.H. Firth, ed., *Memoirs of Edmund Ludlow* (2 vols, Oxford, 1894), vol. 1, p. 373.

4 Q. Skinner, 'Conquest and consent: Thomas Hobbes and the Engagement controversy' in G.E. Aylmer, ed., *The Interregnum: The Quest for Settlement 1646–60* (London, 1972), pp. 81–2.

5 A. Hughes, *Politics, Society and Civil War in Warwickshire, 1620–60* (Cambridge, 1987), p. 300.

6 C. Egloff, 'John Hobart of Norwich and the politics of the Cromwellian Protectorate', *Norfolk Archaeology*, 41, 1994, p. 45.

7 See chapter 3.

8 Quoted in S.R. Gardiner, *The Commonwealth and Protectorate* (4 vols, London, 1903), vol. 4, p. 41.

9 See, for example, Samuel Richardson, *Plain Dealing … In Answer of Several Things Affirmed by Mr Vavasour Powell*, January 1655, British Library, E 865/3.

10 A. Fletcher, *A County Community in Peace and War: Sussex, 1600–60* (Harlow, 1975), p. 301.

11 F. Bamford, ed., *A Royalist Notebook* (London, 1936), pp. 110–11.

12 S. Roberts, 'Godliness and government in Glamorgan 1647–60' in C. Jones, M. Newitt and S. Roberts, eds, *Politics and People in Revolutionary England* (Oxford, 1986), p. 226; P. Jenkins, *The Making of a Ruling Class: The Glamorgan Gentry 1640–1790* (Cambridge, 1983), pp. 109–10.

13 Hughes, *Warwickshire*, p. 272. See A. Fletcher, *Reform in the Provinces: The Government of Stuart England* (New Haven and London, 1986), pp. 15–18 for the composition of the Bench in the 1650s in general.

14 J. Morrill, *Cheshire, 1630–60: County Government and Society during the English Revolution* (Oxford, 1974), p. 224.

15 G. Aylmer, 'Who was ruling Herefordshire from 1645 to 1661?', *Transactions of the Woolthorpe Naturalists' Field Club*, 40 (part 2), 1970; A.R. Warmington, *Civil War, Interregnum and Restoration in Gloucestershire 1640–72* (London, 1997), chapter 4 (the quotation is from p. 99).

16 For a table that shows the increase county by county, see B. Coward and C. Durston, *The English Revolution: An Advanced*

Sourcebook (London, 1997), pp. 72–3.

17 The gross figures are from J.S. Wheeler, *The Making of a Great Power: War and the Military Revolution in Seventeenth-Century England* (Stroud, 1999), p. 213.

18 Michael J. Braddick, *The Nerves of State: Taxation and the Financing of the English State, 1558–1714* (Manchester, 1996), pp. 10–11.

19 See chapter 5.

20 J.T. Rutt, ed., *The Diary of Thomas Burton Esquire* (4 vols, London, 1828), vol. 1, p. 137, quoted in Barry Reay, *The Quakers and the English Revolution* (London, 1985), p. 57.

21 Alan Macfarlane, ed., *The Diary of Ralph Josselin 1616–38* (London, 1976), pp. 379–80, quoted in Ann Hughes, 'The pulpit guarded: confrontations between orthodox and radicals in revolutionary England' in A. Laurence, W.R. Owens and S. Sims, eds, *John Bunyan and His England 1628–88* (London, 1990), p. 34.

22 See, for example, J.L. Latimer, ed., *The Annals of Bristol in the Seventeenth Century* (Bristol, 1900), p. 254 (report of a riot against Quakers by apprentices, December 1654), and the many pro- and anti-Quaker pamphlets that grew out of the Quakers' presence in Bristol, such as *Satan Inthron'd*, 1657 (Bodleian Library, 110 j 131(1)) and *The Cry of Blood*, 1656 (British Library, E 884(3)).

23 Reay, *Quakers*, p. 52.

24 See chapter 3.

25 H.M. Reece, 'The military presence in England 1649–60' (unpublished DPhil thesis, University of Oxford, 1981).

26 A. Fletcher, 'Oliver Cromwell and the localities: the problem of consent' in Jones, Newitt and Roberts, eds, *Politics and People*, *passim*.

27 Christopher Durston, *Cromwell's Major-Generals: Godly Government during the English Revolution* (Manchester, 2001), p. 139.

28 This was a temptation to which I succumbed just over a decade ago when writing *Oliver Cromwell* (Harlow, 1991), p. 163.

29 Durston, *Cromwell's Major-Generals*, p. 75.

30 *Ibid.*, p. 76.

31 *Ibid.*, p. 78.

32 *Ibid.*, p. 107; J.T. Cliffe, ed., 'The Cromwellian decimation tax of 1655: the assessment lists' in *Seventeenth-Century Political and Financial Papers* (Camden Society, 5th series, vol. 7, 1996), *passim*.

33 Durston, *Cromwell's Major-Generals*, p. 108.

34 *Ibid.*, p. 113.

35 Christopher Durston, 'Puritan rule and the failure of cultural revolution' in C. Durston and J. Eales, eds, *The Culture of English Puritanism 1560–1700* (Basingstoke, 1996), *passim*. The following paragraphs rely very much on this excellent article and also *idem*, 'The lords of misrule:

the Puritan war on Christmas', *History Today*, 39, 1989, and 'Unhallowed wedlocks', *Historical Journal*, 31, 1988.

36   Christopher Durston, '"For the better humiliation of the people": public days of fasting and thanksgiving during the English Revolution', *The Seventeenth Century*, 7, 1992.

37   Hughes, *Warwickshire*, pp. 283–4: D. Hirst, 'The failure of godly rule in the English republic', *Past and Present*, 132, 1991, p. 56.

38   C.D. Gilbert, 'Magistracy and ministry in Cromwellian England: the case of King's Norton, Worcestershire', *Midland History*, 2, 1998, pp. 71–83.

39   For example, in Dorchester, David Underdown, *Fire From Heaven: Life in an English Town in the Seventeenth Century* (London, 1992), chapter 7.

40   Durston, *Cromwell's Major-Generals*, pp. 50–1.

41   A. Fletcher, 'The religious motivation of Cromwell's major-generals' in D. Baker, ed., *Religious Motivation* (Studies in Church History 15, 1978), *passim*; Durston, *Cromwell's Major-Generals*, pp. 156–7, 175; Jean Mather, 'The moral code of the English Civil War and Interregnum', *The Historian*, 44, 1982, pp. 207–28.

42   Durston, *Cromwell's Major-Generals*, chapter 8; Durston, 'Puritan rule', *passim*; Hirst, 'The failure of godly rule'; Ronald Hutton, *The Rise and Fall of Merry England: The Ritual Year 1400–1700* (Oxford, 1994), chapter 6.

43   Fletcher, *Reform in the Provinces*, pp. 229–81.

44   Durston , 'Puritan rule', p. 224; Hughes, *Warwickshire*, p. 324.

45   Morrill, *Cheshire*, p. 253.

46   A.M. Coleby, *Central Government and the Localities: Hampshire, 1649–89* (Cambridge, 1987), p. 53; Warmington, *Gloucestershire*, p. 135. See also G.C. Forster, 'County government in Yorkshire during the Interregnum', *Northern History*, 12, 1976.

47   A.L. Beier, 'Poor relief in Warwickshire 1630–60', *Past and Present*, 35, 1966, pp. 96–7; Hughes, *Warwickshire*, pp. 278–81.

48   S. Roberts, 'Local government reform in England and Wales during the Interregnum' in Ivan Roots, ed., *'Into Another Mould': Aspects of the Interregnum* (Exeter, 1998) and 'Initiative and control: the Devon quarter sessions and grand jury, 1640–70', *Bulletin of the Institute of Historical Research*, 57, 1984; Morrill, *Cheshire*, chapter 6; Hughes, *Warwickshire*, pp. 280–1.

49   Hughes, *Warwickshire*, p. 282.

50   J. Morrill and J. Walter, 'Order and disobedience in the English Revolution' in A. Fletcher and J. Stevenson, eds, *Order and Disorder in the English Revolution* (Cambridge, 1985).

51   C.H. Firth, 'The royalists and the Protectorate', *English Historical*

Review, 52, 1937.

52 J. Broad, 'Gentry finances and the Civil War: the case of the Buckinghamshire Verneys', *Economic History Review*, 2nd series, 32, 1975.

53 Joan Thirsk, 'The sale of royalist lands during the Interregnum', *Economic History Review*, 2nd series, 5, 1952–53; *idem*, 'The Restoration land settlement', *Journal of Modern History*, 26, 1954; H.J. Habbakuk, 'Landowners and the Civil War', *Economic History Review*, 2nd series, 18, 1965; *idem*, 'Public finance and the sale of confiscated land during the Interregnum', *Economic History Review*, 2nd series, 15, 1962; P.G. Holliday, 'Land sales and repurchases in Yorkshire after the Civil Wars 1650–70', *Northern History*, 5, 1970.

54 B. Coward, *The Stanleys, Lords Stanley and Earls of Derby 1385–1672: The Origins, Wealth and Power of a Landowning Family* (Manchester, 1983), chapter 6.

55 Braddick, *The Nerves of State*, p. 96.

56 David Underdown's suggestion to that effect in 'Settlement in the counties, 1653–58' in G.E. Aylmer, ed., *The Interregnum: The Quest for Settlement 1646–60* (London, 1972), pp. 176–8, has been confirmed by more recent studies.

57 Morrill, *Cheshire*, p. 261; Hughes, *Warwickshire*, p. 301.

58 Quoted in M. Coate, *Cornwall during the Great Civil War and Interregnum 1642–60* (Oxford, 1933), p. 298.

59 For suggestive remarks about the changes on the country's social and intellectual life in the 1650s, see Derek Hirst, 'Locating the 1650s', *History*, 81, 1996, pp. 371–6. In particular, see Charles Webster, *The Great Instauration: Science, Medicine and Reformation, 1626–60* (London, 1975) for the schemes of intellectual and technological reforms that flourished during the Protectorate.

60 See chapter 4.

61 Although its treatment of the relationship between Interregnum governments and towns is generally excellent, P.D. Halliday, *Dismembering the Body Politic: Partisan Politics in England's Towns 1650–1730* (Cambridge, 1998) seems to me to play down too much the active role of the Protectorate in municipal affairs; see, for example, p. 65. R. Howell, 'Resistance to change: the political elites of provincial towns during the English Revolution' in A.L. Beier, David Cannadine and J.M. Rosenheim, eds, *The First Modern Society: Essays in English History in Honour of L. Stone* (Cambridge, 1989) also has a different assessment from mine.

62 Gardiner, *Commonwealth and Protectorate*, vol. 4, pp. 157–78; J.H. Round, 'Colchester during the Commonwealth', *English Historical Review*, 15, 1900; Halliday, *Dismembering the Body Politic*, pp. 64–5; William A.H. Schilling, 'The central government and the municipal corporations in England, 1642–63' (unpublished PhD thesis, University of Vanderbilt, 1970), pp. 97–9.

63   Schilling, 'Central government and municipal corporations', pp. 94–5, 99–102; Clive Holmes, *Seventeenth-Century Lincolnshire* (Lincoln, 1980), p. 204; Durston, *Cromwell's Major-Generals*, pp. 87–91; Halliday, *Dismembering the Body Politic*, pp. 56–7.

64   Ian Roy, 'The English Republic, 1649–60: the view from the town hall' in H. Koenigsberger, ed., *Republiken und Republikenismus in Europa der fruhe Neuzeit* (Odenburg, 1989), pp. 236–7.

65   Halliday, *Dismembering the Body Politic*, p. 64.

66   For example R. Cust, 'News and politics in early seventeenth-century England', *Past and Present*, 112, 1986; P. Croft, 'The reputation of Robert Cecil: libels, political opinion and popular awareness in the early seventeenth century', *Transactions of the Royal Historical Society*, 6th series, 1, 1993; A Bellany, '"Rayling rymes and vaunting verse": libellous politics in early Stuart England 1603–28' in K. Sharpe and P. Lake, eds, *Cultural Politics in Early Stuart England* (Basingstoke, 1994).

67   Some recent examples are Mark Goldie, 'The unacknowledged republic: office-holding in early modern England' in T. Harris, ed., *The Politics of the Excluded c1500–1850* (Basingstoke, 2001); S. Hindle, *The State and Social Change in Early Modern England c1550–1640* (Cambridge, 2000), chapter 1; M.J. Braddick, *State Formation in Early Modern England c1550–1700* (Basingstoke, 2000), chapter 1.

68   John Morrill, 'The impact on society' in John Morrill, ed., *Revolution and Restoration: England in the 1650s* (London, 1992), p. 110.

69   Hughes, *Warwickshire*, pp. 302–4.

70   L.L. Knoppers, *Constructing Cromwell: Ceremony, Portraits and Print 1645–61* (Cambridge, 2001), chapters 3 and 4.

71   S. Pincus, 'Coffee politicians does create: coffeehouses and Restoration political culture', *Journal of Modern History*, 67, 1995, pp. 111–12.

72   Peter Lake, *The Boxmaker's Revenge: 'Orthodoxy', 'Heterodoxy' and the Politics of the Parish in Early Stuart London* (Manchester, 2001). See the references in this book to David Como's unpublished 1998 University of Princeton PhD thesis and to a forthcoming article by Como and Lake in the *Journal of Ecclesiastical History*.

73   Dagmar Freist, *Governed by Opinion: Politics, Religion and the Dynamics of Communication in Early Stuart London 1637–45* (London, 1997).

74   R. O'Day, 'Immanuel Bourne: a defence of the ministerial order', *Journal of Ecclesiastical History*, 27, 1976; Ann Hughes, 'The pulpit guarded: confrontation between orthodox and radicals in revolutionary England' in Laurence, Owens and Sims, eds, *John Bunyan and his England*.

75   Jeffrey R. Collins, 'The church settlement of Cromwell', *History*, 87, 2002, pp. 29–31.

76   Blair Worden, 'Toleration and the Cromwellian Protectorate' in *Persecution and Toleration* (Studies in Church History 21, 1984).

77   R.S. Bosher, *The Making of the Restoration Settlement: The Influence of the Laudians 1649–62* (London, 1951), pp. 9, 11–12, 23–4, 27.

78   B.R. White, 'The organisation of the Particular Baptists 1644–60', *Journal of Ecclesiastical History*, 17, 1966; G.F. Nuttall, 'The Baptist Western Association 1653–58', *Journal of Ecclesiastical History*, 11, 1960; Hughes, *Warwickshire*, pp. 317–19.

79   On the problem of religious labels before 1660, see P. Collinson, 'Towards a broader understanding of the early dissenting tradition' in his *Godly People: Essays in English Protestantism and Puritanism* (London, 1983) and J.C. Davis, 'Cromwell's religion' in John Morrill, ed., *Oliver Cromwell and the English Revolution* (Harlow, 1990), p. 184.

80   R. O'Day and Ann Hughes, 'Augmentation and amalgamation: was there a systematic approach to the reform of parochial finance 1640–60?', in F. Heal and R. O'Day, eds, *Princes and Paupers in the English Church* (Leicester, 1981).

81   Quoted in A. Hughes, 'The frustrations of the godly' in Morrill, ed., *Revolution and Restoration*, p. 80.

Conclusion:
'the persistent grin'

One final question needs to be raised by way of conclusion. What was the long-term impact of the Cromwellian Protectorate on the way Britain developed in the years after 1659? It seems to me that historians have generally exaggerated its impact. The 1650s (together with the 1640s) have often been regarded as one of the key 'turning points' in the country's history. This period, some have claimed, saw 'the end of the Middle Ages', and the beginnings of modern constitutional monarchy, of religious tolerance and even of the nation's rise to a position of commercial and imperial supremacy in the world.[1] This view needs to be greatly modified.

Within twelve months of the Cromwellian Protectorate the Stuart monarchy was unconditionally restored to power. Given the despondency of royalists at the lack of support they enjoyed during Richard Cromwell's Protectorate in 1658–59 and the small numbers who actively supported Sir George Booth's rebellion in favour of a 'free parliament' in August 1659, Charles II's restoration in May 1660 was remarkable. Why did it come about? The answer lies partly in the fact that between May 1659 and March 1660 all three regimes that followed the Cromwellian Protectorate – the restored Rump (May–October 1659), government by an army-dominated council of state (October–December 1659) and the re-restored Rump (December 1659 – March 1660) – failed to provide effective stable government. All three failed to produce a leader of the stature of Oliver Cromwell, able to contain the divisions between civilian Commonwealthsmen and Cromwellians that had appeared in the 1650s, let alone to bridge the gulf between the varying aspirations that had deeper roots in the period before 1649. None of the civilian politicians of 1659 had the ability, maybe not even the ambition, to do this. Of the politicians within the army, Fleetwood and Desborough had shown their limited abilities as politicians during Richard Cromwell's Protectorate, and Lambert, the general who might have had the ability to fill Oliver Cromwell's boots, failed to rise to the occasion in 1659. Monck is the army leader who played the most crucial role in 1659–60, bringing an English army from Scotland to London, and eventually backing the final expulsion of the Rump. But the outcome (as he must have known) was the calling of a new Convention Parliament which would (as it did) declare for the restoration of monarchy very soon after it met. Monck's role in these events was very clever, but his career both before and afterwards suggests that he possessed none of the qualities necessary to cope constructively with the problems that were left after the collapse of the Cromwellian Protectorate.

What also ensured that the outcome would be the restoration of monarchy was that by the end of December 1659 many believed that this was the only viable alternative to what looked like a descent into not only political anarchy, but also social and religious chaos as well. As Ronald Hutton has persuasively argued, these fears outran by some considerable margin what was actually happening. Only very briefly in the two weeks or so after the army council of state abdicated power at the end of December 1659 were there in fact any signs of a real breakdown of order. In some counties there were reports of irregular troops being raised and not all acted as vigilante forces; some behaved more like bandits. But order was quickly restored and (as Hutton writes) 'compared with the havoc of the civil wars, the disruptions of the later Interregnum were slight'.[2] Government did not break down at the end of 1659, but to some it seemed as if this was happening.

For many propertied people especially in the winter of 1659–60 (as was to be the case 30 years later in 1688–89) panic and fear drove them to demand the establishment of a viable government as quickly as possible; there was no time to negotiate detailed constitutional conditions. Many persuaded themselves also that there was no need to do so, especially since Charles II's Declaration of Breda in April 1660 had made general promises that the King would not rule arbitrarily, and that he would respect property rights and 'tender consciences' regarding religion. Charles II was restored on the crest of a wave of opinion that cried out for stability. Not only was he restored without any formal limitations on his power, but when his first parliament met – the Cavalier Parliament – in 1661 it set about passing legislation that made illegal some of the claims made by parliaments in the 1640s, including the right to legislate without the King and to call parliaments without the King's consent. The King was also given sole control of the army and massive powers of censorship, and the Triennial Act of 1664 had none of the guarantees of regular parliaments laid down in the constitutions of the Cromwellian Protectorate. The powers of the restored monarchy were not exactly the same as those possessed by monarchs before 1641, but there is no doubt that the Cromwellian Protectorate had not put Britain on a high road that led inevitably to the development of a constitutional monarchy limited by parliaments.

Moreover, what further weakens the case that the Cromwellian Protectorate marked a 'turning point' in Britain's history is that much that was done by the regime was swept away in the early 1660s. As has been seen, the Protectorate had largely failed to bring about a hoped-for godly reformation, but the Cromwellian Church settlement, a broad Church with a disciplinary framework of triers and ejectors, had been set in place. Despite attempts at conferences between politicians and divines in London in 1660–61 to retain some elements of this settlement (supported by Charles II and his chief minister, Sir Edward Hyde, Earl of Clarendon), the Restoration Church settlement decided on by the Cavalier Parliament dismantled the Cromwellian settlement and erected a national Church with bishops, a Book of Common Prayer and a liturgy that had been outlawed in the 1640s and 1650s. The broad Cromwellian Church was replaced by a very narrow one, and ferocious penalties were devised in the so-called Clarendon Code for all those who refused to conform to it. The Clarendon Code created a system of religious apartheid, which reserved political office and a university education only for card-carrying members of the Church of England, and condemned Dissenters to the status of second-class citizens, liable (at best) to exclusion from political life and (at worst) to suffer imprisonment or transportation. As has been seen, the 'toleration' allowed by the Cromwellian Church settlement was far from unlimited, but it was much wider than that envisaged by the legislators who drafted the Clarendon Code. It is difficult to see the Cromwellian Protectorate as a 'milestone' on the country's 'road' to 'modern' toleration.

Two other achievements of the Cromwellian Protectorate also proved to be short-lived. The union of all the British Isles, which was a key feature of the history of the 1650s, ended in 1660. Charles II was King of Great Britain and Ireland, but, despite the title, the Cromwellian union of Scotland was not continued and the Scots rejoiced in their freedom from English rule. The extent to which hopes of an Anglo-Scots union survived in 1660 is not known, but it is highly likely that the history of the union in the 1650s did not strengthen the cause. Not only did the Cromwellian Protectorate not mark a turning point on the 'road' to 'the making of Great Britain', but much of the Cromwellian Protectorate's achievement in making Britain a great power in Europe disappeared in 1660. The country's foreign policy under Charles II and James II reflected a step back towards the kind of weak, relatively minor role it had played in European affairs before the 1650s. Not until 40 or 50 years after the end of the Cromwellian Protectorate would contemporaries again begin to see Britain as a major European power.

Yet, even though the idea of the 1650s as 'a turning point' is misleading (perhaps the concept of a 'turning point' should be abandoned?), it would be wrong to suggest that the Cromwellian Protectorate did not leave a legacy other than a negative reaction against the regime, its leaders and what they had tried to do. It is true that in the early 1660s those aspects were most apparent, typified by events on 30 January 1661, the anniversary of the execution of Charles I, when the decayed bodies of Oliver Cromwell, Henry Ireton and others were exhumed and hung on the gallows at Tyburn. But the British Isles of the later seventeenth century and beyond were affected in more positive ways by what had happened during the Cromwellian Protectorate. Adapting a phrase used by Ivan Roots, like Alice in Wonderland's Cheshire cat, the Cromwellian Protectorate disappeared but it left a persistent grin behind.[3] What was 'the persistent grin'?

There were five major ways in which the Cromwellian Protectorate left a long-term permanent impact on Britain and Ireland. All have been discussed in chapters 6, 7 and 8, and are briefly noted here.

The first is the Protectorate's impact on Ireland, where there took place a major revolution that permanently transferred social and political dominance in that country from the Irish Catholic landed elite to the Protestant landed classes. This Protestant Ascendancy, which was to be a constant feature of Irish life in the future, came about as a result of a deliberate act of policy by the Cromwellian Protectorate.

This is not true of the second major legacy of the Protectorate to the future development of Britain. The financial and administrative developments of the Protectorate (and the innovations of the parliamentary regimes on which they were based) had not been prompted by an intention to restructure the State, but had their origins in the need to raise large amounts of men and money to fight wars and maintain large standing armies and a navy. But in the long run the outcome was to help to transform and strengthen the British State. James Scott Wheeler is in danger of exaggerating the point when he writes that 'the military and fiscal developments of the mid-century were the seismic fault lines between semi-feudalism and modern England'.[4] But most of the taxes (principally assessments and the excise) developed during the Protectorate, on lines laid down by the parliamentary regimes of the 1640s, were continued after 1659. Taxation levels, too, remained high. The annual national revenue (now largely from taxes granted by parliament) fell only slightly from its average of £1,719,910 p.a. in the 1650s to £1,642,640 p.a. in the next 25 years, before rising again to £1,975,000 p.a. in the reign of James II.[5] Direct taxation, pioneered in the 1640s and 1650s, became the basis for the emergence of what historians like Mike Braddick and John Brewer have called 'the fiscal-military state', with the means for the first time ever of tapping the country's wealth, so helping to transform Britain into a major world power after the end of the seventeenth century.[6]

The third and fourth, interlinked legacies were the effects of the Cromwellian Protectorate on the political culture of Britain. Historians of late seventeenth- and early eighteenth-century Britain have shown how politics in Britain became increasingly influenced by public opinion and shaped by the emergence of political parties.[7] Chapter 8 identified some ways in which the 1650s contributed to these developments, especially as furious debates raged about religion and the controversial issue of whether a wide range of Protestant views could be tolerated, leaving a legacy of growing political awareness, popular participation in political debates and divisive religious issues.

This points to the final and most important legacy of the Cromwellian Protectorate. Ever since the Reformation English Protestants had differed about the nature of the reformed Church. During the 1640s and 1650s these differences widened as different kinds of Protestantism emerged. Not all of them can be neatly categorised with labels like Presbyterians, Independents and Congregationalists, but all of them had competing prescriptions for the nation's religious settlement. The Cromwellian Church settlement was a heroic attempt to comprehend most, if not all, of these Protestant groups, with the aim of maintaining a united English Church. Whether or not that could have been sustained will never be known. What is certain (with the benefit of hindsight) is that, after the attempt was abandoned in the early 1660s by the architects of the Clarendon Code, a broad national Church was never again established. The result was to exclude many Protestants from the restored Church and thereby to create Protestant Nonconformity. It was not what those at the centre of the Cromwellian Protectorate had wanted, but there is no doubt that what they had done when in power had made a major contribution towards making the division between Church and Chapel a feature of British life that has lasted until our own day.

Notes

1   See, for example, L. Stone, *The Causes of the English Revolution, 1529–1642* (London, 1972), pp. 146–7; C. Hill, *From Reformation to Industrial Revolution* (London, 1968), *passim*.

2   R. Hutton, *The Restoration: A Political and Religious History of England and Wales, 1658–67* (Oxford, 1986), p. 83.

3   Ivan Roots, *The Great Rebellion 1642–60* (London, 1966), p. 257. See B. Coward, 'Cromwell and the Restoration: "a persistent grin"', *Cromwelliana*, 1982–83, reprinted in Peter Gaunt, ed., *Cromwell 400* (The Cromwell Association, 1999). John Morrill, 'Introduction' to his *Revolution and Restoration: England in the 1650s* (London, 1992), p. 14, adapts the same idea but writes about the English Revolution vanishing, 'leaving

only a scowl behind'.

4   J.S. Wheeler, *The Making of a World Power: War and the Military Revolution in Seventeenth Century England* (Stroud, 1999), p. 198.

5   Michael J. Braddick, *The Nerves of State: Taxation and the Financing of the English State, 1558–1714* (Manchester 1996), p. 10.

6   *Ibid.*, *passim*; J. Brewer, *The Sinews of Power: War, Money and the English State, 1688–1783* (London, 1989), *passim*.

7   For example Tim Harris, *Politics under the Later Stuarts: Party Conflict in a Divided Society, 1660–1715* (London, 1993); Mark Knights, *Politics and Opinion in Crisis, 1678–81* (Cambridge, 1994).

Selected documents

Apart from document 12, I have not reproduced documents that are already accessible in collections like J.P. Kenyon, ed., *The Stuart Constitution: Documents and Commentary* (2nd edn, Cambridge, 1986). Many sources from this period are very long. The following documents are brief extracts. I have retained the original spelling throughout and have added only occasional explanatory material in square brackets. Comments on the context in which these documents appeared and on their significance are made in the text of the book.

Document 1: A justification for the establishment of the Protectorate, 1654

Extracts from Marchamont Nedham, *A True State of the Case of the Commonwealth of England, Scotland, and Ireland, And the Dominions thereto belonging; In reference to the late established Government by a Lord Protector and a Parliament etc.* (London, 1654; reprinted by the Rota at the University of Exeter, 1978), pp. 3–4, 8–11, 13–14, 22–3, 28–9, 30, 40, 43.

> We have thought meet, in all meekness and moderation, to present our Judgment to the publike view, and offer such Particulars to others, as may (through the blessing of God) be a ground of satisfaction to them, as well as to our selves; being fully perswaded in our own breasts, as to the present Form of Government, that such Cautions and Limitations are therein described, as make due and full provision for the Peoples Liberties, and those just Rights, the

maintenance whereof hath been so religiously prosecuted in the late War ...

After a survey of the events during the rule of the Rump from 1649 to 1653, *A True State* comments on the alleged deficiencies of rule by parliament alone.

The Government then of this Nation being (through necessity) alter'd, and at length established in the way of a Free-State or Commonwealth in the hands of the Parliament, both the Army and People were content to acquiesce therein, and continued languishing year after year, in hope at last to have tasted those Fruits of Freedom, which seemed to shoot forth and flourish in the Bud, at the beginning of that Establishment: But ... after the incurrence of divers years, all our hopes were blasted, in regard particular Members became studious of Parties and private Interests, neglecting the publick; and by reason of the dilatory Proceedings in the House, and unlimited arbitrary decisions at Committees, wholly perverted the end of Parliaments ... they brought on their Bill for a new Representative ... the evil consequences thereof both in respect of freedom and safety, are discernable to every eye, and would have proved a remedy worse than the disease. For besides the infinite number of Laws which would have bin Enacted by the constant sitting of the supreme Authority, that in a few years no man could have told how to have behaved himself, either in respect of his life or estate, (as is known by experience of the last Parliament, who have made more Laws then had been in some hundreds of years before), the Supreme Powers of making Laws, and of putting them in execution, were by that Bill to have been disposed in the same hands, which placing the Legislative and executive Powers in the same person, is a marvellous In-let of Corruption and Tyranny: whereas the keeping of these two apart, flowing in distinct Channels, so that they may never meet in one (save in some transitory extraordinary occasion) there lies a grand Secret of Liberty and good Government ...

A True State continues by describing Barebone's Parliament, in words that Oliver Cromwell was to use in speeches in the first Protectorate Parliament.

... it so fell out in a short time, that there appeared many in this Assembly of very contrary principles to the Interest aforesaid; which led them violently on to attempt and promote many things, the consequence whereof (however it might not be intended by the generality of them) would have been A subverting the Fundamental Laws of the Land, the destruction of Propriety, and an utter extinguishing the Ministry of the Gospel. In truth, their principles led them to a pulling down all, and establishing nothing: So that instead of the expected Settlement, they were running out into meer Anarchy and confusion ...

After explaining that allegation, *A True State* goes on to justify why the Instrument of Government placed the executive and legislative powers in different hands. Here are two key passages on that theme.

To have returned back again to Representatives, as the Parliament had propounded in their Biennial Bill, and so to have governed these Nations by Parliaments always sitting, not only clear reason, but experience evinceth, that neither Safety or Liberty could be expected therein. Parliaments always siting are no more agreeable to the temper of this People, than it is to a natural Body to take always Physick instead of Food ...

... If we take a survey of the whole together, we find the Foundations of this Government laid in the People. Who hath the power of altering old Laws, or making new? The people in Parliament; without them nothing of this nature can be done; they are to be governed only by such Laws as they have chosen or shall chuse, and not to have any imposed upon them. Then, who is to administer or govern according to those Laws, and see them put in execution? Not a person claiming an hereditary Right of Soveraignty, or power over the Lives and Liberties of the Nation by birth, allowing the People neither Right nor Liberty, but what depends upon Royal grant or pleasure, according to the tenor of that Prerogative challenged heretofore by the Kings of England; under whom, if the Commonalty enjoyed anything they might call their own, it was not so much to be esteemed a matter of Right, as a Boon and effect of grace and favour. But the Government now is to be managed by a Person that is elective, and that Election must take its rise originally and virtually from the People, as we shall fully evince by and by, in particular, and shew that all power both Legislative and Executive, doth flow from the Community; than which there cannot be a greater Evidence of publike Freedom.... Consider what care is taken for succession of Parlaments. A Parlament is to be called every three years at least, not leaving it to the pleasure of the chief Magistrate to do it or not to do it; but other persons, in case of his Failer, are impower'd and required to issue forth Summons without him ...

Later, *A True State* explains how the Instrument of Government

> fully answers likewise the main ends of the Parlament and Army, in
> reference to matters of Religion; wherein the Rights and Liberties
> of the People are duely fenced and provided for, as in all the princi-
> pal Points of Civil Interest and Freedom.... we conceive it is high
> time for our Governours to lay a healing hand to these mortal
> wounds and breaches, by holding forth the Truths of Christ to the
> Nation in some solid Establishment, and not quite to lay aside or let
> loose the golden reins of Discipline & Government in the Church;
> but yet to order them in such a way that they might not tie up all
> mens Consciences, who profess Truth in sobriety, to any one par-
> ticular Form, nor be laid as snares and chains upon conscientious
> and zealous men (as it was wont to be in the dayes of Popery and
> Prelacy;) the summ of all that is intended by way of Coercion, being
> only to restrain such as shall abuse their Liberty to the Civil injury
> of others, and to the actual disturbance of the publick Peace, or such
> as under the profession of Christ hold forth and practise
> Licentiousness.

Document 2: Local support for the Protectorate from the godly of Coventry, 1654

An extract from an address from Coventry: *To His Highness Oliver Lord Protector of the Commonwealth of England, Scotland and Ireland, The Humble Address and congratulation of the Maior, Recorder, Alder-men, Ministers, Sheriffs, Common councill, and other Inhabitants of the City of Coventry.* From *Mercurius Politicus*, 30 March – 6 April 1654, pp. 3384–5.

> As we bless God for, so we canot but with glad hearts, represent to
> your Highness, how clearly we have of late beheld, that holy Prov-
> erb fulfild (*In the Mount of the Lord it shalbe seen*) for when we feared
> the life of Religion, Magistracy, Ministry, Laws & Liberties (the dear
> concernments of Gods people) would have expired, and bin found
> by Posterity covered with Ashes, through the inadvertency of some
> Men, it pleased the Lord above and beyond our foresight and pro-
> vision, hapily to repose, and make your Higness eminently a mean
> to prevent the danger; and raised you up to save us from these our
> fears; so we cannot but expect, that the same will also make you
> instrumental to accomplish these our hopes; that religion and all
> ordinances of Christ are moving towards purity and power; that
> the building of the Lords house may now rise to the top-stone, and

all his people cry *Grace, Grace,* unto it: That Magistracy and Ministry will be secured from the violation of prophane and irregular pens and tongues; and that henceforth men fitly qualified may be set apart for both callings: that the laws will receive life, & common liberties toeir [their] maintenance, and that we shall have no self advantage, solemnly to bless the Lord for your Highness protecting of us, and our affairs civil, then we of this City have had for the fruit of your power whilst it was martial. These are our hopes, which under God have their foundation in your Highnesses constancy, to contend for, & adhear to the knowne and undoubted interest of God and this Nation, so well of late secured in the provision made for future Parliaments. Now that your Highness may be the hand of the Lord to do all these things, and fulfil his good pleasure; we shall not be wanting, or neglect any duty incumbent on us, which may conduce to the Nations protection and your Highness, or your Highness protection under God, and we shall ever pray and remain, Your Highness most humble servants.

Document 3: Speeches in the first Protectorate Parliament

Extracts from the debates in parliament on 11 September 1654 on whether the government should be by a single person and a parliament, as laid down in the Instrument of Government. A defence of this type of government was made in Marchamont Nedham's *A True State* (document 1). This document is Guibon Goddard's summary of some of the arguments that supported the opposite case. From J.T. Rutt, ed., *The Diary of Thomas Burton Esquire* (4 vols, London, 1828), vol. 1, pp. xxix–xxi.

The arguments on the other side, were,
First upon reasons.
1. That the supreme power was originally in the people.
2. That to join any thing in co-ordination with it, would be to set up two supremes, that would always check one the other, and have several interests, and several affections, and ends, and, by consequence, would never be at peace.
3. That so great a power could no where be so safely trusted, as in a Parliament, which is the representative of the people.
4. That the former government, by King and Parliament, was but an usurpation upon the common right.
5. That the experience of the inconvenience of that government had caused the nation to alter it, and to settle it in the Parliament; and that they have been in possession of this government by a

Parliament, in the way of a Commonwealth, for some years last past.

6. That the providences of God are like a two-edged sword, which may be used both ways; and God in his providence, doth often permit of that which he doth not approve; and a thief may make as good a title to every purse which he takes by the highways.

7. That if the titles be measured by the sword, the Grand Turk may make a better tittle than any Christian princes.

8. That the addresses and approbation of the country were not in reference to the present government, as formerly established, in a single person and a Parliament, but to congratulate the present deliverance out of those extremities and confusions, which the little convention of assembly [Barebone's Parliament] were putting upon us, as being sensible that any government for the present were better, until it shall please God, in his due time, to bring through many shakings to a steady foundation: wherein, they looked upon him [Oliver Cromwell] generally, as great instrument; but not as the root or fountain of a steady and fixed government....

10. Lastly ... That the foundation of the government of this nation was laid long since, and asserted in the late Parliament, by which so many things were built and destroyed, as it would not find an east faith in another age; and if that foundation were not good, the Parliament, and all that acted with it, were the greatest and most infamous regicides and murthers, and villains in the world. That no man that sat that had acted in any capacity, especially the soldiery, (who were most violent for the contrary opinion), could be justified upon any other account.

Document 4: Petition of the three colonels, 1654

An extract from the petition of Colonels Thomas Saunders, John Okey and Matthew Alured to the Protector, November 1654. From *Calendar of State Papers, Domestic Series*, 1653–54, pp. 302–4, where the date is wrongly given as 1653.

As members of the army, we solemnly declared (14 June 1647) that we engaged as mercenaries but in conscience for the liberties of our country, yet from our confidence in you, who engaged with us in the same quarrel, we waited your counsels to the utmost extremity.

But finding you engaged in transactions whereupon the life and death of the cause bought with our blood hangs, we are obliged to remind you of the tyranny against which we are engaged, and of the fundamental rights and freedoms we intend to redeem out of the tyrant's hands, and to this the whole army agreed, not only before but after the exemplary justice done on the late king. We then declared his tyranny to consist in his opposition to Parliament, concerning the people's safety in their absolute command of the militia, and of their power to call officers of justice and ministers of State to account, which he said could not be done without him, and that whatever he did, no power could meddle with his sacred person.

We then declared that we must have constant Parliaments, freely chosen by the people, which should have the supreme power in making laws, removing grievances, determining peace or war, etc., and that no person should be exempt from punishment by the people's Parliament ... [the petitioners then explain that they oppose the power given to the Protector in Instrument of Government on the grounds that a future Protector might use the army] to destroy Parliament, and bring us into vassalage ... Such a militia commander will be master of all Parliaments ... so that all provisions for liberty of conscience or freedom would thus be made void.

Document 5: The impact on the Protectorate's leaders of the Vaudois massacres, 1655

An extract from *A Declaration of His Highness, with the Advice of His Council, Inviting the People of England and Wales to a Day of Solemn Fasting and Humiliation*, 25 May 1655. From British Library, E1064/54.

The Poor Inhabitants of the valleys of Lucern, Angrone, and other within the Dominions of the Duke of Savoy, professing the Reformed Religion, and refusing to abandon the same, which hath been transmitted unto them from their Ancestors (the old Waldenses, those famous Martyrs, who with their Lives and Fortunes hath born their frequent Testimonies to the Truth) were by an Edict from the said Duke enjoyned in the hardest season of Winter, to quit their habitations, upon penalty of Loss of Life, and Confiscation of their Estates unless they should within twenty days after Publication of the said Edict make it appear, that they have embraced the Roman Religion, which hard and rigorous Command was soon after most severely put in execution by an Army sent amongst them, which by continual Slaughters, Massacres and other intolerable Violence daily exercised upon them, inforced them to retreat to the Mountainous Parts of their Countrey ... This being the sad condition of Our Brethren and Fellow Members in the Body of Christ, should those of the same Faith and Hope with them (who through the Strecht-out hand of God, enjoy Deliverence and Protection from the like Fury and Violence) neglect or disregard them in this Day of their Distress for the testimony of Jesus, Assistance and Relief would arise to them some other way; But we should be little able to give an Accompt with Chearfulness of the Call of God that is now upon Us, for the exercise of Mercy and Compassion: God who hath given them to suffer for Christs sake, hath given the Liberty of the Gospel in that measure, with those Attendances of Peace and Plenty, as we must now look upon it as a great Contempt of his Distinguishing Mercy, should not we improve our utmost Interest in him, and lay out what he hath intrusted Us withal as We have opportunity for their Relief. Out of Our deep sence therefore of the said calamitous Estate of Our poor Brethren, as also of the future Danger upon all the Protestant Churches in general ... [14 June 1655 was appointed as a day of humiliation and fasting, and ministers were to encourage their congregations to contribute to a fund for the relief of the Vaudois].

Document 6: Godly comradeship reinforced by the crisis of 1655

An extract from the newspaper *Perfect Proceedings of State Affairs in England, Scotland and Ireland*, 29 March – 5 April 1655, p. 4568. From British Library, E831/6.

Glocester 26 March. God still owns the dispised interest of his holy people. It were the dispised ones that appeared with us, now to suppresse the Cavaliers, Col. Richard Aylworth [and other named people] all Justices of the Peace. These are all of them honset men, most of them of the Congregational way, or such as wish will be the same: Hand in hand with these went divers Ministers of our Country, whom the Country doth indeed hate and call Independent, but 'tis manifest in our Country, whose fidelity there is most reason to confide in.... Some formerly would have put out these our Justices for factious men, & those Ministers before hinted must have expected no better then to be turned out, but God hath been mercifull to our Country in honouring them that honour him. And I hope the Lord wil incline the heart of my Lord Protector to watch against those wicked men, that are still nibling to get our Godly Justices out of Commission. In great haste, I rest.

Document 7: A proclamation on religion, 15 February 1655

From W.C. Abbott, ed., *The Writings and Speeches of Oliver Cromwell* (4 vols, Cambridge, Mass., 1937–47), vol. 3, pp. 626–7.

By His Highness: A Proclamation prohibiting The Disturbing of Ministers and other Christians in their assemblies and Meetings.

It having pleased the Lord, by the manifold Mercies and Deliverances which he hath wrought in and for these Nations of late Years, and the Blessings wherewith he hath blessed the Endeavors of the Good People thereof, in making them Successful against His and their Enemies, to crown Us with this, is not the least Token of His favor and Good Will to Us, That there is a free and uninterrupted Passage of the Gospel running through the midst of Us, and Liberty for all to hold forth and profess with sobriety, their Light and Knowledge therein, according as the Lord in his rich Grace and Wisdom hath dispenced to every man, and with the same Freedom to practice and exercise the Faith of the Gospel, and to lead quiet and peaceable Lives in all Godliness and Honesty, without any Interruption from the Powers God hath set over this Commonwealth, nay with all just and due Encouragement thereto, and Protection in so doing by the same; A Mercy that is a Price of much Blood, and till of late years denied to this Nation, as at this day it continues to be most of the Nations round about Us, and which all that fear God amongst Us ought duly to consider and be thankful for in this Day, wherein God hath so graciously Visited and Redeemed his People; His Highness, as He reckons it a Duty Incumbent upon Him, and shall take all possible Care to Preserve and Continue this Freedom and Liberty to all Persons in this Commonwealth fearing God, though of differing Judgements, by protecting them in the sober and quiet exercise and profession of Religion, and the sincere worship of God, against all such who shall, by imposing upon the Consciences of their Brethren, or offering violence to their Persons, or any other way, seek to hinder them therein; So likewise doth He hold himself equally obliged to take Care, That on no pretence whatsoever, such freedom given should be extended by any beyond those bounds which the Royal Law of Love and Christian Moderation have set us in our walking one towards another; Or that thereby occasion should be taken by any to abuse this Liberty to the disturbance or disquiet of any of their Brethren in the same free Exercise of their Faith and Worship, which himself enjoyes of his own. And His Highness cannot but sadly lament the wofull distemper that is fallen upon the Spirits of many professing Religion and the Fear of God in these dayes, who instead of a suitable return to the Lord our God for this Liberty, and all our other Mercies, and appearing in an answerable carriage by a Spirit of tenderness and forbearance one towards another, and provoking one another to Love and all good Works, are found in a spirit of bitterness towards their Brethren, biting and devouring, hatefull and hating one another, and provoking one another to Love and good Works, are found in a spirit of bitterness towards their Brethren, biting and devouring, hatefull and hating one another, and whilest they pretend the Liberty which Christ hath purchased for his People, do openly and avowedly, by rude and unchristian Practices, disturb both the publique and private meetings for preaching the Word, or other Religious Exercises, and vilifie, oppose, and interrupt the Publique Preachers in their Ministery, whereby the Liberty of the Gospel, the profession of Religion, and the Name of God is much dishonoured and abused, and the spirits of all good men much grieved. His Highness therefore, having had many informations from divers men lately risen up under the names of Quakers, Ranters, and others, who do daily both reproach and disturb the Assemblies and Congregations of Christians, in their Publique and Private Meetings, and Interrupt the Preachers in dispencing the Word, and others in their Worship, contrary to just Liberty, and to the disturbance of the Publique Peace, doth hold himself obliged by His Trust, to Declare His dislike of all such Practices, as being contrary to the just Freedome and Liberties of the People, which by the Laws and Government of this Commonwealth they ought to be Protected in; And doth hereby strictly Require and Command all Persons whatsoever, That they forbear henceforth all such irregular and disorderly Practices. And if in Contempt hereof, any Persons shall presume to offend as aforesaid, We shall esteem them as Disturbers of the Civil Peace, and shall expect, and do require all Officers and Ministers of Justice to proceed against them accordingly.

Given at White-Hall the 15 day of February 1654 [5].

Document 8: A local demand for godly reformation, 1655

This is report of a petition from the mayor, five aldermen and 118 inhabitants of Harwich, Essex, to the Protector, 19 February 1655. From *Calendar of State Papers, Domestic Series*, 1655, p. 46.

God has set you over these nations for his honour and our unexpressible happiness, and fitted you to further the Gospel by advancing painful and powerful preachers for which all reformed churches are your daily orators, and especially all the inhabitants of our British Jerusalem.

In our borough are 1,000 persons capable to attend worship, beside strangers flocking to one of the greatest shipping ports, yet we have no established preacher. In the corrupt times of the late King, we were joined to Dovercourt, a mile off, and the vicar preached at each place once on the Lord's Day, but this has led to profaneness, tippling, and gaming in both places. We beg to have a godly divine of our own choice settled among us.

Document 9: A measure to prevent royalist delinquents being elected to municipal offices, 1655

An extract from a Protectorate proclamation, 21 September 1655, giving the reasons why the decision was made to continue the provisions of an act of 1652 which had made it illegal for anyone guilty of supporting the royalist cause to take part in town elections or be elected to municipal offices. From British Library, 669f20/15.

> His Highness the Lord Protector in His great Care and Wisdom, considering the premisses and foreseeing the dangers this Commonwealth must necessarily be exposed unto, if such Malignant and disaffected persons should be in offices of Trust and Power in the Commonwealth, and calling to mind the late horrid Treason and Rebellion, contrived and carried on by the inveterate and restless malice of that party to involve these Nations in blood and confusion, who have avowedly and with open face professed their end was, and still is (though in the utter ruin and desolation of these Nations) to set up that Power and Interest, which Almighty God hath so eminently appeared against ...

Document 10: An eyewitness's account of proceedings in Cony's case, 1655

Walter Zanchy wrote these comments after attending one day of the trial. From *Calendar of State Papers, Domestic Series*, 1655, pp. 167–8.

> I was at the Upper Bench last Saturday when Mr. Cony's business came on. I went out for his Highness' counsel, and when I returned, the room was filled, so that I heard but little. Serjeant Twisden, one of Cony's counsel, excepted against the formal part of the return of the *habeas corpus*, and said that customs were payable

by an Ordinance of Parliament of Dec. 1647, whereby, and by subsequent Acts, they were continued to March 1653 only, and the customs are due by no law since. He insisted much on the taking away the Star Chamber, and urged that subjects were not to be imprisoned, nor their goods attached, but in a legal way on trial by jury ... Mr. Attorney-General, in his reply, wondered the serjeant should speak so much against the present authority, being that by which the Court sat, and by which Mr. Cony's expected justice. Serjeant Maynard, also of Cony's counsel, spoke little, but I could not well hear what he or others of Cony's counsel said.

Document 11: A proclamation of 31 October 1655

Extracts from a *Declaration of his Highness in Council, showing the reasons of their proceedings for securing the peace of the Commonwealth, on occasion of the late insurrection.* From *Calendar of State Papers, Domestic Series*, 1655, pp. 405–11.

After God had so clearly decided the contests with the late king and his party that they were wholly vanquished, and their persons and estates subjected to those whom they designed to enslave, it was hoped they would have been convinced of their errors, and lived in peace, especially if they and their estates were made free from punishment. They were therefore admitted to compound, on terms so easy that many were in better condition than the Parliamentary party, who had to make large payments to maintain the war ... their reformation, not their ruin, was designed. Thus after the battle of Worcester, on 3 Sept. 1651, though the party was utterly dispersed in England, and had lost their strength both in Scotland and Ireland, endeavours were made to unite the people and compose their spirits ... So great respect we had to this sort of men in the settlement of the present Government that, after 3 Parliaments, they were to be admitted to sit in the supreme councils of this nation.... but they have proved themselves implacable, and never to be drawn from that cursed interest which has occurred the shedding of so much innocent blood, and almost the ruin of these lands. Therefore we are obliged in duty to proceed in another way ... No magistrate should show favour to those who only refrain from outward acts, but remain enemies at heart. The late king's party have notoriously shown that they appear to these old principles, and have been all along hatching disturbances by secret assassination or open force. Therefore it will not be thought strange that we have seized many who were not in open arms in the late insurrection, nor that we have laid a burden on the estates of the rest, to defray the charge they have occasioned....

There then follows an account of various royalist plots, and a reprint of a letter from Charles II – 'the pretended king' – encouraging rebellions.

It is therefore evident that, unless we would give up all for which so much blood has been spilled, and the hope of reforming the nation from the spirit of prophaneness, we must secure the peace by additional forces, the charge of which ought not to be put on those who have borne the heat and burden of the day, but on those who were the occasion of all our dangers. We have therefore erected a standing Militia of horse in all counties, under such pay as may encourage them and get not to be burdensome, and land the charge on such of those who were engaged in the late wars as are liable to bear it. It may seem great severity to tax the whole party, when few have been convicted or detected, in which case their whole estates had been confiscated, but we appeal to all indifferent men whether the party was not generally involved in the business ... If the supreme magistrate were in such cases tied to the ordinary rules, and could not proceed against the suspected, there would be no safety from conspiracy. But supposing some are innocent, yet as they avow, and love and glory in the cause, it is but just that they should share in the charge of securing the State against the dangers of which they are the authors ... We publish these things chiefly that the well affected may be encouraged, and not suffer themselves to be divided by artifices and factions from that settlement and reformation which every good man longs for.

Document 12: Instructions to the major-generals, October 1655

These extracts are from the final instructions given to the major-generals in October. Protector and Council had been drafting them since August. From J.P. Kenyon, ed., *The Stuart Constitution: Documents and Commentary* (2nd edn, Cambridge, 1986), pp. 322–4.

1. They are to endeavour the suppression of all tumults, insurrections, rebellions or other unlawful assemblies which shall be within the said counties respectively, as also all invasions from abroad, and to that purpose shall have power to draw together the said forces or troops, and march in such places as they shall judge convenient in England and Wales.

2. They are to take care and give order, that all Papists and others

who have been in arms against the Parliament, or assisted the late King or his son in the late wars, as also all others who are dangerous to the peace of the nation, be disarmed, and their arms secured in some adjacent garrisons, or otherwise disposed of, as may be for the public service.

3. [Thieves and highwaymen to be prosecuted.]

4. They are to have a strict eye upon the conversation and carriage of all disaffected persons within the several counties; and they shall give the like direction to all the said captains and officers at their meetings, to be watchful and diligent in the same kind. As also that no horse-races, cock-fighting, bear-baiting, stage plays, or any such unlawful assemblies be suffered or permitted within their counties, forasmuch as treason and rebellion is usually hatched and contrived against the State upon such occasions, and much evil and wickedness committed.

5. They and the aforesaid officers shall labour to inform themselves of all such idle and loose people that are within their counties who have no visible way of livelihood, nor calling or employment, and shall consider by what means they may be compelled to work, or be sent out of the Commonwealth ...

6. They shall in their constant carriage and conversation encourage and promote godliness and virtue, and discourage and discountenance all profaneness and ungodliness; and shall endeavour with the other justices of the peace, and other ministers and officers who are entrusted with the care of those things, that the laws against drunkenness, blaspheming and taking of the name of God in vain, by swearing and cursing, plays and interludes, and profaning the Lord's Day, and such like wickedness and abominations, be put in more effectual execution than they have been hitherto.

7. They shall take an exact account of what proceedings have been put upon the ordinance for ejecting of ignorant, insufficient, and scandalous ministers and schoolmasters, and take care that the same be put in execution for the time to come....

17. That no house standing alone and out of a town be permitted to sell ale, beer or wine, or give entertainment, but that such licenses be called in and suppressed....

19. And for the effecting more particular a reformation in the city of London and Westminster, that all gaming houses and houses of ill fame be industriously sought out and suppressed within the cities of London and Westminster and all the liberties thereof.

20. That all house keepers within the same who have no trade or calling, or do not labour in such trade or calling, or have no other

visible estate, but are observed generally to lodge and harbour loose and dissolute persons, be bound to their good behaviour and compelled to work, and for want of security be sent to Bridewell.

21. That all alehouses, taverns and victualling houses towards the outskirts of the said cities, or either of them, be suppressed, except such as are necessary and convenient to travellers; and that the number of alehouses in all other parts of the town be abated, and none continued but such as can lodge strangers and are of good repute.

Document 13: Opposition to the exclusion of MPs in the second Protectorate Parliament, 1656

An extract from *A Narrative of the late Parliament (so called), their Election and Appearing; the Seclusion of a great Part of them ... published for Information of the People; by a Friend to the Common-wealth, and to its dear-bought Rights and Freedom*, 1657. From *The Harleian Miscellany: A Collection of Scarce, Curious and Entertaining Pamphlets and Tracts* (ed. Walter Scott, 6 vols, London, 1809), vol. 3, pp. 449ff.

Upon this breach made in the House, and giving up the rights and interest of the English nation in parliament, to be judged without doors, by an inferior power; divers gentlemen then sitting in the house, who being endued with principles of justice and righteousness, and love to the nation's freedoms, immediately withdrew; and others would not enter into the house at all, but departed to their several habitations.

Upon all which it is proposed and queried:

1st. Whether since the Conquest there was ever such a blow given (by a people owning themselves a Parliament) to the interest and freedom of the English nation, as the suffering to be secluded from them (by an inferior power) so great a number of members chosen by the people to sit, as their representatives in parliament; without any cause shewn for such a proceeding?

2. How this upstart Protector and his council, of little more than three years standing, should come to be empowered to do those things, which a King and his council, of more than four-hundred years descent, could not, nor durst not do? And whether the late, together with the former force, put upon the House, by excluding so many of their members, be not a crime twenty-fold beyond that of the late King's; in going about to seclude the five members, so highly dis-resented in that day by the people, and afterwards attended with so great feud and bloodshed?

Document 14: Parliamentary speeches in the second Protectorate Parliament

Extracts from the parliamentary debates on (a) the case of James Nayler and (b) the Militia Bill. From J.T. Rutt, ed., *The Diary of Thomas Burton Esquire* (4 vols, London, 1828), vol. 1, pp. 24–6, 46–7, 54–5, 56, 62, 69, 78, 230, 233, 237–8, 240.

(a) The case of James Nayler:

5 December 1655.

Major-General [Philip] Skippon.
... It has been always my opinion, that the growth of these things [Quaker ideas] is more dangerous than the most intestine or foreign enemies. I have often been troubled in my thoughts to think of this toleration; I think I may call it so. Their great growth and increase is too notorious, both in England and Ireland; their principles strike both at ministry and magistracy.... I am as tender as any man, to lay impositions upon men's consciences, but in these horrid things. I have been always against laws for matters ex post fact; but in this, I am free to look back, for it is a special emergency. You would extend to punishment. This offence is so high a blasphemy, that it ought not to be passed. For my part, I am of opinion, that it is horrid blasphemy ...

Major-General [William] Boteler.
Though my indisposition might plead for my silence, yet I should go out with a troubled conscience, if I should not have borne witness against it. We all sit here, I hope, for the glory of God. My ears did tingle, and my hear tremble, to hear the report. I am satisfied that there is too much of the report true. I have heard many of the blasphemies of this sort of people; but the like of this I never heard of. The punishment ought to adequate to the offence. By the Mosaic law, blasphemers were to be stoned to death. The morality of this remains, and for my part, if this sentence should pass upon him, I could freely consent to it.

6 December 1656.

James Nayler being brought to the bar, refused to kneel or to put off his hat. The House agreed beforehand that they would not insist upon his kneeling, being informed that he would not do it, and that he might not say that was any part of his crime. They would not give him that advantage; but commanded the serjeant to take off his hat.
[Nayler was then cross-examined:]

Question. King of Israel; assumed you thus?

Answer. As I have dominion over the enemies of Christ, I am King of Israel spiritually....

Q. Why did you ride into Bristol in that manner?

A. There was never any thing since I was born so much against my will and mind as this thing, to be set up as a sign in my going into these towns; for I knew that I should lay down my life for it.

Q. Whose will was it, if not yours?

A. It was the Lord's will, to give it into me to suffer such things to be done in me; and I durst not resist it, though I was sure to lay down my life for it.

Q. How were you sure?

A. It was revealed to me of my father, and I am willing to obey his will in this thing.

...

Q. Are there any more signs than yours?

A. I know no other signs. There may be other signs in some parts of the nation; but I am set up as a sign to this nation, to bear witness of his coming. You have been a long time under dark forms, neglecting the power of godliness, as bishops. It was the desire of my soul, all along, and the longing expectation of many godly men engaged with you, that the nation should be redeemed from such forms. God hath done it for you, and hath put his sword in the hands of those from whom it cannot be wrested. The sword cannot be broken, unless you break it yourselves, by disobeying the voice, the call, and rejecting the sign set up amongst you to convince them that Christ is come.

8 December 1656.

Major-General [John] Disbrowe [Desborough].
We must not proceed without rules; though the offence be heinous enough. We must either take the law of God, or of man, to regulate the judgements herein.... I speak not to extenuate Nayler's offence, but, if we judge by Christian rule, the other persons are more guilty of blasphemy. He is a great sinner, a vile sinful man; but, to call him a horrid blasphemer, I shall not give my vote.

Lord [Walter] Strickland.
I look upon him as a man exceeding scandalous, proud and sinful; but to say he is a blasphemer I cannot agree. He does not blaspheme God ... He believes that more of Christ is in him than in any other creature; but he showed no malice to Christ, or envy.

If you have any rule, I would have you proceed against him as a seducer, and to let none to be allowed to come to him: to shut him up as one that has the plague upon him. Haply you have some persons here, that you will find you out a law to secure him from doing further hurt; to act rather as a magistrate than by another power, whereby you have not a rule to proceed.

Lord President [Henry Lawrence].
If you hang every man that says, Christ is in you the hope of Glory, you will hang a good many. You shall hear this in every man's mouth of that sect, and others too, that challenge a great interest in Christ.

I do not believe that James Nayler thinks himself to be the only Christ; but that Christ is in him in the highest measure. This, I confess, is sad. But if, from hence, you go about to adjudge it, or call it blasphemy, I am not satisfied in it. It is hard to define what is blasphemy.

Colonel [William] Sydenham.
These Quakers, or Familists, affirm that Christ dwells personally in every believer. That which I fear, is to draw this down into precedent, for, by the same ground, you may proceed against all that sect. Again, what sticks with me, is the nearness of this opinion to that which is a most glorious truth, that the spirit is personally in us. The precedent in this case will be the most dangerous to posterity.... If some of those Parliaments were sitting in our places, I believe they would condemn most of us for hereticks.

Colonel Holland.
I hope he may speak now that has spoken nothing in this business. Consider the state of this nation, what the price of our blood is. Liberty of conscience, the Instrument [of Government] gives us. We may remember how many Christians were formerly martyred under this notion of blasphemy; and who can define what it is. I am wholly against the question. I may transgress your orders, it being the first day I sate here.

(b) The Militia Bill:

25 December 1656.

Major-General Disbrowe.
I have a short Bill to offer you, for continuance of a tax upon some people, for the maintenance of the militia. It will be for the security of your peace. It can fall upon no persons so fitly as those that occasion the charge. Let us lay the saddle upon the right horse. Your friends and enemies have hitherto borne an equal share. There ought to be a discrimination; for if your enemies should have prevailed, they would have freed themselves.

Mr [Luke] Robinson.
This motion is very properly offered. The Cavaliers are the cause of
this war [against Spain], considering how near they are a kin to the
Spaniard. You protect them. They do not protect you. They keep
together, waiting an opportunity to supplant you. In the late
insurrection few of that party but had a younger brother, or some
relation engaged in the plot, at that time in every family, especially
in the North parts.

Colonel Sydenham.
… It is well enough known what plots were laid; how implacable
and inveterate that party are against you; how they separate themselves to this day. They have not relinquished their party; not one
of them declared against Charles Stewart. The tax was laid upon
good consideration, and I hope this Parliament will never think it
unreasonable to continue it.

Mr. [Thomas] Bampfield.
… If I were satisfied in my conscience, that this tax could be laid
without a violation of the Act [of Oblivion], without breach of your
faith, I should not say a word on it. I have as little to plead for the
Cavaliers as any man. I believe some are as bad as can be. Admit
they be bad as can be, we ought to be honest to them…. It was told
you that Acts of Oblivion were never broken in Parliament. Admit
some have been actually in the insurrection against us: but to draw
the whole party under punishment for the offence of some, is a
justice I cannot understand…. While the general tax continued
they had no justice against us, but now God will plead for them, in
regard we have violated those rules, and exceeded that square of
justice, which ought to bind all men. In Samuel xxi.1, we read that
there was a great famine for three years. The reason being inquired,
it was because Saul 'slew the Gibbeonites'. This may run parallel
with the case of the Cavaliers. There was deceit used to gain that
league.
   More so is the Cavaliers' case. We had advantage by it as well as
they. In the Gibeonites' case no removing of the judgment, till justice was done upon Saul's sons. They increased, and Saul in great
prudence slew them, in zeal to the house of Israel, in regard of their
enmity, and increase of them; but we find God of another mind. If
we keep our promise, our greatest safety is to keep faith. It is God's
rule; David's precept. Most honest to keep the public faith to those
that have not actually broke that faith. I have heard that it was
Machiavel's policy to place honesty only in safety, but God's rules
are otherwise. Let us pursue those and we may expect a blessing.
Otherwise God will punish us as he did Saul's sons. It is best to deal

plainly with God in those things. I hope that this Parliament will never think fit to exceed those rules. We are upon a sure foundation if that be done....

Lord [John] Lambert.

I am as guilty of the Act of Oblivion as any man. I have laboured to oblige that party; to win them, as much as may be; but find it impossible till time wear out the memory. They are as careful to breed up their children in the memory of that quarrel as can be. They are, haply, now merry over their Christmas pies, drinking the King of Scots' health, or your confusion. The Gibeonites' case is not a parallel with this.

Document 15: A report of Oliver Cromwell's interrogation of Major Packer and five captains, February 1658

An extract from a letter from Secretary John Thurloe to General George Monck, 12 February 1658. From C.H. Firth, ed., *Selections from the Papers of William Clarke* (Camden Society, new series, vols 49, 54, 61, 62, 1891–1901), vol. 61, p. 140.

... his Highness sent for the Major and five Captaines, and discoursed with them at large, who all declared their dislike of the present Government [the Humble Petition and Advice], and made severall objections to it, and semed to speake of the goodness of a Comonwealth. His Highness tooke much paines with them to satisfie their scruples, and gave them tyme to thinke upon what he had said to them; and after three or four dayes consideration, he sent for them againe, and spake with them in the presence of above twenty officers, and wished them to propound the grounds and reasons of their dissatisfaction in the presence of their fellow officers, but Major Packer said they had already propounded them, and had considered what his Highness had said to them, but that their dissatisfactions did still remaine with them; which is all the answer they would give at that tyme, and at two other tymes after wherin his Highness laboured to satisfie them, save that they all said that they were willing still to continue in the army, and follow his Highness upon the grounds of the good old cause, but would not expresse what they meant by the old cause. After four or five tymes discourse in this manner, his Highness being utterly unsatisfied with their answers, dismist them all from their commands, vizt. Major Packer, Captain Gladman, Captain Malyn, Captain Barrington, Captain Spinage, and Capt. Leut. Hunter; these are all Anabaptists.

Document 16: Viscount Saye and Sele's reasons for
refusing to sit in the Other House, December 1657

An extract from a letter from Viscount Saye and Sele to Lord Wharton, 29 December 1658. From C.H. Firth, 'A letter from Lord Saye and Sele to Lord Wharton, 29 December 1658', *English Historical Review*, 10, 1895, pp. 106–7.

> For the Goverment of this Kingdome according to the right consti-tution thearof and execution agreable thearunto, I think it to be the best in the worlde; beinge a mixture of the 3 lawfull governments in that manner that it hath the quintessence of them all, and thearby alsoe the one is a boundery unto the other, whearby they are keapt from fallinge into the extreames which eather apart are apt to slippe into, Monarchy into Tyranny, and Aristocracy into Oligarchy, Democracy into Anarchy; now the cheefest remedie and prope to opholde this frame and building and keape it standinge and steady is, and experience hath shewed it to be, the Peeres of the England, and theyr power and priviledges in the House of Lords, they have bin as the beame keepinge both scales, Kinge and people, in an even posture, without incroachments one uppon another to the hurt and dammage of both.... This being soe, will it not be as most unjust, most dishonourable and most unworthy, for any antient Peere of England to make himself a felo de see [a self-murderer] to the Nobilyty of Englande and to just and rightly constituted Gov-ernment of the Kingdome by being made a partye and indeed a stalkinge horse and vizard to carry on the designe of over-throwinge the House of Peeres, and in place thearof to bringe in and sett up a House chosen att the pleasure of him that hath taken power into his own hands to doe what he will, and by this House that must be carryed on as picked out for that pourpose, and altered and newe chosen as tyme and occasion shall require, some 5 or 6 Lords called to sitt with them whoe may give some counte-nance to the designe, which for my part I am resolved neaver to doe....

Document 17: Andrew Marvell on the
accession of Richard Cromwell

From Andrew Marvell, *On the Death of Oliver Cromwell.*

> And Richard yet, where his great parent led,
> Beats on the rugged track: he virtue dead
> Revives, and by his milder beams assures:

And yet how much of them his grief obscures.
He, as his father, long was kept from sight
In private, to be visited by better light:
But open'd once, what splendour doth he throw!
A Cromwell in an hour a prince will grow.
How he became that seat, how strongly streigns,
How gently wonds at once the ruling reins!
Heav'n to this choice pepar'd a diadem,
Richer than any Eastern silk, or gemm:
A pearly rainbow, where the sun inchas'd,
His brows like an imperiall jewell grac'd
We find already what these omens mean,
With ne'er more glad, nor Heaven more Serene.
Cease now our griefs, calm peace succeeds a war.
Rainbows to storms, Richard to Oliver.

Document 18: Richard Cromwell's speech, 18 October 1658

Extracts from 'The speech of the protector Richard to the officers of the army: in the hand-writing of secretary Thurloe, and corrected by him'. From Thomas Birch, ed., *A Collection of the State Papers of John Thurloe Esquire* (7 vols, London, 1742), vol. 7, pp. 447–9.

Takeing notice, that there are in towne very many of the officers of the army both of English and Scottish army, and some alsoe from Ireland, and probablie more then are like to be againe for some tyme, I had a desire to see you together, and thought myselfe obliged to speake some things to you, which I judge the present state of affaires makes it necessary for me to say.

I need not to observe to you, in what conjuncture of tyme and affayres I am come to the government. You all knowe it, and you know the difficulties my father all this tyme wrestled with; and I beleeve noe man think that his death hath lessened them. I am sure that our enemies thinke they are much encreased and that now is their tyme to devoure us all at once; and they have their instruments in every corner, and in all shapes, to manage their designes that way. Their main work is to divide. It's the work of their day to divide you from me, and me from you, whom God and the law hath joyned together, and you amongst yourselves. And if they can effect this, they thinke they effect their desires …

Then if their work be division, our worke is union. And if there be union in principles and ends, it is more than probable wee shall be united in our affections and actions.

Soone after my accession to the government, I receaved from the whole army an addresse, as you knowe, wherein you expressed your affection and fidelity to me, and engaged to be with me, as you had been with my father ... And this I suppose you did to strengthen my hands against the opposition I am like to meet with in carryinge on the Lord's worke in this land, and in preserving the good cause my father and the honest men of this nation hath engaged in. And the army did in that addresse expresse those particulars, wherein they conceived the life and spirit of that cause to consist, which in a few words are,

1. The liberty of the nation, as wee are men:
2. The liberty of conscience, as wee are Christians:
3. The keepinge of the army in the hands of godly men:
4. A godly magistracy, and godly ministrie.

All that the army sayd in their addresse to me, and all that is in the hearts of honest men touching our cause, is reducible to these 4 heads. And if it be soe, if in truth this be all that lyes in the bottom of men's spirits, I doe not see, wherupon any differences shall growe amongst us. All these things are in my heart to promote, and to venture my life, and all I have, and am, in the defence of; soe that soe farr as you have exprest yourselfe in your addresse, I can truly say, I am as you are, and you are as I am....

It is to my disadvantage that I have been soe little amongst you, and am no better knowne to you. I hope a little tyme will remove that disadvantage ... For my owne part, I have an entire confidence in you, as those who were my father's companions in all his daungers and difficulties, and who were witnesses of all the wonders God wrought for him, and you, and these nations; and I knowe his soul clave to you; and I am perswaded soe did you to hym. God hath raised me up in my father's stead and put me in the same relation towards this nation and you, as he stood in ...

The government I can assure you, is not that I take pleasure in. If my lott by beinge here be cast amongst the people of God to serve them, yea to suffer with them, I shall rejoice therein....

It might have pleased God, and the nation too, to have chosen out a person more fitt and able for this worke then I am. I am sure it may be sayd of me, nor for my wisdom, my parts, my experience, my holiness, hath God chosen me before others; there are many here amongst you, who excell me in all these things; but God hath done herein as it pleased him; and the nation, by his providence, hath put things this way. Beinge then thus trusted, I shall make a conscience, I hope, in the execution of this trust, wherein I see not how I should doe, if I should parte of the trust, which is committed to me, unto any other, though they may be better men then myselfe....

[Richard Cromwell then firmly refused to abandon control of the army to any other, and his speech continued:] I have made my brother Fleetwood lieutanent-generall of all the army, and soe by consequence commander in cheife, and I am sure I can doe nothinge, that will give him more influence in the army then that title will give him, unless I should make him generall; and I have told you the reasons why I cannot doe that....

Document 19: A contemporary critique of the foreign policy of the Protectorate

Extracts from Slingsby Bethel's *The World's Mistake in Oliver Cromwell; or a short Political Discourse, Shewing That Cromwell's Maladministration (during his Four Years, and Nine Moneths pretended Protectorship,) layed the Foundation of our present Condition, in the Decaye of Trade* (1668; reprinted by the Rota at the University of Exeter, 1972), pp. 3–4, 5, 8–9.

This Nation being in this flourishing and formidable posture, Cromwell began his Usurpation, upon the greatest advantages imaginable, having it in his power to have made peace, and profitable Leagues, in what manner he had pleased withall our Neighbours, every one courting us then, and being ambitious of the friendship of England; But as if the Lord had infatuated, and deprived him of common sence and reason, he neglected all our golden opportunities, misimproved the Victory God had given us over the United Netherlands, making peace (without ever striking stroak) so soon as ever things came into his hands, upon equal tearms with them. And immediately after, contrary to our Interest, made an unjust Warr with Spain, and an impollitick League with France, bringing the first thereby under, and making the latter too great for Christendom; and by that means, broke the ballance betwixt the two Crowns of Spain, and France, which his Predecessors the Long Parliament, had wisely preserved.

In this dishonest Warr with Spain, he pretended, and indeavoured, to impose a belief upon the world, that he had nothing in his eye, but the advancement of the Protestant Cause, and the honour of this Nation; but his pretences, were either fraudulent, or he was ignorant in Forreign affairs (as I am apt to think, that he was not guilty of too much knowledge in them) ...

And whereas, it had in all Ages been the policies of the Northern

States and Potentates, to keep the Dominion of the Baltick Sea, devided amongst several pettie Princes and States, that no one might be the sole Master of it ... Cromwell contrary to this wise Maxime, endeavoured to put the whole Baltick Sea into the Sweeds hands ...

Bethel then summarised the alleged consequences of these policies.

First, in his sudden making a Peace with Holland, so soon as he got the Government, without those advantages for Trade, as they who beat them did intend to have had, as their due, and just satisfaction for their Charges in the War.

Secondly, in his War with Spain, by the losse of that beneficial Trade to our Nation, and giving it to the Hollanders, by whose hands we drave (during the War) the greatest part of that Trade which we had of it, with 25. in the hundredth profit to them, and much losse to us.

Thirdly, by our losse in the War with Spain, of about 1500 English ships, according as was reported to that Assembly, called Richards Parliament.

Fourthly, in the disgracefullest defeat at Hispaniola that ever this Kingdom suffered in any age or time.

Fifthly, and lastly, in spending the great Publick stock he [f]ound, and yet leaving a vast Debt upon the Kingdom....

Document 20: Two Swedish diplomats' views of the Protectorate's foreign policy, 1655

Extracts from the reports of Peter Julius Coyet and Christer Bonde, Swedish ambassadors in London, to their master, King Charles X, of the situation in England in the mid-1650s. From Michael Roberts, ed., *Swedish Diplomats at Cromwell's Court, 1655–56: The Missions of Peter Julius Coyet and Christer Bonde* (Camden Society, 4th series, vol. 36, 1998), pp. 83–4, 135.

(a) Coyet's report, 22 June 1655:

He [Oliver Cromwell] spoke much also of his late majesty King Gustav the Second and Great, of glorious memory; saying among other things that, being then a private person, he nevertheless had always followed his great campaigns with the greatest pleasure, had many times thanked God, with tears of joy in his eyes, for His gracious mercies, and when the tidings came of his death, had so mourned it that he could scarcely believe that any Swede could mourn it more bitterly; for he saw that a great instrument to quell the power of the papists had been taken away. But he hoped now that Y[our] M[ajesty] would repair that loss, and follow the late King Gustav's laudable example; and that with all the more fruit and benefit to the common cause, since he made no doubt that on his side there was a readiness to contribute all possible means to the seconding of the work; which before had not been properly attended to by this state, and much good thereby neglected.

(b) Bonde's report, 23 August 1655:

And he [Oliver Cromwell] said that he certainly believed that Y[our] M[ajesty] would not limit himself to his present plans, but rather hoped that the beneficient design whose execution in Germany Almighty God had seemed to destine to the hand of King Gustavus (of illustrious memory), but by him could be no more than begun, might by the great King Charles be completed, and achieve its ends to the glory of God; and to this he was ready to contribute what he could.

Document 21: A foreign policy debate on the Western Design, 1654

These extracts are from some brief notes among the papers of the Earl of Sandwich. From C.H. Firth, ed., *Selections from the Papers of William Clarke* (Camden Society, new series, vols 49, 54, 61, 62, 1891–1901), vol. 61, pp. 203–8. R. Hutton, *The British Republic* (Basingstoke, 1990), p. 137, disputes Firth's attribution of these notes to Edward Montague.

July 20, 1654. – We cannot have peace with Spain out of conscience to suffer our people to go thither and be idolators. They have denied you commerce unlesse you be of theire religion.

Lambert.
1. The work is improbable.
2. To farre off, having greater concernments of setli[n]ge at home.
3. Not like to advance the Protestant cause; or gaine riches to us or vent [for] troublesome people in England, Ireland, or Scotland.
4. The case at first wrong stated. The charge not well considered. The regulation of our lawe and other concernments not well taken care of it.
The settlement of Ireland in its government. Transplantation or

not transplantation? Better wayes of vent for our people may be found then it.

Oliver Cromwell's reply:

Wee consider this attempt because wee thinke God has not brought us hither where wee are but to consider the worke that wee may doe in the world as well as at home, and to stay from attemptinge untill you have superfluitye is to putt it off for ever, our expenses being such as will in all probabilitye never admitt that.

Now Providence seemed to lead us hither, haveing 160 ships swimminge: most of Europe our enemyes except Holland, and that would be well considered also: we thinke our best consideration had to keep up this reputation and improve it to some good, and not lay them up by the walls. Thence wee came to consider the two greate crownes, and the particular arguments weighed, we found our opportunitye point this way.

It was told us that this designe would cost little more then laying by the shipps, and that with hope of greate profitt.

Document 22: Hopes of profits from the occupation of Jamaica dashed, 1655–56

Extracts from two documents that give varying estimates of the value of possessing Jamaica. From W.C. Abbott, ed., *The Writings and Speeches of Oliver Cromwell* (4 vols, Cambridge, Mass., 1937–47), vol. 3, p. 816 and vol. 4, pp. 193–5.

(a) A proclamation of the Protector relating to Jamaica, 31 August 1655:

Whereas, by the good providence of God, our fleet, in the late expedition into America, have possest themselves of a certain island, called Jamaica, spacious in its extent, commodious in its harbours and rivers within itself, healthful by its situation, fertile in the nature of its soyl, well stored with horses and other cattel, and generally fit and worthy to be planted and improved, to the advantage, honour and interest of this nation....

(b) The Protector and Council's letter to the chief commanders in Jamaica, 7 June 1656:

Gentlemen, We have received your letters ... whereby you give an account of the state and condition of the forces both at land and sea, and of our other affairs at Jamaica, which is such as doth still administer unto us further cause to be humbled before the Lord, and to search out what His mind may be in this His sad dispensation. And we do observe, that the hand of the Lord hath not been more visible in any part of this rebuke, than in taking away the hearts of those, who do survive amongst you, and in giving themselves up to so much sloth and sluggishness of spirit, that they care not to take pains, either for their security against the enemy, or for providing food for themselves, choosing rather to die with hunger, or expose themselves to be devoured by the Spaniard, than to labour for their own preservations in any kind ...

Document 23: A Dutch view of the Protectorate's foreign policy, 1655

A Dutch medallion, 1655. The French and Spanish ambassadors in the background are rivals for the privilege of kissing the bare posterior of Oliver Cromwell, whose head is on Britannia's lap. © The British Museum.

Document 24: Part of the Declaration of the Parliament of the Commonwealth of England, concerning the Settlement of Scotland, October 1651

From C.S. Terry, ed., *The Cromwellian Union: Papers Relating to the Negotiations for an Incorporating Union Between England and Scotland, 1651–2* (Scottish Historical Society, vol. 40, Edinburgh, 1902), pp. xxi–xxiii.

[After the appointment of commissioners, the Declaration proceeds:]

1. As to what concerns the advancement of the glory of God, that their constant endeavours shall be, to promote the Preaching of the Gospel there, and to advance the power of true Religion and holinesse, and that God may be served and worshipped according to his mind revealed in his Word …

2. They doe declare, as to what concernes the freedome to be established to the people there, and the security to this Commonwealth to be had from time to come, that Scotland shall, and may be incorporated into, and become one Common-wealth with this of England …

[3. All who aided the royalist cause are to have their estates confiscated.]

4. The Parliament doe declare, That all such persons of the Scottish Nation as are not comprehended within the former Qualifications, but have kept themselves free from the guilt of those things which have compelled this War, and shall now upon the discovery of their own true interests, be disposed to concur with, and promote the ends formerly and now declared by the Parliament, shall be taken into the protection of the Parliament, and enjoy the Liberties and Estates, as other the free people of the Common-wealthe of England.

And forasmuch as the Parliament are satisfied, That many of the people of Scotland who were Vassels, or Tenants to and had dependency upon the Noble-men and Gentry (the Chief Actors in these invasions and wars against England), were by the influence drawn into and have been involved with them in the same Evils, it is hereby declared, That all those [who have already or shall within 30 days acknowledge the power of the English Commonwealth] shall not only be pardoned for all Acts past, but be set free from their former dependencies and bondage-service, and shall be admitted as Tenants, Free-holders, and Heritors, to farm, hold, inherite, and enjoy from and under this Common-wealth, proportions of the said confiscated and forfeited Lands, under such easie Rents, and reasonable conditions, as may enable them, their Heirs and Posterity, to live with a more comfortable subsistence then formerly, and like a free People, delivered (through Gods goodnesse) from their former slaveries, vassalage, and oppressions.

Document 25: Preamble to the Act for the Settlement of Ireland, 12 August 1652

From C.H. Firth and R.S. Rait, eds, *Acts and Ordinances of the Interregnum, 1642–60* (2 vols, London, 1911), vol. 1, pp. 598–9.

Whereas the Parliament of England, after the expence of much Blood and Treasure for suppression of the horrid Rebellion in Ireland, have by the good Hand of God upon their undertakings, brought that Affair to such an issue, as that a total Reducement and Settlement of the Nation may, with Gods blessing, be speedily effected; To the end therefore that the People of that Nation may know that it is not the intention of the Parliament to extirpate that whole Nation, but that Mercy and Pardon, both as to Life and Estate, may be extended to all Husbandmen, Plowmen, Laborers, Artificers, and others of the Inferior sort, in maner as is hereafter Declared; they submitting themselves to the Parliament of the Commonwealth of England, and living peaceably and obediently under their Government; And that others also of higher Rank and Quality may know the Parliaments intention concerning them, according to the respective Demerits and Considerations under which they fall; Be it Enacted and Declared by this present Parliament, and by the authority of the same, That all and every person and persons of the Irish Nation, comprehended in the following Qualifications, shall be lyable unto the Penalties and Forfeitures therein mentioned and contained; or be made capable of the Mercy and Pardon therein extended respectively, according as is hereafter expressed and declared.

Document 26: A Scot's view of the union with England

These extracts are from the letters of Robert Baillie, a Presbyterian Scot, whose letters and journal are a major primary source for Anglo-Scottish relations in the mid-seventeenth century. From David Laing, ed., *The Letters and Journals of Robert Baillie* (3 vols, Edinburgh, 1842), vol. 3, pp. 317–18, 387.

For Mr. Spang at Middleburgh, September 1st 1656.

Our State is in a very silent condition: strong garrisons over all the land, and a great armie, both of horse and foot, for which there is no service at all. Our Nobles lying up in prisons, and under forfaultries, or debts, private or publict, are for the most part either broken or breaking ... The great Seall of Scotland (with Cromwell's large statue on horseback, *Oliverus Dei Gratia Reip. Angliae Scottiae et Hiberniae Protector*, under the arms of Scotland *Pax Quaeritur Bella*,) is given to Desborough, the Signet, with the great fees of the Secretar's place, to Colonel Lockhart, the Register's to Judge Smith, and the rest of the places of State to others. The expences, delays, and oppressions in law-sutes, are spoken of to be as great as was ever.

The Spanish warre has wracked many of our merchands ... They say the excise will be double, so that the revenue will be above three hundred thousand pounds a-year, the halfe whereof is never together among us. The trueth is, money was never so scarce here, and groweth dailie scarcer, and yet it's thought this Parliament in September [the second Protectorate Parliament] is indicted mainlie for new taxations. What England may bear, to whom the Protectour remitted the halfe of their monethlie maintenance of one hundred and twenty thousand pound sterling, I know not; but Scotland, whose burthen has been triple, besides the fynes, forfaulters, debts, and other miseries, seems unable to bear what lyes on already. Wise men think the Protector wiser than to desire the emptie title of a King, when he has much more already than the King. No man looks for any good of this Parliament, but fears evill; yet all who are wise thinks that our evills would grow yet more if Cromwell were removed. They think his government, as it is, will be farr better than a Parliament, or any thing else they expect, and only think this warre with Spain needless and hurtfull, and hope by the Parliament it will be taken away

For William Spang, Glasgow November 11, 1658.

The Countrey lyes very quiet; it is exceeding poor, trade is nought, the English hes all the moneys.

Document 27: Army demands for wholesale transplantation in Ireland, 1655

Extract (a) presents the first two in a list of nine reasons given in a petition by officers and soldiers in Dublin, Carlow, Wexford and Kilkenny to the Lord Deputy and the Irish Council for the transplantation of all Irish men and women, not just landowners, to Connaught in about March 1655. Extract (b) is from a letter written in Dublin on 23 May 1655. From S.R. Gardiner, 'The transplantation to Connaught', *English Historical Review*, 14, 1899, pp. 724–6, 733.

(a) The petition:

1. The first reason that we shall humbly offer to your honours' consideration for the transplanting of the Irish, as aforesaid, is to prevent those of natural principles their becoming one with those Irish as well in affinity as idolatry, as many thousands did who came over in Queen Elizabeth's time, many of which had a deep hand in all the late murders and massacres; and shall we join in affinity with the people of these abominations? ...

2. The second reason is grounded on the law of nature which teacheth self-preservation, which we can in ways expect, so long as they live within our bowels; it being consistent to their principles to destroy the enemies of their holy faith ...

(b) The letter:

The officers of the army here are very sensible of that horrible cruelty in the massacre of the poor protestants in the duke of Savoy's dominions; they intend to make application to his highness about it. It was less strange to us when we heard that the insatiable Irish had a hand in that blood. If our transplantation go not on, they may give us the dregs of that cup to drink as the kindness of their neighbourhood. The Lord grant our own iniquity may not be an occasion of delivering us our children into the hand of so cruel an adversary!

Document 28: The transplantation policy in Ireland in action

An extract from a letter from T. Herbert (on behalf of the Irish commissioners) to Colonel Francis Foulke, Governor of Drogheda, 27 April 1654. From R. Dunlop, ed., *Ireland under the Commonwealth, Being a Selection of Documents Relating to the Government of Ireland, from 1651 to 1659* (2 vols, Manchester, 1913), vol. 2, p. 422.

The Commissioners of the Commonwealth have received your letter of 25 inst., declaring that several persons, removing from your parts into Connaught, desire some time of stay for their wives, children, and stock, for the better enabling them to travel, and that it is your judgment that, by their short stay, the contribution and other public taxes will be the better secured and paid, they have commanded me to signify their pleasure accordingly, which is, that notwithstanding any former Rule, you may suspend the transplantation of such wives and children (whose husbands and parents are to go into Connaught) for such time as you shall judge fitt (not exceeding 1st of July next) and may permit the stay of their cattle until they be in condition to drive, allowing but one servant to look unto the respective herds or flocks, and such servants to be neither proprietors, nor such as have been in arms against the Commonwealth.

Document 29: Godly magistrates in action in England

These two extracts come from the papers of two godly magistrates, who did their utmost to bring about godly reformation in the areas under their control. Extract (a) is from the diary of Robert Beake, who was mayor of Coventry in 1655–56. From L. Fox, ed., 'Diary of Robert Beake, mayor of Coventry, 1655–56' in R. Bearman, ed., *Miscellany One* (Dugdale Society, vol. 31, 1977), pp. 114–15, 1301. Extract (b) is from the notebooks of Captain John Pickering, who was a JP in Pickering in Yorkshire in the 1650s. From G.D. Lumb, ed., 'Justice's Note-Book of Captain John Pickering, 1656–60' in *Miscellanea* (Thoresby Society, vol. 11, 1904), p. 73.

(a) Robert Beake's diary:

1655

15, 16: November. I sate at Crowne and made an order for the outing of Walford, minister of Wishaw, for scandal in life....

18 November A man for travelling from Alsley, being the Lord's day, was set in the stockes.

A man travelling from Righton to Exhall to be a godfather was distrained and paid 10s.

19 November 3 Quakers for travelling on the Lord's day were set in the cage. Memorandum: it greieved me that this poore deluded people should undergoe punishment of such a nature.

20 November By order of the magistrates this day was kept afast for diseases and the smale pox that raigned in the citty. The observation of it was very great among all sorts....

21 November Henry Walsmeley and Frances Rotten confessed they had carnal knowledge of each other, for which the one was sent to goal, the other to the house of correction.

1656

2 March I sent 3 troopers towards Dunchurch and 3 towards Meriden by order of the commissioners to take up such as travel on the Lord's day and pass by Coventry....

6 [March] The constables were summoned to appeare before me this day to returne the names of al alehouse keepers that were put downe that still sel without license.

(b) Captain John Pickering's notebook:

JAMES AUSTWICK, per SWEARING. Saturday, 23th August (56) James Austwick, senr, of West Ardsley was convicted upon the oath of Will. Cotton of the same ffor swearing two prophane oathes & one prophane curse, wch is the first, second & third offences & warrant given to the Constable to punish him accordingly.

JOHN SMITH, per DRUNK: & SWEARING. Memorand: That John Smith of West Ardsley, collier, was convicted before Mr. Ward, of Pomfrett, upon the oaths of Willm Cotton & Thos. Kidson of West Ardsley, the 30th of August last, ffor being drunk the 13th of ye same month & did then also prophanely sweare six oathes one after another; ffor wch offences he forfeited one & forty shillings eight-pence; & warrant giuen by me to the Constable to leuy the same, & for want of distressse to set him in the stockes for the space of thirty-nine howers....

JONAS TETLEY: MARRIED. Md: that Jonas Tetley & Elizabeth Thornton, both of Bradford were duly married before me on the eleaventh day of Sept: 1656

Document 30: Indifference to catechising

An extract from the diary of Adam Martindale, minister of Rostherne in Cheshire. Here Martindale described the popular reaction to his campaign of religious education by using cat-echisms. From R. Parkinson, ed., *The Life of Adam Martindale* (Chetham Society, 1st series, vol. 4, 1845), p. 122.

Within the compasse of this septennium, in the yeare 1656, the min-isters of our Classis and many others of our neighbours agreed upon some propositions about the worke of personal instruction (as many in other counties did). Multitudes of little catechismes we caused to be printed, designing one for every family in our par-ishes, and to all, or most, they were accordingly sent. But when we actually set upon the worke, even such as had but (comparatively) small parishes or chappelries to deal with met with great discouragements, through the unwillingness of people (especially the old ignoramusses) to have their extreme defects in knowledge searched out, the backwardnesse of the prophane to have the smart plaister of admonition applied (though lovingly) to their sores, and the businesse (reall or pretended) left as an excuse why the persons concerned were gone abroad at the time appointed for their instruction.

Document 31: Troops used to suppress a service using the Book of Common Prayer, 1657

John Evelyn described in his diary what happened when he went to a church service using the Book of Common Prayer at the chapel in Exeter House, occupied by the Earl of Rutland, on 25 December 1657. From E.S. de Beer, ed., *The Diary of John Evelyn* (6 vols, Oxford, 1955), vol. 3, pp. 203–4.

I went with my Wife etc: to Lond: to celebrate Christmas day. Mr. Gunning preaching in Excester Chappell on 7: Micha 2. Sermon Ended, as he was giving us the holy Sacrament, The Chapell was surrounded with Souldiers: All the Communicants and Assembly surpriz'd & kept Prisoners by them, some in the house, others carried away: It fell to my share to be confined to a roome in the house, where yet were permitted to Dine with the master of it, the Countesse of Dorset, Lady Hatton & some others of quality who invited me: In the afternoone came Colonel Whaly, Goffe & others from Whitehall to examine us one by one, & some they committed to the Martial, some to Prison, some Committed: When I came before them they tooke my name & aboad, examind me, why contrarie to an Ordinance made that none should any longer observe the superstitious time for the Nativity (so esteem'd by them) I durst offend, & particularly be at Common prayers, which they told me was but the Masse in English, & particularly pray for Charles Stuard, for which we had no Scripture: I told them we did not pray for Cha: Steward but for all Christian Kings, Princes & Governors: The[y] replied, in so doing we praied for the K. of Spaine too, who was their enemie, & a Papist, with other frivolous and insnaring questions, with much threatning, & finding no colour to detaine me longer, with much pitty of my Ignorance, they dismiss'd me: These were men of high flight, and above Ordinances: & spake spitefull things of our B: Lords nativity: so I got home late the next day, blessed be God: These wretched miscreants, held their muskets against us as we came up to receive the Sacred Elements, as if they would have shot us at the Altar, but yet suffering us to finish the office of Communion, as perhaps not in their Instructions what they should do in case they found us in that Action.

Document 32: Richard Baxter's aims for religious 'unity'

An extract from a letter from Richard Baxter, minister of Kidderminster in Worcestershire, to Colonel Edward Harley, on 15 September 1656. From N.H. Keeble and Geoffrey F. Nuttall, eds, *Calendar of the Correspondence of Richard Baxter* (2 vols, Oxford, 1991), vol. 1, pp. 224–5.

For unity we desire

1. that you doe not only (as before) authorize Associations in order to Unity but earnestly perswade & press ministers thereto … & let the united pastors & Churches have countenance of the State …

2. Let some further meanes be tryed for the reconcilinge of the Presbyterians, Independants & Prelaticall. A free chosen Convocation is best in its season: but at present I feare they would be so divided amonge themselves, as would rather widen than close the wound. The same I feare if you should call but a dozen Ministers of severall Judgments to a Consultation. What if you tryed but this much first? Let the Committee [that Baxter proposed should be set up by the forthcoming parliament] send their desires to one or two of the most moderate Byshops, & to one or two of the most moderate & best esteemed Presbyterians, & as many of the Congregationall way, that (without any consultation with the differinge partyes) they would send in 1. Their concessions as to as narrow a compass as possibly they can for the Peace of the Church: 2. And their Judgments how the closure must be made. And withall that you send to one two or 3 moderate, able men, that are addicted to Pacification, & are for the closure of all partyes, being engaged in none of them; & desire their Judgement in briefe, on what termes the severall partryes may close so far as to hold a Comfortable Communion without deserting any of their Principles? … This is no impossible worke to be done. I prove it by experience.…

Bibliographical essay

The following is not comprehensive; it is primarily meant to provide starting points for studying the Cromwellian Protectorate. Other works are listed in the chapter notes, and many of the following works contain useful bibliographical guidance.

Austin Woolrych, *England Without a King, 1649–60* (London, 1983), Toby Barnard, *The English Republic, 1649–60* (2nd edn, Harlow, 1997) and Ronald Hutton, *The British Republic, 1649–60* (Basingstoke, 1990) are brief introductions to the period, designed for readers who know little or nothing about it. Roger Hainsworth, *The Swordsmen in Power: War and Politics Under the English Republic, 1649–60* (Stroud, 1997) has more information, but a much better overview for those who want to get more deeply into the history of the 1650s is chapter 12 in Derek Hirst, *England in Conflict 1603–60* (London, 1999) and chapters 16–28 in Ivan Roots, *The Great Rebellion 1640–60* (London, 1966; 2nd edn, Stroud, 1995). The latter has stood the test of time very well. This is also true of the magisterial books by S.R. Gardiner, *History of the Commonwealth and Protectorate, 1649–56* (4 vols, London, 1903) and C.H. Firth, *The Last Years of the Protectorate 1656–58* (2 vols, London, 1909). (Godfrey Davies, *The Restoration of Charles II* (San Marino, Calif., 1955) completed the history to 1660.) Some of their judgements are outdated, but most of them are still thought-provoking, and the research on which they are based is awesome. No serious student of the period can afford not to have these books constantly at hand. Two articles that touch on many of the questions and developments that are central to the history of the period are Austin Woolrych, 'The Cromwellian Protectorate: a military dictatorship?', *History*, 75, 1990, and Derek Hirst, 'Locating the 1650s', *History*, 86, 1996. Among the best collections of essays on various aspects of the Protectorate are G.E. Aylmer, ed., *The Interregnum: The Quest for Settlement, 1646–60* (London, 1972), Ivan Roots, ed., *'Into Another Mould': Aspects of the Interregnum* (Exeter, 1998), John Morrill, ed., *Oliver Cromwell and the English Revolution* (Harlow, 1990) and John Morrill, ed., *Revolution and Restoration: England in the 1650s* (London, 1992).

Of the major figures in the Protectorate, Oliver Cromwell has attracted more attention than anyone else by far. There are some excellent essays on Oliver Cromwell as Protector by Derek Hirst, 'The Lord Protector, 1653–8', J.C. Davis, 'Cromwell's religion' and Anthony Fletcher, 'Oliver Cromwell and the godly nation' in Morrill, ed., *Oliver Cromwell and the English Revolution* (above). There have also been recent studies of him by Barry Coward (Harlow, 1991), Peter Gaunt (Oxford, 1996) and J.C. Davis (London, 2000); they provide details of many earlier biographies. L.L. Knoppers, *Constructing Cromwell: Ceremony, Portraits and Prints, 1645–61* (Cambridge, 2000) is splendid on the way Cromwell was perceived by contemporaries, as is John Morrill, 'Cromwell by his contemporaries' in Morrill, ed., *Oliver Cromwell and the English Revolution* (above). Others have attracted much less attention. The best studies of Richard Cromwell are by R.W. Ramsey, *Richard Cromwell* (London, 1935) and Earl M. Hause, *Tumble-Down Dick: The Fall of the House of Cromwell* (New York, 1972). Major figures like Charles Fleetwood and John Desborough are still very shadowy in the absence of scholarly biographies of them. Philip Aubrey, *Mr Secretary Thurloe 1652–60* (London, 1990) is disappointing on Thurloe, and, though both are useful, neither W.H. Dawson, *Cromwell's Understudy* (London, 1935) nor David Farr, 'The military and political career of John Lambert, 1619–57' (unpublished PhD thesis, University of Cambridge, 1996) unravel Lambert's enigmatic character. What can be done is shown by Patrick Little, 'The political career of Roger Boyle, Lord Broghill, 1630–60' (unpublished PhD thesis, University of London, 2000) and N. Matthews's useful study of a second-ranking figure in the Protectorate, *William Sheppard: Cromwell's Law Reformer* (Cambridge, 1984). G.E. Aylmer, *The State's Servants: The Civil Service of the English Republic, 1649–60* (London, 1973) lacks a clear overall theme, but is packed with information about the men who served the Protectorate and how government worked during the period.

More recently, Peter Gaunt has done more than most to illuminate the workings of Protectorate government. Some of his seminal work on the Protectorate Council remains relatively inaccessible in his unpublished thesis, 'The councils of the Protectorate from December 1653 to September 1658' (unpublished PhD thesis, University of Exeter, 1989), but he has published some of his major findings in '"The single person's confidants and dependants"? Oliver Cromwell and his protectoral councillors', *Historical Journal*, 32, 1989, and other articles that are mentioned below. The financial aspects of Protectorate government have been in the doldrums since the publication of Maurice Ashley, *The Financial and Commercial Policy of the Cromwellian Protectorate* (London, 1934). But two recent works have breathed new life into the subject: M.J. Braddick, *The Nerves of State: Taxation and Financing the English State, 1558–1714* (Manchester, 1996) and J.S. Wheeler, *The Making of a World Power: War and Military Revolution in Seventeenth-Century England* (Stroud, 1999). Peter Gaunt's article, 'Oliver Cromwell and his Protectorate Parliaments: co-operation, conflict and control' in Roots, ed., *'Into Another Mould'* (above) is a good survey of the role of parliaments in the Protectorate. This provides a corrective to H.R. Trevor-Roper's once-influential interpretation, originally published in 1956, reprinted in Ivan Roots, ed., *Cromwell: A Profile* (London, 1973). There is also a valuable critique of this by Roger Howell, 'Cromwell and his parliaments: the Trevor-Roper thesis revisited' in R.C. Richardson, ed., *Images of Oliver Cromwell* (Manchester, 1993). David Smith includes a chapter and much bibliographical information on Protectorate parliaments in his *The Stuart Parliaments, 1603–89* (London, 1999).

Though they largely cover the period before December 1653, Blair Worden, *The Rump Parliament, 1649–53* (Cambridge, 1973) and Austin Woolrych, *From Commonwealth to Protectorate* (Oxford, 1982) are essential reading for anyone interested in the establishment of the Protectorate. Woolrych's account of the way the first Protectorate constitution emerged is supplemented by G.D. Heath, 'Making the Instrument of Government', *Journal of British Studies*, 6, 1967, and Peter Gaunt, 'Drafting the Instrument of Government: a reappraisal', *Parliamentary History*, 8, 1989. Ivan Roots, 'Cromwell's ordinances: the early legislation of the Protectorate' in Aylmer, ed., *The Interregnum* (above) is still the only major study of the work of the Protectorate government in its early months. Peter Gaunt, 'Interregnum government and the reform of the post office, 1649–59', *Historical Research*, 66, 1987, provides a case study that illuminates what was done at that time. The first Protectorate Parliament is well covered in two articles by Peter Gaunt, 'Law-making in the first Protectorate Parliament' in C. Jones, M. Newitt and S. Roberts, eds, *Politics and People in Revolutionary England* (Oxford, 1986) and 'Cromwell's purge? Exclusion and the first Protectorate Parliament', *Parliamentary History*, 6, 1987, and David Smith, 'Oliver Cromwell, the first Protectorate Parliament and religious reform', *Parliamentary History*, 19, 2000.

On the political history of the Protectorate's middle years, Blair Worden, 'Oliver Cromwell and the sin of Achan' in D. Beales and G. Best, eds, *History, Society and the Churches* (Cambridge, 1985) is essential reading for an understanding of the crisis of confidence that affected many of the regime's leaders in the mid-1650s. There are studies of the royalist rebellion in 1655 by Austin Woolrych, *Penruddock's Rising* (Historical Association pamphlet, London, 1953) and Andrea E. Button, 'Penruddock's rising, 1655', *Southern History*, 19, 1997. As is often the case, though, one should not ignore the contribution of C.H. Firth. His

'Cromwell and the insurrection of 1655', *English Historical Review*, 3, 1888, is still very useful. Until recently, the best works on the rule of the major-generals were articles by D.W. Rannie, 'Cromwell's major-generals', *English Historical Review*, 10, 1895, Ivan Roots, 'Swordsmen and decimators: Cromwell's major-generals' in R.H. Parry, ed., *The English Civil War and After, 1642–58* (London, 1972) and Anthony Fletcher, 'The religious motivation of Cromwell's major-generals' in D. Baker, ed., *Religious Motivation* (Studies in Church History 15, 1978). But these and John Sutton, 'Cromwell's commissioners for preserving the peace of the Commonwealth: a Staffordshire case study' in Ian Gentles, John Morrill and Blair Worden, eds, *Soldiers, Writers and Statesmen in the English Revolution* (Cambridge, 1996), though still useful, leave much about this subject unexplained. This historiographical gap has now been splendidly filled by Christopher Durston's authoritative *Cromwell's Major-Generals: Godly Government during the English Revolution* (Manchester, 2001).

On the later years of the Protectorate the best recent works are Carol S. Egloff, 'The search for a Cromwellian settlement: exclusion and the second Protectorate Parliament, parts 1 and 2', *Parliamentary History*, 17, 1998 (her 1990 Yale University PhD thesis, 'Settlement and kingship: the army, the gentry and the offer of the crown to Oliver Cromwell' is still unpublished), Christopher Durston, 'The fall of the major-generals', *English Historical Review*, 113, 1998, and Ruth E. Mayers, 'Real and practicable, not imaginary and notional: Sir Henry Vane, *A Healing Question* and the problems of the Protectorate', *Albion*, 27, 1996. But earlier work is still useful. See, for example, P.J. Pinkney, 'The Scottish representation in the Cromwellian parliament of 1656', *Scottish Historical Review*, 66, 1967, and Peter Gaunt's article on Oliver Cromwell and Protectorate Parliaments in Roots, ed., *'Into Another Mould'* (above). C.H. Firth (again) should not be ignored. His 'Cromwell and the crown', *English Historical Review*, 17, 1902, is still very valuable. On the parliament held during Richard Cromwell's Protectorate there are useful articles by Derek Hirst, 'Concord and discord in Richard Cromwell's parliament', *English Historical Review*, 107, 1988, G. Davies, 'The election of Richard Cromwell's parliament, 1658–9', *English Historical Review*, 63, 1948, and G. Nourse, 'Richard Cromwell's House of Commons', *Bulletin of John Rylands Library*, 60, 1977–78. But the essential works on the last period of the Protectorate are two articles by Austin Woolrych, 'The Good Old Cause and the fall of the Protectorate', *Cambridge Historical Journal*, 13, 1957, and 'Last quests for settlement' in Aylmer, ed., *Interregnum* (above), his long mini-book-length 'Historical introduction' in R.W. Ayers, ed., *The Complete Prose Works of John Milton, vol. 7* (New Haven and London, 1980), chapter 1 of Ronald Hutton, *The Restoration: A Political and Religious History of England and Wales, 1658–67* (Oxford, 1986), and Earl Hause's biography of

Richard Cromwell (above).

Of the many works on the religious beliefs and aspirations of those at the centre of power during the Protectorate, Blair Worden's three articles, 'Toleration and the Cromwellian Protectorate' in W.J. Shiels, ed., *Persecution and Toleration* (Studies in Church History 21, 1987), 'Providence and politics in Cromwellian England', *Past and Present*, 109, 1986, and 'Oliver Cromwell and the sin of Achan' in Beales and Best, eds, *History, Society and Church* (above) come into the 'essential reading' category, as do Anthony Fletcher, 'Oliver Cromwell and the godly nation' in Morrill, ed., *Oliver Cromwell and the English Revolution* (above), J.C. Davis, 'Cromwell's religion' in *ibid.*, and J.C. Davis, 'Against formality: one aspect of the English Revolution', *Transactions of the Royal Historical Society*, 6th series, 3, 1993. Chapter 8, 'Puritans in power', of John Spurr, *English Puritanism 1603–89* (Basingstoke, 1998) is a good overview of the topic. Derek Hirst, 'The failure of godly rule in the English Republic', *Past and Present*, 132, 1991, Ronald Hutton, *The Rise and Fall of Merry England: The Ritual Year 1400–1700* (Oxford, 1994), chapter 6, and Jeffrey R. Collins, 'The Church settlement of Oliver Cromwell', *History*, 87, 2002, provide assessments of the impact that the Cromwellian Church settlement and the drive for godly reformation had on the country. But it is Christopher Durston who has been most productive in recent years in writing on this topic. His 'Puritan rule and the failure of cultural revolution' in C. Durston and J. Eales, eds, *The Culture of Puritanism, 1560–1700* (Basingstoke, 1996) is the best survey of it and should be supplemented by other articles by him: 'Lord of misrule: the Puritan war on Christmas, 1642–60', *History Today*, 35, 1985, 'Unhallowed wedlocks', *Historical Journal*, 31, 1988, and '"For the better humiliation of the English people": public days of fasting and thanksgiving during the English Revolution', *The Seventeenth Century*, 7, 1992. See also the interesting contribution by Jean Mather, 'The moral code of English Civil Wars and Interregnum', *The Historian*, 44, 1982. The 'failure' of godly aspirations and popular opposition to them are the themes of many of these works. That these need to be qualified is suggested by the evidence of popular engagement with and enthusiasm for religious reform in Ann Hughes, 'A pulpit guarded: confrontation between orthodox and radicals in revolutionary England' in A. Laurence, W.R. Owens and S. Simms, eds, *John Bunyan and his England, 1628–88* (London, 1990), Ann Hughes, 'The frustrations of the godly' in Morrill, ed., *Revolution and Restoration* (above), Ann Hughes and Rosemary O'Day, 'Augmentation and amalgamation: was there a systematic approach to the reform of parochial finance, 1640–60?' in their *Princes and Paupers in the English Church* (Leicester, 1981) and Rosemary O'Day, 'Immanuel Bourne: a defence of the ministerial order', *Journal of Ecclesiastical History*, 27, 1976.

Index